UNCOMMON COURAGE

AN INVITATION

REVIEWS

These reviews are by people who've actually read this book. Some are authors and other celebrated people; a few are from the toughest audience, my family.

"The book combines a rare combination of captivating storytelling and truly insightful lessons about how you and I become an ever-better version of ourselves! My favorite takeaways were the simplifications of the complex and the honesty which so often is replaced with a facade these days."

—**David JP Philips, founder JP University, the Reinventor of Communication**

"Passionate. Inspirational. Powerful. This incredible compilation of stories and insights is down-to-earth and engaging and helps us play our part in the world. Written from the depths of her soul, Andrea's vulnerability encourages us to reflect on how we are living our lives. This is a great read that will inspire everyone to become a better human and make the world a better place."

—**Shirley Taylor, CSP, author, *Connecting the Dots – To Inspire the Leader in You***

"In this book, Andrea Edwards honestly and openly shares with us her inner journey as she has traveled the world and faced the complexities of relationships, parenting, business and social media. This is not a quick-fix self-help book, but rather travel guide from which you can pick up useful-tips, plan some must-sees, and avoid being ripped off at the market. Finding meaning and purpose can be elusive, but as you read this book you will be inspired by one woman's life that is full of purpose. Uncommon, uncompromising, and sometimes, uncomfortable purpose."

—**Andrew Bryant, CSP, author, *Self-Leadership: How to be a More Successful, Efficient and Effective Leader from the Inside Out***

"I challenge you to come away from this book without being changed in how you see yourself and the world around you. Accept Andrea's invitation to find your own truth to guide you forward."

—**Dr. Tanvi Gautam, author, *The Spark Lies Within: And other secrets of women leading inspired and authentic lives***

"Reading *Uncommon Courage* is like going to a dinner party and being seated with an experienced CEO, a spiritual guru and a wise old grandma. While they say you have to learn your own lessons, with this book you might just graduate 'the school of a beautiful life' with more magical moments and fewer scars."

—**Tara Moody, marketing and culture speaker, strategist, content creator**

"I started reading thinking, 'Oh I've probably heard all this before,' and yet once I began, I couldn't put the book down. Time and time again, *Uncommon Courage* nails it. You can't avoid thinking, laughing, even shouting out loud as you read this book."

—**Lindsay Adams OAM CSP, author, *The DNA of Business Relationships***

"Andrea brings herself straight from the heart fully into the world—wisdom, courage, and love. This book is food for the unsettled heart to find peace, for the discouraged heart to stir with hope again, and for the love in our hearts to flow from ourselves to the world."

—**Wendy Tan, author, *Wholeness in a Disruptive World***

"This goes deep into the human heart. Written with genuine rawness, it had me engaged, start to finish. I found myself constantly reflecting on my own self-discovery, while feeling enlightened to continue to embrace my journey to self-love and internal abundance."

—**Wendi Stewart, financial markets analyst and trader**

"Using very personal insights this book brings you practical everyday tips for a better life, more courage and even approaches to solutions for global issues. It's a plea for more civil courage and personal development."

—**Dr. Frank Hagenow, CSP, psychologist, author,**
Leadership Without Mind Games

"Need a little more courage? Read *Uncommon Courage*. Andrea takes you step-by-step through her extraordinary AND ordinary moments that create turning points. The experience, research and insights raise our awareness of the difference we can all make as we continue to learn, listen and take action. Whether we take small or radical steps, we can all create significant and positive change in our world."

—**Kerrie Phipps, author,** *Do Talk to Strangers: How to Connect with Anyone Anywhere*

"When I read *Uncommon Courage*, I felt like I was peeling an onion—so many layers, so SO inspirational. I love this book and Andrea because she makes me want to be a better person, for myself and for Mother Earth! This booked helped me with a few of my demons, helped me with compassion, as well as showing compassion for people that I feel do not deserve forgiveness—but it's not for them, it's for me. Always the key message. Definitely a must-read in today's crazy world. It will shift how you think, live and love."

—**Vicky Coburn, wellness consultant**

"As an amateur and professional performing musician spanning 20 years to serial social media conversationalist who's achieved guru status among her loyal "tribe," Andrea's life journey takes us through the streets of Calcutta where she meets Mother Teresa to being chased, robbed and *nurtured* in some of the most dangerous countries on the planet—to learning unconditionally how to say YES. *Uncommon Courage* is nothing short of epic. A feverish read to say the least."

—**John Vincent Gordon, CEO Expat Choice Media**

"*Uncommon Courage* is unconventional, unapologetic and undoubtedly a gem that everyone must read. Combining real-life stories with powerful questions, this book makes you stop, reflect, and want to take action towards being the person you want to be. So, if you're feeling stuck, grab this book, dig deep and go be magnificent!"

—**Sha En Yeo, the Happiness Scientist**

"*Uncommon Courage*—wisdom from a woman wise beyond her years—will compel you to find what is meaningful to you and spur you on the journey to living an impactful life. A must read for anyone who wants to create a better world around them."

—**Anupama Singal, author,** *SYZYGYmoments*

"This package of valuable nuggets of wisdom gives you recipes on how you can lead a happy life true to yourself while making a positive impact on others. Her keen insights build upon her personal and professional experiences in her lifelong and curiosity-driven quest to find her purpose. While Ms. Edwards does not shy away from the challenges presented by social media, her message is ultimately one of hope in that a more constructive online discourse can be found if more of us find the courage to speak our minds and help others."

—Niklas Myhr, the Social Media Professor

"Filled with inspirational stories and provocative questions, this book takes you on a journey of self-discovery. Through entering Andrea's world, you enter yours; not only to re-evaluate what you believe and why, but to have self-compassion and the courage to embrace change, act with kindness and step into committed action."

—Natalie Turner, author, *Yes, You Can Innovate*

"Good books are meant to be read and then re-read; *Uncommon Courage* falls slap bang into this select list, it's a keeper. Full of wise and humane anecdotes, woven into a rich tapestry of plain and simple life lessons, this is one of those addictive can't-put-down-read-through-in-no-time gems."

—Ferenc Nyiro, artist and yogi

"This book is a humorous and evocative treasure trove of insights on how to live your best life—minus the 'woo-woo.' It is akin to having a wise, non-judgmental friend help you dig a little deeper into the *how* and the *why* of who you are and where you are heading. This is the book to buy for everyone in your life who is oozing promise and potential and just needs a nudge to tap into their own #UncommonCourage."

—Samantha Gayfer, strategic marketing and crisis communications leader

"Written as a journey of self-discovery, the life lessons come from the love of travel, a deep curiosity about life and the world, and passion for humanity and the environment. This is no ordinary book, it's an adventure with an invitation to growth and self-acceptance."

—Sally Foley-Lewis, author, *The Productive Leader*

"I feel like I'm sitting around a bonfire when I read Andrea T Edwards' reflective, raw, grounded and highly enlightening new book *Uncommon Courage*. Andrea's stories beg me and, I believe, you, to go inside and focus on what is truly important, while getting rid of the 'noise' that surrounds us all, often stopping our true voice in this world. So, grab her book, light a fire if you can, and settle in for a great journey full of surprises, wisdom and courage. *Uncommon Courage* rocks!"

—Kevin Cottam, author, *The Nomadic Mindset: Never Settle . . . for Too Long*

"I love this book. Andrea has experienced a lot—good and bad—and I love how she draws on these experiences to explain how she reflects, always with the aim to become the best version she can be for the sake of herself, her community and the planet. She does this while inviting the reader to think and reflect on their versions of their life and how they might consider doing the same. It is a great read and a great exercise on reflection."

—Rebecca Kynaston, athlete, mother, eternal student

"When you learn from osmosis, it lasts longer! The trials, experiments and playing with fire: a journey travelled vicariously and a partner who shows how to care. Care, for yourself, others around you, and the earth that we live in. *Uncommon Courage* spurs us to keep our naivety in the right place and work towards creating a better world, within and without. A book that I can go to every time I feel a little nudge, to show a bit of courage."

—Pravin Shekar, author, *Throne Wars: Marketing Lessons from the Art of War*

"Andrea always had the single-minded desire to live her very best life. To be more than was expected of her and to experience more of life than most of us could ever believe possible. She had the courage to break free from the comfort and routine of her upbringing, the courage to live her best authentic life, and now, the courage to share her stories, warts and all. A great set of wisdoms for readers of all ages and stages."

—Phillipa Edwards, producer, conductor, composer
and the toughest audience—her sister

UNCOMMON COURAGE

AN INVITATION

ANDREA T EDWARDS

Copyright © 2021 by Andrea T Edwards
Edited by Joanne Flinn, Authority Services
Graphics by Tim Hamons
Layout by Karl Hunt
Cover by Arewa Lanre
Published by Courageous Publishing

This publication is presented to provide competent and reliable information regarding the subject matter presented. However, the author and publisher are not engaged in offering it as legal, financial, health or other professional advice.

The contents of this book are personal opinions and observations, based on the author's personal experience. Neither the author or the publisher shall be held liable or responsible to any person or entity with respect to any loss, incidental or consequential damages caused, or alleged to have been caused, directly or indirectly, by the information or programs contained herein. The advice and strategies contained herein may not be suitable for your situation. No one should make any decision without first consulting his or her own professional and conducting his or her own research and due diligence. You are solely responsible for the consequences of your use of this material.

First edition: June 2021

The publisher is not responsible for the websites (or their content) that are not owned by the publisher.

Library of Congress Cataloging-in-Publication Data.
Names: Andrea T Edwards, author
Title: Uncommon Courage, An invitation
Identifiers: ISBN 978-1-7372944-0-5 (international print edition)
          ISBN 978-1-7372944-1-2 (digital edition)
Subject: Personal Development, Sustainability, Career Advice

This book is dedicated to my two sons, Lex and Jax.

All I want for you boys (and all children) is a life where you can fully express yourselves and love the world you live in. A world in balance with Mother Nature. I want you to swim in clean oceans and rivers, walk trash-free mountain paths, and breath in crystal-clean air. I want for you to see and experience animals flourishing in the wild, to know peace and harmony, and understand that we must work together for the good of all. I want yours to be a world where all have the opportunity to live with dignity. I hope you'll feel the deep love that must exist within you and within all of us to make this possible. I love you guys. Go and be spreaders of love in the world and never stop fighting for what is right for all life on this planet xxxx

For every book you buy, I plant a tree!

CONTENTS

Foreword   xix

Welcome   xxiii

#1 Get out of your life!   1

#2 Open your mind up   8

#3 Never be ashamed of the music you love   12

#4 Do you have voices in your head?   15

#5 Worry is a waste of time   21

#6 Let people be dicks sometimes   26

#7 Embrace social media, we need you!   29

#8 Integrity and values   35

#9 Aim past the top of the hill   39

#10 Watch out for projection   42

#11 Control your own narrative   46

#12 From judgment to compassion   50

#13 My recipe for true love   54

#14 Find your purpose   61

15 Mind your jealousy   65

#16 Rejecting the unattainable   67

#17 Find your voice   71

#18 Exude love   74

#19 It's time to honor Mother Earth   77

#20 Trust your own counsel   84

#21 You've just got to do you   88

#22 What you resist persists   91

#23 Trust first   96

#24 Be an exciti-pants   100

#25 It's OK to walk away   102

#26 Epiphanies on anger   107

CONTENTS

#27 Use time well, especially during a crisis   111

#28 The one-minute meditation   113

#29 Unleash your voice for equality   119

#30 Don't be a maybe   122

#31 Manbassadors   126

#32 Seize your moments   131

#33 Watch out for negative Nellies   135

#34 Be a Queen   139

#35 Beware the victim mindset   143

#36 Givers and takers   147

#37 Have you met your soul yet?   151

#38 Forgiveness is for you   156

#39 Consequences   160

#40 What is suffering for?   163

#41 Take time off and think   169

#42 Focus on the best in people   174

#43 The beauty of abundant thinking   176

#44 Join the giving economy   180

#45 Hold your cynicism   **183**

#46 How's your brand rage?   **187**

#47 Breath in love, breath out hate   **192**

#48 Listen to the quiet ones   **195**

#49 It's time to speak up   **197**

#50 Get outside your success echo chamber   **201**

#51 There is enough to go around   **205**

#52 Positivity ain't all it's cracked up to be   **208**

#53 Let's talk about femininity   **213**

#54 Refuse to play small   **216**

#55 How to deal with eco-anxiety   **219**

#56 The habit of courage   **225**

#57 Why be so hard on yourself?   **229**

#58 Lead with compassion   **231**

#59 Don't be so overawed by power   **239**

#60 What do you really want from your career?   **242**

#61 Give yourself permission to dream   **245**

#62 Please don't disengage   **249**

CONTENTS

#63 Break the rules   253

#64 Don't lose yourself in challenging times   256

#65 Unleash the yearners   269

#66 Stuff isn't important, people are   273

#67 Let's make MX the new X   276

#68 Self-protection and the circle of trust   283

#69 Be generous   287

#70 Be kind   290

#71 Be a person of your word   295

#72 Roller coaster or merry-go-round?   299

#73 Seven tips for handling social media trolls and not accidentally becoming one   302

#74 Support the young fighters   307

#75 When they go low, we go . . .   311

#76 Explore all perspectives   314

#77 Domestic violence and fear   319

#78 Invest in memories   323

#79 A time for reflection   326

#80 Reconsidering work   331

#81 Different speeds, different agendas   335

#82 The gift of all experience   338

#83 Speak truth with love to your partner   343

#84 Beware drama kings and queens   347

#85 Beg your pardon, Dolly Parton   349

#86 Mothering is weird   353

#87 Going with the flow   357

#88 Other people's business   359

#89 Wine time   365

#90 Stand up for yourself   367

#91 Get future-ready   371

#92 No regrets   375

#93 When did we turn into complainers?   379

#94 Let's address shallowness   381

#95 Death reflection   385

#96 The ripple effect   389

#97 In good times and bad, look to serve   393

#98 Let's address powerlessness   398

CONTENTS

#99 Spend time alone, in silence   401

#100 Were you taught to hate someone you never met?   404

#101 Principles have a price   409

#102 Calm down, slow down   411

#103 Remember to seek awe   413

#104 Just say yes   419

#105 Cheers   423

#106 Live large and have fun   426

#107 Wisdom from my 100-year-old grandma   429

#108 Let's show up   432

Afterword   439

Acknowledgements   441

About Andrea T Edwards   447

A tree is planted for every book you buy.

FOREWORD

- What will your life be remembered for?
- Will you be missed when you are gone?
- Did you leave those around you better for knowing you?
- Have you found your purpose?

Rarely in a human lifetime do we experience the entire world being forced to stop. When it happens, though, we have an opportunity to reflect upon important questions. The global pandemic, with all its challenges and tragedy, is also the kind of *big reset* that can force us into a pause for intense learning and personal growth.

This is one of the reasons I was delighted when Andrea asked me to write a foreword for *Uncommon Courage.* As I read her book, I knew that Andrea's experience and wisdom could help so many people who are facing struggles through a period that is challenging for all of us.

Ultimately, life is about having the courage to say **this is the kind of person I want to be.** And to be who we aspire to be, we need to go deep into sometimes difficult conversation with ourselves. *Uncommon Courage* takes us on a personal journey, one that digs into the important questions of working out who we are and who we want to be—for ourselves, our loved ones, our communities, and the world.

Courage requires continual maintenance and effort—there is no final destination. I used to talk about this during one of my keynotes, "Building your Confidence Muscle," when I was a guest speaker for companies around the globe—this is when I first had the pleasure of meeting Andrea, over a decade ago. You have to work on your courage, just like you build muscles at the gym. Some days you get sore, other days you can tell how much progress you have made, and yet there is never a question—if you want to stay in shape, you have to keep using those muscles no matter what. With courage as with staying healthy, there are no shortcuts!

I got a reminder of the importance of working my courage muscles at the beginning of the pandemic. There I was, comfortable and strong in my work presenting on stages around the world, and overnight, I had to recreate the entire atmosphere in my "home office." How do you show up with a lot of excitement to no audience interaction? The silence when I Zoomed onstage was deafening, and facing it took a new kind of courage. So, like everyone else who was suddenly forced to work from home, I was definitely challenged professionally. I struggled to find my rhythm, but I can definitely say I trusted my own counsel, as Andrea so wisely advises us to do in these pages. Building my courage muscles in new ways brought new opportunities. In 2020 I did 187 keynotes and customer engagements, almost twice as many as I did in 2019, and I haven't been on a plane for work since March 2020!

Uncommon Courage peels away at questions of how to live with purpose and courage in today's world like layers of an onion. Through Andrea's loving, curious attention to the world around her, we are taken deep within ourselves. When you set off on this journey with Andrea, you'll have to trust the process, explore your mindset and your ideas, and be willing to reflect on how they have shaped who you are today. This is a path of recognizing and embracing opportunities, of seizing your moments with courage for the results you deserve.

As I always tell people I'm mentoring, opportunities sometimes show themselves as "whispers" and we need to have the courage not only to hear them but to act on them as well. Sometimes these whispers come from within, and sometimes they come from those who inspire you, the great people around you. Sometimes they will come to you while reading a book like this one.

It doesn't matter how successful we are right now—there will always be times we need courage, there will always be times it feels uncomfortable, and there will always be times a whisper comes from within or without at the right time to guide us forward. We must simply be open to hearing it.

Some of the chapters in this book will be gentle whispers, some may stop you in your tracks. It depends on how open you are to working on yourself, how willing you are to lean on your intuitions and the subtle—or not so subtle—whispers around you.

Enjoy this journey—let it inspire you to live your life with courage, reflection, purpose, and truth. #BeBold

Allow *Uncommon Courage* to be your invitation to have the courage to step into all you aspire to be.

TIFFANI BOVA
Global Growth and Innovation Evangelist

Author of the *Wall Street Journal* bestselling book *Growth IQ: Get Smarter About the Choices that Will Make or Break Your Business*

WELCOME

ON THE FIRST OF JANUARY 2020, I turned 50. It was the start of a new decade and a milestone birthday for me. The feeling in the air that night as the clock turned to midnight and the fireworks lit up the sky was one of hope for the future. It was a beautiful celebration with friends near and far.

Boy, am I glad I celebrated—because not long afterward, news started to break of the emergence of a new coronavirus.

Living in nearby Thailand, we had the first case confirmed outside of the Chinese mainland. Things got tense quickly and kept getting tenser by the day. We were all paying close attention to the news (especially those of us in Asia), hoping it would be under control quickly, like what we saw with SARS in 2003.[1] Then *bam*—by Chinese New Year, the real 2020 had started, and you don't need me to tell you *that* story.

In the lead-up to my 50th birthday, I decided to record and release a series of original videos, *50 Wisdoms in 50 Days*. It's quite an effort doing a project like this (I had to put on make-up every day!). Many people listened to them and have since told me that I should get those wisdoms out into the wider world, as the messages of encouragement and hope would help people going through today's challenging times.

---

1   https://www.history.com/news/sars-outbreak-china-lessons

So that's how this book came to be. Written from my heart to yours, it's here to help you embrace your best life, regardless of what is going on around you. No matter how good or how bad things are, this is about the mindset that helps you live your best life all the time. It's not easy, and it takes constant vigilance, but it works. It really does.

However, one thing I've learned since the pandemic began: times like these teach more wisdom, so the original set of 50 has expanded significantly. To be honest, it was hard to stop writing new ones.

A principal lesson I've learned during this journey of life is that once you fully embrace the deeper wisdoms of peace, love, and joy, well . . . you need to embrace them all the time, regardless of external influence, and especially not just when the going is good.

Because real wisdom means connecting deeply to who you are from a place of profound love—for self, for community, for the world. Love really is all there is.

My awakening to this idea began more than three decades ago. I love reading and travelling. I've devoured ideas and philosophies from many cultures, religions and movements. On top of that, I spent my 30s committed to reading all the books on business, self-help, and spirituality that I could get my hands on. I wanted to understand: what made a book successful? What made a book a best seller? What did I enjoy and what did I hate to read? After this, my quest morphed into studying speakers, influencers and social media more broadly.

As I was reading/watching/analyzing, I gathered together the common threads running through all these books, and the people who made an impact on me. From what started as an exercise to understand the different genres, I began to weave new ideas and life goals for myself: the idea of the power of mindset, the importance of deep self-awareness, and a deeper understanding of self-love, positive thinking, generosity, abundance, and so much more.

I learned many ideas and practices that I could apply to myself, and I decided to make myself a case study of many of these ideas.

I didn't talk about it. I just did it. I wanted to test the effect of these ideas in my own life to see if they helped me create a good life and a better world. I wanted to see if they actually delivered on their promise. However, to really succeed, I had to fully sink into it, I couldn't just do it on the surface. You might say I surrendered to these ideas because it was the only way to really know if they were true. No pessimism, doubt or judgment allowed. Just sink into it, Andrea! So, I did.

This collection of writing is drawn from my 30-year case study on what worked in the real, day-to-day life of a young woman growing into a corporate creature who became an entrepreneur and then a speaker, trainer, and author, as well as a traveler, wife, mother, and friend. It's a story of personal growth, but it's also a story of resilience and a deepening of empathy and compassion towards all—even those I don't like. Spoiler alert: if you want to transform your life, it starts deep inside, and it requires long-term commitment, no matter what.

I'm sharing these insights from an understanding that for many of us, committing to self-growth is very challenging indeed. Some of us start, grow, and then pause for a breather because it's intense. Or we find it too hard to keep going because we're clashing with people in our life who are at odds with the bigger, fresher version of ourselves we're becoming. It's not an easy process to commit to and it's definitely OK to say *enough for now*, because change is not easy and shouldn't be rushed. I absolutely respect that.

Personally, I go through periods of amazing growth and then I stall, sometimes going into a downward spiral or funk for a while. What I've learned is that these moments, too, are part of the journey to growth.

For 30 years, no matter how good or bad life got, I committed to holding these wisdoms true. It wasn't easy to keep believing, especially when things weren't going well. While there were days, weeks, and even months where I felt my anchor come lose, I always returned to these ideas. This was because I felt better, more at peace, and more in love with life—all of it, even when times were bad!

This is why I'm sharing these principles with you. They got me through tough financial times—really tough, like knocked-down-on-our-knees tough. They got me through the adjustment to parenthood. The stress of jobs lost. The challenges of a child needing special care and the pressure that creates on a marriage. A career that no longer lifted me. The pressure of creating a new life and career in new countries, time and time again. In other words, they got me through the tough stretches that life can dish out, and I'm confident they'll do the same for you.

I talk a lot about my husband, Steve Johnson, in this book. He's been on this journey with me for more than half of the case study I'm discussing. Since I was well on my way when we met, it meant he had to accept the ride, too. That was part of loving me, right?

Steve has been an absolute legend in so many ways. When we met, and even today, I share ideas and ways of life or thinking that are not natural to how he sees the world. I've always appreciated how Steve challenges me when he doesn't agree (which helps me challenge my own thinking) and we've had to talk through many ideas, adapting and refining as we went to ensure we were always together. And yes, by sticking together, it might mean it takes longer to grow, but it's worth it if we are committed to going forward, together.

If you read this and are inspired to follow these ideas or indeed find your own path to contentment, I definitely recommend bringing your loved ones or circle of friends with you. It will make it much easier to succeed, because when you are not in alignment with those closest to you, you can risk losing friendships or stalling your personal growth, because evolving as a person can result in clashing with those closest to you. Avoid that if you can. Go together.

Back to Steve. A really important contribution he has always made is giving me the full space to be me. He never tried to change who I was or how I wanted to grow. He never tried to stop me doing the work I felt was important, either—even when there was no financial gain attached. More importantly, because he's so good at what he does (which is very different to my work), he gave me the space to live my life and grow my business how I wanted to—which gave me real confidence and space to know if these ideas are actually workable. I knew I could never surrender to these ideas completely and test them fully if I was overwhelmed with day-to-day pressure as well. So, thank you so much, my love, for this gift of time and headspace. You gave me the opportunity to really test, so I could know if these ideas were really true. This is a gift of unimaginable value. Thank you for everything you do—for me and our boys.

Dear reader, while you may not get the same space as Steve gave me, hopefully my ability to fully experiment proves the results enough, because if you can embed many of these ideas deep in your psyche, it will make your life better, more enjoyable and, yes, even more successful. This is about a deep and foundational change, which will leave you lighter, more in love with the world, and more in love with life.

HOW TO USE THIS BOOK

Given that these wisdoms function as my philosophy for a good life, it's natural that they are interconnected. Whenever you see a **#hashtag**, you're looking at a reference to another related wisdom in this book. One way to navigate the book is by following the hashtags as links to connected wisdoms. Another is to read straight through, or you can even pick a wisdom by asking yourself a question, then opening this book at random.

As you make your way through these pages, you might encounter bits of wisdom that you've uncovered and conquered already—awesome! Celebrate!

You might find some of these ideas too far out for you; maybe you just don't relate to or resonate with them, and that's cool, too.

I've learned that sometimes I'm not ready for a certain idea, but just a few years on, I'll interpret the same words or ideas in a completely different way. We are always growing and evolving.

We are all unique and different, too. If everyone loved everything I've written here, then I wouldn't be saying anything you haven't heard before. So yes, you may find a few of your buttons (lovingly) pushed.

And if some of these ideas even make you angry, this is also normal. Anytime something makes me angry, I look at it as an opportunity and I dig into why I am angry. What is it that made me feel so strongly? Ask yourself this question, for when you answer it honestly you are your own best teacher. Anger is part of life, something we need to understand and embrace more deeply, as we'll discuss in these wisdoms.

And finally, I don't pretend to have all of the answers. This book is simply my perspective, which I hope contributes to making the world a better place. And I hope that at least one of these wisdoms turns out to be exactly what you need to read right now.

WHO THIS BOOK IS NOT FOR

This book is not for someone facing extreme poverty or famine. According to the World Bank, the impact of COVID-19 will push 200 million people into extreme poverty,[2] and the World Food Program claims 30 million people face imminent famine.[3] Humanity's growing inequality is something that we must start addressing. All of us.

I'm also not writing for those in the midst of war zones or refugee camps or for those drowning in the world's oceans while escaping atrocities or climate disasters.

And I'm not necessarily writing this for those who've retained the ancient wisdoms, though everyone is welcome to dip in and see what resonates. The Aboriginals and other indigenous peoples the world over, the elders, the wise—they already know and live these truths or are fighting to bring them back to the center of their communities.

It's also not for people who need professional help to deal with mental health issues or crippling addictions. It's not for people living in desperation, who are incapable of breaking free, while the societies we've built continue to keep a noose around their necks. No, they do not need these words, but we do.

Because if we can hear them, if we can deeply embrace the wisdoms shared here, which ultimately come from sages across the arc of history, we can elevate ourselves to create a world that puts dignity at the heart of all societies everywhere on earth. We can raise our consciousness and start to see that if we care for the least of us, everyone benefits. That is my goal. But it begins with us.

ARE YOU ONE OF THE LUCKY ONES?

If you are, this book is for you. Those of us who have shelter, a roof over our head to protect us from the weather, and a comfortable one at that. With reliable energy sources we can harness to create an environment that's appropriate to where we live and that allows us to do the things we need to do.

---

2   https://www.worldbank.org/en/news/press-release/2020/10/07/covid-19-to-add-as-many-as-150-million-extreme-poor-by-2021
3   https://www.wfp.org/news/un-food-agencies-warn-rising-levels-acute-hunger-potential-risk-famine-four-hotspots

It's for those who know there will be food on the table two to three times a day. Those whose children have access to a good education, to sports and physical development, to the kind of technology that can enhance their educations. It's for those who have the things they need— like fridges to store food, for example. Up to 80% of the world's population do not have a fridge!

If we can afford to drive a car or fly on a plane, we are the lucky ones. Life is very good in the comfort zone, and it's easy to take things for granted. However, while growing inequality has been an issue for decades, the pandemic has been a wake-up call.

We're waking up to the fact that though we have all the stuff in the world, and so much knowledge about how to live, what truly matters is human connection. We've been building a world where we've never felt more disconnected or been more unhappy. We've also never been more divided. Our things and our knowledge are not serving us the way we thought they would. The path we've been on is the wrong one and the start of the '20s shook us all wide awake.

We're waking up to the fact that we have a massive opportunity to change our course and that if we can become genuinely kinder, more compassionate, more open, more self-aware and (constructively) self-critical, we can change the direction of the world.

Together, we really *can* move mountains and make real change for good.

What we are not considering deeply enough is that this change starts *within* each of us. And it begins with moving away from fear, anger, hatred and the negative emotions that create the division that's been rolling around our world for too long.

If enough of us can step up to the challenge of our times, we can reach the tipping point to real change, which will see us understanding the need for balance with all life on earth. This can happen rapidly with enough of us in the director's seat.

When we achieve this, we can help everybody rise—especially our fellow-travelers who are less comfortable, less fortunate. This is our challenge and our collective responsibility, and I truly believe we can do it!

Truly, this book is for those who are lucky enough to be comfortable, even if life is not perfect, because you can, with this book in your hands and a deep commitment to be the most beautiful version of yourself, make a better life and a better world—for yourself, your community, and all humanity.

Thank you for choosing to read my book. I am truly humbled you want to spend this time with me.

ANDREA T EDWARDS

SETTING THE SCENE

THIS BOOK COVERS THOUGHTS AND IDEAS I've pondered over the years, from managing emotions and being at peace with yourself to love, work, life skills, owning your voice, the environment, and so much more.

As I was compiling it, one of the challenges was how to pull it together. I struggled with this until my dear friend John Vincent Gordon said, "Give it rhythm!" Well, this appealed to my musical and composing background. While I would have loved it to be the rhythm of my favorite symphony, Stravinsky's *Rite of Spring*, instead it has become more of a waltz. A waltz is definitely more consistent rhythmically than Stravinsky.

I wrote each wisdom to be capable of standing alone. I didn't want to clump similar topics together, as each piece feeds into a bigger overall picture. I wanted this to matter more.

So, I hope you feel its rhythm.

I have broadly categorized the wisdoms into seven kinds:

1. **Self-awareness**

2. **Self-empowerment**

3. **Empower others**

4. **External influence**

5. **Social leadership**

6. **Career thoughts**

7. **Climate courage**

Each category may have different meaning or importance for you at this moment, based on where you are in your life today.

NOT EVERYTHING IS FOR EVERYONE

Through the book, I've added questions or mini projects to certain wisdoms for those of you keen to dig deeper into an idea. I've set these "home-play" questions or activities in grey outlined text boxes.

For people whose minds don't work like this, I encourage you to keep moving and skip the mini projects. Don't get annoyed by them, because they're not for you, but rather for the people who love to engage this way.

Answer the questions or commit to the projects if that is your style, or just read the wisdoms and see what you take away from them, skipping past the activity pages if that's your preference. There is never one way to please everyone and I'm doing my best to create this information for as many people as possible, while understanding you can't win them all!

Anyhoo, let the journey begin!

Scan the QR code below and you download a printable version of the workbook. No email address required.

andreatedwards.com

#1

GET OUT OF YOUR LIFE!

SELF-EMPOWERMENT

MY OWN PERSONAL-GROWTH case study started in 1992 in Egypt. I was 22, blonde, and an army musician. It was the first country I landed in outside my home country of Australia, and an incredible experience of personal growth and awakening. This is where everything I've written in this book began, which is why I've chosen to start telling my story here.

It was my first real opportunity to face my thoughts, as well as deal with the loneliness, the dangers, the unknowns of travel, and the discomfort too—yes, all of it.

The glory of traveling this beautiful world has been my greatest privilege, not to mention top-of-the-pops in regard to what I've learned about living the best possible life.

When we explore the world, it's not only about confronting external differences—sometimes on such an epic scale it scares the life out of us—it's the personal and internal deep changes that matter even more. Even if we start off pretty happy with ourselves, travel changes us profoundly and deeply, for the better.

Now, it's important to recognize that we don't all need the same experiences to grow. Not everyone was born with an insatiable desire to explore the world. Many people find the space for silence, thought, and growth in their home landscape. This is really about getting out of your day-to-day way of seeing things, in whatever way that makes sense to you. We are all different and must honor ourselves rather than feeling an obligation to do something everyone says we must do to be whole.

For me it was definitely travel, and my time in the Middle East was the beginning of a love affair with otherness that changed everything about who I was.

This was my first journey, and I haven't stopped since. I've spent half my life away, exploring our glorious world. I'm completely addicted to it and I never feel more alive than when I'm in a new, unknown place.

Many developing countries can be uncomfortable to travel in, especially for basic things—like access to suitable toilets. But it's important to see beyond this to the raw beauty and humanity operating at a different level to what we've always known in our comfortable lives. There is something primal in these experiences, and I couldn't help but get drawn in when I began traveling.

It also makes it really hard to go home, because being comfortable loses its appeal. That's the downside of this experience: disconnection from your roots. It's worth it, though.

Most of my adventures in the early days were solo, and this gave me weeks and months of silence to confront my own thoughts. When you meditate or work with a spiritual teacher, the number one thing they recommend is shutting the external noise down, so you can face yourself. This process can be frightening, intense, and lonely. It's also very liberating, which is why I did it and did it again and again.

There was a lot of stuff in my mind that I came to understand wasn't mine at all, programming I'd undergone that left me misaligned to who I wanted to be. I knew I needed to face these things in order to become who I wanted to be, and that I could only do this work through the kind of transformative silence I found in travel.

Those solo months on the road saw me pulling down tendrils of my own thoughts, ideas, and opinions, and gave me the chance to look at them and ask myself, is this my idea? Do I want to continue owning it or does it need to get tossed out?

So many ideas went to the scrap heap. The religious education I had all through school got broken down, jumbled around, and mostly rejected. It wasn't all bad, but there were many ideas I did not buy into, now that I had the opportunity to question them.

There was family stuff, too; this time of reflection helped me understand that everyone was just trying their best in their own unique way.

My parents' divorce and the anger I held onto for years afterwards: also sent to the scrap heap.

I also really started to understand the gift of the experiences of my childhood. Every part of my childhood experience shaped who I am, and I finally appreciated that I should be grateful for it all—the good, the bad, the ugly—because without all that, I wouldn't be me.

I reflected on politics, business, the world—asking myself which were my opinions and which were the opinions of others. Which ones should I keep, which ones should I reject? It was the ultimate detox for my brain and heart.

And all the way through this painful and lonely process—which does not seem to stop once you start, by the way—I discovered me and, in that discovery, I opened myself up to new possibilities, new ideas, and other ways to look at things. I even started to like different sorts of music! Yes, even my music tastes were more adventurous after I began my journey of self-discovery.

I went from black and white in my thinking to seeing everything in many layers of gray. I learned to listen to new ideas and questioned them from every angle. I took nothing as truth, and today I tell my boys that there is no single truth. There are only ideas, and you've got to discover your truth and then be ready to change your mind again and again.

Nobody on this planet knows it all. I've discovered that if you try to see the world from other people's viewpoints as well as your own, it changes the game.

It wasn't just the silence that helped me, it was the experiences I was having every day too. I witnessed other people's lives, lived differently, but still, so much beauty everywhere. I saw alternative lifestyles I would have shunned before and realized how narrow my thinking was. As long as you're smiling and doing no harm, enjoy!

Those long months of silence and incredible experiences, often digging deep into ancient history (a true passion), gave me the opportunity to gain so much more clarity. And it's a path I continue to travel, because I never stop learning if I stay open.

That ability to step away from everything I'd ever known, and not only confront differences externally, but to face up to the silence and the thoughts in my head—such a gift. I am forever grateful I took myself out there and in return, discovered a better version of myself, a less judgmental, more open, more forgiving version.

When you travel, you constantly see the kindness of strangers. And I saw the kindness in humanity everywhere, from fellow travelers helping me out when I got in a bind to the incredible kindness of locals every place I visited. This vision of humanity is addictive.

I'll always remember the Egyptian lady in Cairo who gently showed me how to cross one of their crazy roads when I first arrived. I'm now a master road crosser anywhere. Or a chemist in Cairo, who took me into his shop, gave me water, and took care of me because I'd lost my way in this maze of a city, and he didn't think it was a safe place for a young woman to be walking alone.

Or another stranger in Shanghai in 1995, who took me to some of the best off-the-beaten-track places to visit just to show me her amazing, beloved city.

Or the gorgeous hearing- and speaking-impaired man in Calcutta who sold me toilet paper and kept an eye out for me, along with a hunchbacked man with a huge smile, who got me taxis any time I needed them. These two men were everything to me as I fell in love with that city.

And the small, curious children everywhere, fascinated by this person who looked different to anything they'd known before. Did that interaction with me have an impact on them, too? It certainly changed me.

Or the people learning to speak English in China, back in the mid-'90s, chewing loudly in my ear and spitting tea on the floor, as we all cramped in together on a horrible train ride for hours and hours and hours. I'll never forget the lady who lost her shoe down the toilet on that trip. The spit from the tea was swishing back and forth on the floor by the end of this journey. You certainly didn't want to be without shoes.

Or the boy in Mexico, who wanted to have his way with me, in his little hut nearby, and somehow, his eyeballs pulsed when he looked at me. I didn't know eyeballs could pulse until that point.

So many people, from all walks of life, all faiths, all cultures—just human beings at their best, helping, guiding, showing and expecting nothing in return (except maybe the boy in Mexico—bless him). I always met so many more amazing people than I did people wanting to do me harm. I saw laughter everywhere.

When you travel, you have to learn to trust others when you are out there, facing the world alone. You learn to become vulnerable and to accept your own vulnerability, because you must.

Equally, you learn to pay attention to your intuition and trust yourself when you believe someone is a threat. My intuition is very, very good, and I could spot and feel danger a mile away.

I learned to handle myself on many levels. On that first trip to Egypt, Jordan, and Israel as a 22-year-old blonde woman, I was almost raped several times. I was mauled, groped, and stared at relentlessly. Because I'm a fighter, I punched a number of men during that time. I was still in the army after all, so they didn't scare me. Let's just say, no one was grabbing me and getting away with it! Guatemala City, Tegucigalpa in Honduras and Managua in Nicaragua—three of the most dangerous cities in Central America apparently—and yet I never had a moment of fear as I wandered the streets alone at night. I had to. I was by myself and I needed to eat. As a woman, solo travel teaches you that you don't need a man looking after you.[4]

Travel's ultimate gift is strength in yourself. When you travel alone, you learn to fight and stand up for yourself. You learn how to get around with barely any language at all. You learn how to cope, and you learn how to thrive as you get fully connected with yourself.

I personally believe the only thing that matters in life is doing the work to get to the best version of ourselves. Everything else is just a distraction from that. The journey is different for all of us, and the destination too, but if we can find our path without to that joy within—wow, that's a life worth living. Travel was the beginning of my quest for deep self-awareness, and everything you'll read within these pages is an extension of that journey.

If travel isn't your thing, there are other ways to make sure you face yourself from outside your life. Comfort is a beautiful thing, but it is never where personal growth lies. You've got to get a whole lot of uncomfortable to achieve that.

Globally, we're all in a lesson in discomfort because of this pandemic. It's a wonderful opportunity to prioritize working out how to take the time and space to get out of your life, to hear the silence inside and to work out what is really you. I hope we all take advantage of this powerful and

---

4   Which isn't to say that it isn't awesome to be taken care of by someone you love. Travel taught me all of the above, but my husband, Steve, taught me another layer of true vulnerability. Thank you, my love. It's so nice to share the journey with you and to be loved by you xxx.

yet uncomfortable time for growth. There are life lessons everywhere, if we choose to see them.

"Travel isn't always pretty. It isn't always comfortable. Sometimes it hurts, it even breaks your heart. But that's okay. The journey changes you; it should change you. It leaves marks on your memory, on your consciousness, on your heart, and on your body. You take something with you. Hopefully, you leave something good behind."

—Anthony Bourdain, *No Reservations: Around the World on an Empty Stomach*

#2

OPEN YOUR MIND UP

SELF-AWARENESS

STEPPING BACK IN TIME: the young person I was at 17, when I left my family home and went out into the world, had a very closed mind. I was completely closed off to so many ideas—partly owing to my Catholic upbringing. Friends from that time are surprised by how different I am today.

Because today, in terms of what I'll consider with an open mind, well—absolutely nothing is off limits. Nothing.

It started with my travel, where I met people so different to me, and whose experiences didn't resemble mine at all. I'm grateful for the many different ways these people opened my eyes.

I also started to learn that when I react negatively to a behavior or idea, it's time for me to dig into it. This means digging within myself and asking: Why do I oppose it? Is there any upside to this idea? Is this black and white, or is there room for gray? What do people who agree with this idea think? What am I missing?

Of course, this internal archaeological dig doesn't mean I'll accept the idea or behavior that made me conduct the search in the first place. But going through this process helps me view everything from multiple angles, so I can be sure of my position on the idea or behavior I'm looking into, and usually strongly opposed to.

I am not as black and white in my thinking as I was, because when you open your mind, you definitely see that the world is grey. Or, even better, it's technicolor!

Opening my mind helped me move away from judgment of others, and it opened me up to wide and beautiful acceptance. I realized that no one on this planet is right or wrong. We are all just people—with our own experiences, pain, stories, and desires—and when we see this, our compassion for each other deepens. We can focus more on the bigger challenges that need to be addressed. This is the kind of thinking we need in order to evolve, as a collective, to a higher level of consciousness.

CHECKING YOUR MINDSET

It's hard to recognize that you have a closed mindset. It's something you hold onto and justify tightly, but here are some ways to open your mind, if you have enough courage to try:

1. Consider the strength of your feelings on issues that matter to you. Dig deep. Find the original source of that opinion. Is it yours, or was it given to you by your family, community, media or elsewhere? If you know someone who is involved in an issue you are against, ask them to join you for a tea or coffee. Talk to them. Be open to understanding their point of view. See if you want to revise your strong feelings. If you don't, that's ok. At least you dug into the opinions you carry. Many simply don't.

2. Look around and consider the diversity of the community you are part of. If everyone looks like you, make the effort to find people who don't—people of a different skin color, race, religion, way of life, or sexuality. Have a cup of tea or coffee with them, too.

3. Listen to other people's points of view with complete openness. At the beginning it might be hard, because you might find some ideas revolting or repulsive, but try to listen and see if you can accept them a little more.

4. Travel to foreign places and immerse yourself. Some places you visit may challenge your sensibilities, but even when the going is rough, you will start to see the beauty underneath—the genuine smiles of

the people you meet. Beauty is everywhere when you go with an open heart.

5. Read and watch opposing views. If you are only open to one channel of communication or one way of thought, widen it a little. It doesn't mean you need to agree with what you hear, but if we work harder to hear and see from each other's points of view, we have an opportunity to reduce the divide between humanity. We will never all be in agreement, but we can be less divided.

NEVER BE ASHAMED OF THE MUSIC YOU LOVE

SELF-EMPOWERMENT

IF YOU WERE STRANDED ON AN ISLAND, what five songs would you select to keep you company?

1. _____

2. _____

3. _____

4. _____

5. _____

And now, imagine living in a society that bans music. You could be marked for death just for playing music! Imagine a society that declares music cannot be a core part of individual and collective joy and liberation. There are societies like that in the world to this day. Shocking, right?

Oh, and there are musical snobs too—who are, in my experience, nearly as bad.

The music we love is a powerful expression of individuality.

Personally, I will *never apologize for rocking out to ABBA.*

My best childhood friend Emma was Frida, and I was Agnetha. We used to sing and dance our hearts out to "Dancing Queen" on my parents' front porch in the 1970s. And yes, of course we were singing into hairbrushes!

More than a decade later, when we were both 24, Emma died in a motorcycle accident. I still miss that crazy, wonderful lady. And to this day, "Dancing Queen" takes me right back to that front porch at 66 Vermont Street, Wodonga.

Music is inextricably associated with so many important moments of our lives—our beautiful memories. It's an integral part of who we are.

And girls reading this, as you grow into your womanhood, don't let the men in your life tell you what's good and what's bad in terms of the music *you* like. You do you, OK?

Whatever you listen to and whatever importance it has in your life, stand your ground. Never be ashamed of the music you love.

Likewise, respect other people's musical passions. Don't mock someone for their taste in music. It has an intimate and powerful meaning to them in ways that are theirs and theirs only. None of us have the right to judge the musical loves of another.

DO YOU HAVE VOICES IN YOUR HEAD?

SELF-AWARENESS

I HAVE VOICES IN MY HEAD. It's the only way I can explain it. Can you relate? Or perhaps you just think that's for crazy people? But we need to be honest with ourselves. Don't you sometimes feel like you are speaking to yourself from several different positions that are so at odds with each other, they could almost be voices?

I've been trying to understand these voices for more than two decades. As I was completing this book, I was introduced to the work of Shirzad Chamine, the author of *Positive Intelligence*. He calls the voices saboteurs. They come from a form of self-protection we develop in childhood. Up to 75% of us have these negative saboteurs, and in order to live to our fullest potential, we must get them under control.

According to Chamine, the saboteur that is universal is the Judge. It appears in three ways: judging self, judging others, and judging circumstances.

I got judging others and circumstances under control decades ago, but the judging self—well, that has definitely been my nemesis. I am truly horrible to myself.

But I recognized this voice and determined it was not my friend about a decade ago, and in my experience, the most important part of getting these negative, judgmental inner voices under control is identifying them for what they are: saboteurs that make our lives a little bit or a lot worse.

Here's something really interesting. Chamine's research confirms my own informal survey—I've basically asked everyone I've ever met—up to

16

25% of people do not experience these voices at all, which means they may find it hard to believe they even exist. However, for those of us who do have them, the challenge we face is that the negative voice(s) are typically in control, and this can be devastating.

Recognizing these voices or saboteurs and acknowledging the damage to you and to your potential is the first step, and then the next challenge is to find the internal reserve of strength to overcome them. Because once you get them under control, life gets a whole lot better.

I know this because I was able to overcome them.

HERE IS HOW I DID IT.

Step 1: Watch what's going on in your mind. For example, if you notice that you have constant negative chatter in your mind bringing you down, telling you *you're hopeless, you're not good enough, you can't do this, you can't do that, you're too ugly, too fat, too useless . . .* you've already taken the first step. You've identified that voice and now you need to separate it from the others. A voice that brings you down and limits you has no right to inhabit your consciousness.

Getting an awareness of the voice is half the battle. Notice how you let it be the boss, and how unkind it is to you. Notice how you believe it. It's now time to look at it as something separate, another consciousness.

Alternatively, the voice can be negative towards others, a voice of judgment or superiority. If you regularly have un-charming, judgmental thoughts about others' inadequacies, it also diminishes you and closes you off to a richer and more beautiful life. And of course, it can also be circumstances. Nothing is ever good enough. You have now succeeded, so it's time to set a new goal and a new goal and a new goal, meaning you're never happy or content. You don't celebrate the unfolding of life, because you are stuck in achievement mode.

Can you see this voice? Yes? Well. . . .

Step 2: Shut it down. My voice was very negative to me and I've learned I must tell it to go away and keep telling it to go until it's gone.

For me personally, I told it to get lost in a very firm voice. I actually said, "F@*# off!" every time it showed up. I'm not trying to be offensive, but after all it's done to me, that nasty voice really needs strong language. Find your own words to tell it to rack off!

This is not easy. It's a cunning, cruel little voice and it's a master gaslighter.[5] It desperately wants to stay. When you close it down, you'll feel its presence lurking in the back of your mind, always seeking to find a way back in. It's very good at it too, and it's truly a horrible piece of work.

If you are full of judgment towards self, others or experiences, shut this voice down. It is not worthy of your attention.

Step 3: Stay on top of it. I'm serious about this part—it can reappear powerfully. It has for me, and boy is it believable when it does. You should hear what it was telling me when I was writing this book! I almost believed it. This voice works really hard to reconvince me of my own worthlessness. If that voice reappears for you, as it may well, identify it again, tell it to go away in strong language, ignore it, and shut it back in its box immediately! Rinse and repeat.

FOLLOW UP ON THAT VOICE

Step 1: Watch what's going on in your head. Identify and separate the negative voice(s).

Step 2: Shut it down. Be firm. Use strong language.

Step 3: Stay on top of it. It's always trying to come back!

Do you have this negative voice? (circle what is true for you)

Yes   No

---

5   Gaslighting is a psychological term long used to describe someone who undermines another person's reality by denying facts, the environment around them, or their feelings. It's manipulation designed to change another person's thinking, their emotions, and who they fundamentally are.

　　For example, if a wife tells her husband that he is shirking childcare responsibilities and he is, and he responds by suggesting that *she* is the problem or refusing to acknowledge that it's even happening, he is gaslighting her. Politicians gaslight too.

What does your voice say to you? Close your eyes and spend time in silence. Ask yourself, what is my negative voice? Work hard to identify it. This can be tricky. The voice may be negative towards self, or it can be negative towards others or circumstances. All three make life worse. Write down what you know.

If not, do you know someone who struggles with it? (circle what is true for you)

Yes   No

If you answered yes, copy this chapter and send it to them (author's permission granted).

Now write what you'll say to that voice every time it appears. *I urge strong language, which can be *very* empowering when used for your own greater good!*

Check in 30 days later. Have you succeeded in identifying that negative voice? Have you shut it down? Remember, if it doesn't serve you, if it makes your life worse (through hatred of self or hatred of others), then break free of it.

Mark your calendar with a monthly check-in for the next 12 months. It will keep trying to come back. It's the very definition of pernicious. DO NOT believe it. It's wrong. If you have an internal voice that makes you feel less or unworthy, it is NEVER right. Shut it down.

Also do check out **PositiveIntelligence.com**. I have been really impressed with what I've seen of the work Shirzad Chamine is doing. His work will help you overcome your personal struggles, which are almost definitely linked to your saboteurs.

#5

WORRY IS A WASTE OF TIME

SELF-AWARENESS

WORRY IS DEBILITATING. It ages you. Faces get hard, lines get deeper, and hair goes gray faster. Worry is a form of stress. It acts like inflammation in our bodies and can lead to a multitude of health problems.

Mostly we worry about the future. Maybe we worry about retirement and that nest egg—or lack of it. Or we worry about job or income uncertainty. If you're like me, you worry about the climate crisis and the general state of the world.

In his self-help book *How to Stop Worrying and Start Living*, Dale Carnegie said that 90% of the things we worry about never come to pass. Personally, I noticed that if I pay deep attention and actually look at what happens next, it's more like 99% of the time that the thing I spent so much time worrying about does not come to pass. This means the only real effect of worry is that it stops us moving forward.

Worry delivers no results; it puts in motion no change. Worry delivers no benefit, and in fact does nothing but leave us in a self-manufactured place of fear. That being said, it's a natural human tendency.

As I've gotten older, and with my case study on myself in full swing, worry was one of the first things I let go. I worry about the big things, like the climate crisis, but the day-to-day worries do not burden me. I let them go.

I discovered that the best thing I can do is put all that energy spent on worry into focusing on changing the situation. Worry won't change the situation—but actions will. Practically speaking, as we move into a decade of heightened uncertainty, our worry levels will tend to increase. Yet worrying won't solve the challenges we face.

Try this experiment. Take a holiday from worry for a month. Focus on action or on simply feeling excited about the future you want to create for yourself. *Excitement is a powerful form of intention, and intention becomes action quite naturally.*

Remember, worry is fear, and fear is like fire. If you take away its oxygen, it naturally dies down. In the absence of worry, you can address those things causing you worry in a more clear-headed and energetic way.

Doing the work to eradicate worry from your consciousness will put you into action-taking mode. Being active makes you feel more in control, which means you'll naturally worry less. It's the opposite of a vicious circle, and it's exactly what we all need to face the future.

Some of my dearest friends have been huge worriers. It has never changed anything, staying in this space. However, as I've witnessed, it's a mind habit that is hard to break. Never ever give up trying to break the worry habit. It is the greatest freedom you will ever give to yourself, and it will move you into a state of mind where you can take action.

YOUR HOME-PLAY

Now take a holiday from worry. Put any and all fears on the shelf for 30 days and let yourself not worry about a thing. If the worry pops up, put it aside and tell it "Later, mate!" Tell yourself you'll think about it once the 30 days are up, but not before.

If 30 days feels too long, begin with a day. Then build up to a week. Then a month.

Write down the top 10 things that you are worried about right now:

1.

2.

3.

4.

5.

6.

7.

8.

9.

10.

At the end of 30 days, you can go back to those worries if you need too. But chances are, you'll find that many of the things you've been really worried about have somehow become less worrisome after being starved of all the oxygen you were giving them.

After your holiday from worrying, write your results here.

How did you do? Were you able to stop worrying? Cross-check your top 10 list of worries.

Did any worries disappear for good or diminish considerably?

Have you changed your thinking on something that was consuming you before your holiday?

#6

LET PEOPLE BE DICKS SOMETIMES

EXTERNAL INFLUENCE

EVERY ONE OF US has been a dick at some point or another. Dickishness is when we act out of character, when we're a bit crabbier or a touch more self-centered, or even when we do or say hurtful things to get a rise. In children, that's negative attention seeking. You could say it's the same thing in adults. It often happens because of stress, anxiety, fear, or other negative emotions. Sometimes we're a dick for a week or a month or even longer, if we're going through a tough patch!

Right now, more people are being more dickish than usual. Being a dick can be a sign of deep fears and insecurities. Suicide rates are rising in every country, in every culture. People today are feeling lost, fearful, misunderstood, under-valued, and vulnerable. They may have eco-anxiety, which leaves them worried about the future or their children's future. Adding to the confusion and uncertainty are the cesspool of politics, misinformation, and Fake News. Plus we've got that pandemic on our hands, too! Jobs lost, no money coming in, no food on the table.

There's a lot going on. All of these issues can bring out the worst in people, so our role is to bring out the best in them.

Now, if someone is a dick all the time, of course it's hard to have them in your life. But if someone is being a dick and it's out of character, ask them what's going on.

Approach them with empathy and non-confrontational intentions, and you'll likely find they are in pain or confused or scared. Sometimes all three. Most often people aren't even aware what's wrong until you actually draw it out of them. Ask if they are all right. Ask if they need help. Give them the space to answer—in their own way, in their own time. Probe gently to see if you can help them identify the cause of their angst.

When they realize that they have, in fact, been feeling out of sorts, they might also realize they've been behaving like a dick—and stop. However, best not to make it your job to point that out to them.

Let's give each other the benefit of the doubt. This is how we make room for grace to enter the equation. When we don't give the benefit of the doubt, we lock people into being their worst selves, even if it was just momentary. In that moment, we don't allow each other to grow and evolve from whatever pain is causing us to act out. It's a lose-lose for everyone involved.

Let's not turn our backs and leave momentarily dickish people in that space! Changing the world for the better starts with the simple step of helping people emerge from a tough moment to become their best selves.

GIVE THEM SOME LOVE

List out uncharacteristic dickish behavior you've seen in people in your community lately and make an appointment to speak (gently) with those people.

What dickish behavior—temporary or perhaps even sustained—do you recognize in yourself?

#7

EMBRACE SOCIAL MEDIA, WE NEED YOU!

SOCIAL LEADERSHIP

LET'S TALK ABOUT SOCIAL MEDIA as a critical tool for connection, engagement and, yes—changing the world.

If you've already had the opportunity to watch it, you'll probably agree that *The Social Dilemma on Netflix* is a very important film. One of the key issues it raises is the potential for utopia or dystopia—both are present right now in our society and we're in a battle for the winner. To me, this was the really important part of this film's argument. It's the bit we can focus on.

However, the film missed a really important message: the human aspect of social media, and the problems with the societies we've built.

Throughout history we've blamed our bad behavior on our tools. In this case, we blame social media. It has a huge influence, there's no denying it. And it can be used to damage, destroy, and diminish. But does it control us?

And more importantly, what do we do about it? Is technology going to solve the problem? I don't think so. I don't think government legislation is the solution, either. Old, predominantly white men who are not fully literate on social media are not the right ones to understand the issue, let alone sort it out. How can they understand the way someone who was born in a digital world uses it? They just can't.

Learning how to think for myself has been my key to protecting myself against control and manipulation by others, including social media algorithms. In teaching young people to think, not conform, our education systems have a huge role to play in helping society better navigate social media.

Yes, the use of social media comes with responsibility and requires us to hone our critical thinking skills, because the upside of social media is magnificent. This is where I've chosen to focus so much of my message professionally. It's why I insist the positives outweigh the negatives.

Each of us can access social media to connect with people around the world; it's not the preserve of the rich or the few.

Each of us, not just media owners, can amplify messages that are important to us. It is the first time in human history that information has been democratized to such an extent. While we haven't done a great job with that freedom yet, we must reflect on its important value to us and to society moving forward!

We must consider that if we get rid of these tools because of their negative potential, we may be throwing the baby out with the bathwater. Are we sacrificing something worth preserving? Our individual power has never been greater, our ability to have a say never more formidable—and that's so important if we want to create massive change.

However, the levels of toxicity on social media need to be addressed. What does this look like for those of us seeking positive change?

First, we must take personal responsibility for what happens on social media. Our silence lets negative voices dominate. It's like staying silent and letting a schoolyard bully do their thing. It is time for us to claim our platforms and raise our voices, demanding the future we want for ourselves and future generations. To speak up, loud and proud, each of us. Let's get out of the passenger seat and take the wheel.

Passivity does not cut it. It costs you your voice and your future. Don't like what you're seeing or hearing? Good, act. Don't sneer. To find and enact sustainable solutions to the problems facing us, we need participation greater than we've ever seen before.

FOUR RECOMMENDATIONS TO GET YOU FOCUSED AND ENGAGED

- Choose to participate. If you don't like the conversation taking place on social media, get involved and change it.

  The negative voices on social media—the trolls, the bots, and those seeking to divide us—have an outsized presence. Such voices would typically represent about 1–2% of the population in a geographic area (think about the size of this community in your town or city). But today, in the digital world, they have grouped together and their voice is organized and strong. They're in recruitment mode too, and they are good at it! Therefore, rather than turning away from this battle, show up and stand for something else. There are more of us than of them, but only if we act like it!

- Don't get into arguments with people on social media, just don't. There is zero point. You won't achieve anything, other than becoming angrier and more cynical. That is not good for you. It's not good for any of us.

  What do you do instead? Move past them! If you think someone is open to another point of view, great—have a conversation. But if they are really far down the rabbit hole, move on. Arguing, diminishing other people, or trying to make them look stupid isn't going to achieve the goal. Let them go. Focus on making a positive impact and connecting in a constructive way.

- *Do* share compelling, factual, useful information across your social media channels. This is how it works. The algorithms feed people the information they are interested in and it also shows them the information shared by people in their community.

  The top five categories of trust on social media are: family, friends, social media connections, bloggers, and colleagues. You are at least one of these to everyone in your community. Share compelling, well-researched, credible, peer-reviewed information, and you'll be ensuring that those trapped in the algorithm nightmare can get a different point of view shedding light on things for them.

- Support people doing good on social media. Amplify people who are sharing a compelling message that should be heard by a wider audience.

  All over social media, people get excited by the latest filter that distorts their look into something they're not, or the latest celebrity post featuring a new haircut, or an influencer sharing a meaningless experience that creates envy in their audience. Enough of the nonsense. Support real voices with real messages that are driving positive change.

What does support look like? Share good posts. Add your own comments. If you are up to it, write a post!

This image represents social media influence bubbles. You influence from within your bubble, and it overlaps into the other bubbles in your communities, and with more than three billion social media bubbles, our influence ripples out across the human digital landscape! There is so much power here. Use it!

Let's focus on what matters and get real. Move away from the nonsense.

We can get things back into alignment. We can use social media channels for their best purpose: to share and drive change.

Because, when you own your voice, you not only own your future, you help define our collective future.

That's on all of us. Step up!

#8

INTEGRITY AND VALUES

SELF-EMPOWERMENT

NTEGRITY IS A WORD that gets thrown around a lot in many different contexts. According to the *Cambridge Dictionary*, it is "the quality of being honest and having strong moral principles that you refuse to change."

Rather than trying to define it any further than that, I'll define the three qualities that stand out to me in someone who strikes me as living with integrity: they know who they are, they commit to their word, and they always speak the truth. Living with integrity means having deep clarity about your personal values. You have to be unwavering in your commitment to them.

Why is it so important to define and then live by your values? When you are anchored in your values, you're less likely to stumble, crossing the rough terrain of life. A person who is deeply connected to their values knows where they will not compromise. The people around them know and respect them as being a person of their word. Even when we disagree with someone, we can appreciate the alignment and commitment they have to their values. That's integrity.

One of life's gifts is that you get to pick *your* values. When you're sure what they are, they light a guiding path ahead for you. They make decisions simpler. Does it fit? Or not? How can whatever it is be adjusted so that it aligns with your values?

They'll lead you through whatever you do for the rest of your life. If you are empowered in them, you won't let anybody shift you away from them. Nobody can make a decision for you or get you to support something if it's against your values.

TIM HAMONS

Being deeply anchored in and committed to your values is how you'll get to be regarded as a person of integrity (or not) by the people around you. For example, here are four people and how I see their values:

Mother Theresa: faith, service, and love

Gandhi: non-violence and respect for others

Merkel: intellectual rigor and a woman of her word

Obama: sincerity and possibility

Which isn't to say that being recognized for having integrity is the point. Integrity is about living a life anchored in values—regardless of external influence, opinions, and accolades.

INTEGRITY IN ACTION

Who in your life, is someone you consider a person of deep integrity? What are the qualities they have that you respect?

Do you see yourself as a person of integrity?

Has life made you slip a bit or compromise on your values in some way? Can you determine what or who did that to you?

What are your foundational personal values? Identify them, work out what they are, define what's important. List them here.

#9

AIM PAST THE TOP OF THE HILL

SELF-EMPOWERMENT

THIS IS A WISDOM I LEARNED from my dad. As a young teenager, I really enjoyed racing bicycles with my dad. We did track racing in the summer and road racing in the winter. The community was great. I loved getting out on my bike anytime the weather allowed and adored the wind in my hair and the strength of my muscles in action. It's a brilliant sport for a young gal.

There was one road loop we used to train on outside Wodonga, Australia. It was just over 30 kilometers long and was a perfect length for afterschool training. On this loop there was one big hill, and it used to hurt like hell riding up that beast. It wasn't on the scale of the Tour de France, but it was steep enough for a teenager. It gave me a good muscle burn every time I rode over it, and it never got easy.

One day, after my dad beat me over that hill *again*, I was frustrated. I asked: "How do you always beat me over it? Why can't I win?"

"It's really simple, Annie," he replied. "You aim to get to the top of the hill. I aim to get *past* the top of the hill. This is the difference between winning and not winning."

I beat him over that hill every time after that. He didn't like it too much 😊.

In life, not many of us even aim for the top—most people quit before they get there. But it's not even about the top, it's about getting past the top.

This became a guiding metaphor in my life: aim past the top of the hill. That's where real glory resides.

REFLECTIONS

What is my metaphorical hill?

When have I given up? Even before I hit the top, let alone over the top of the hill?

What does aiming past the top of the hill look like for me? What could I achieve if I did this?

What three things am I going to do differently to focus on getting over the hill, not just to the top of it?

1.

2.

3.

#10

WATCH OUT FOR PROJECTION

SELF-AWARENESS

SELF-AWARENESS IS ABSOLUTELY KEY to happiness, yet it is not something we are typically taught to be good at. Recognizing the feelings or emotions we hold in our bodies and understanding why we experience them in the first place helps to let the negative ones go, and that can be life changing.

We have a tendency to project feelings onto other people, rather than reflecting on why we feel these emotions in the first place and trying to see where that challenge may reside in ourselves. When you can understand your own thought patterns, you'll see that the negative aspects of your relationships often have nothing to do with other people at all.

Here's an example of something I've come to recognize as others projecting their own struggle for self-awareness onto me. I was told recently that a certain group of women are intimidated by me. I have heard this all my professional life, and in the early days, it upset me a lot because I'm not *trying* to make anyone else feel small. I NEVER want to make anyone feel that way.

However, I also know my voice and presence are big. I'm out there on social media, sharing my views, my life, funny moments, tough moments, and more. One of the things I'm told people find intimidating is my confidence in my knowledge. The irony is that this is the only thing I'm ever truly confident about! I'm crazily curious and back it all up with deep research. I never stop reading and never stop looking at all the angles.

I really believe in the power of changing minds and inspiring curiosity by sharing knowledge. I'm committed to sharing a message of hope and change, as well as to do whatever I can to make the world a better place while I'm in it. I'm aware of my impact.

And yet the comments about how I'm intimidating still come in. What can I do? Backing down or changing who I am won't change other people's feelings of being intimidated. I can't do anything to change hearts and minds on this—and trust me, I've tried.

I can change how *I* feel toward other people, though. I can always be open to changing how I communicate too. Being self-aware to understand my impact while being true to myself is something I can always pay attention to. I don't stay fixed—or I try not to! This is how I've learned to address my self-awareness over the years.

For all of these situations, all I ask is, when you have negative feelings toward someone—anything from vague discomfort to outright rage—check in with yourself to see if what you're feeling falls under one of these reactions:

- Anger. Are you really angry with the person you are directing your ire towards, or frustrated about something this brings up in your own life? (**#Epiphanies on anger**, *see wisdom 26*[6])
- Hatred. Even when it feels justified, this close relative of anger is an ugly emotion to sit in your body. Can you step away and release it? Can you forgive? (**#Forgiveness is for you**, *wisdom 36*)
- Jealousy. Ask yourself. What can you change to stop feeling jealous? (**#Mind your jealousy**, *wisdom 15*) Because jealousy is a waste of time, a distraction from doing what you want to do. Often this is a perception of others having a leg up or a lucky break where opportunity appears to come easy to them. We never have all the story. Resenting someone for what they have situates you in a negative space that does not serve you. You can't grow with resentment or jealousy in your heart.
- Judgement. At its base this is a sense of superiority or thinking we have all the answers or an understanding of someone else's life. When

6   Remember, you can explore more with the cross-reference with a related wisdom.

we judge others, we are showing a deficit in our character. (**#From judgement to compassion**, *wisdom 12*)

No matter what emotions we feel and who or what we believe caused them, what's key to self-awareness is learning how to recognize them and understanding why we have them in the first place. The other person might be the problem, but we all need to work on recognizing when these feelings come from within us and not from external sources—in other words, understanding how we may be projecting when we see them as having external causes. Then, and only then, can we learn how to let negative emotions go. In my life experiment, I have found this level of self-awareness critical to well-being.

Because we are all connected, self-awareness extends beyond the boundaries of our own person. It also means being conscious that others are in pain. People in pain want to be seen—which isn't always pretty. There is always a lot of pain in the world, and right now is no different. We can bear witness, one human to another, with compassion and empathy.

Above all, let self-awareness begin with you. You deserve peace. Letting go is not easy, but *wanting* to be free from anger, jealousy, judgment, or hate is a really good place to start. When you really let the negative emotions go, you are giving a gift to yourself, not to those who have harmed you. As for them, they stop living rent-free in your head, a space they don't deserve.

When you act out of self-awareness, you add to the **#Ripple effect** *(wisdom 96)* . . .

And I know it's not always easy, yet it's important to **#Breath in love, breath out hate** *(wisdom 47)* . . .

And you need to know that **#Forgiveness is for you** *(wisdom 36)*.

#11

CONTROL YOUR OWN NARRATIVE

CAREER THOUGHTS

THIS IS A WISDOM INSPIRED by the late Princess Diana. While none of us can know the truth of her life for certain, this was my impression. As her separation was becoming a foregone conclusion, Diana realized she needed to get her narrative under control. If she didn't, she was at risk of being separated from her boys. She was mother to the heir to the British crown, after all.

Watching her grow from a shy young princess to a self-assured woman showed me what controlling your own narrative could achieve. Despite all the criticism she was subject to, defining herself as an adult under the public eye, she put herself out there to make an impact in areas that princesses don't traditionally talk about. She truly created foundational change in society. Who else was able to cross that chasm of fear towards AIDS patients at the time? Or landmines and children? It was remarkable. Princess Diana decided how she wanted to be perceived and treated, and she took control of her life. Bravo Princess Diana, and RIP.

I saw this closer to home too. You don't need to be a princess to take control of your own story. Another inspiring woman in my life was not famous. She showed me how it was done, up close and personal.

As a woman in the 1970s, working was really important to her and she did it no matter what. She wasn't worried what other people thought either. For a while, she had a stay-at-home husband—unheard of back then. She put herself out there, loved it, and yes, was also a feisty-pants feminist.

If you haven't already figured it out, I'm talking about my mum.

We didn't agree on a lot (and still don't), but in her own unique way, she was an amazing and really influential role model. She didn't tell me—she showed me I could get married and still keep something for myself, that I could be a wife and mother and make something of myself according to my dreams.

This is something that's defined me all my life. I've always done something. I've always been busy. I'm always working towards a goal. Some of it is personal, some of it is professional, but as the years go on, it's all coming together and feeling like a coherent story.

Controlling your own narrative is fundamentally about not getting lost in someone else's story—be it your husband, wife, friend, or anyone else. This is a path society tends to tell us to take. And then one day, finding ourselves alone, we don't know our own story because we haven't been the one telling it. We've been a supporting actor all along in another person's story.

Keep something for you. Support your partner's career but don't get lost in it. If supporting them means you can't work, focus on a passion, or work for a charity, focus on education, become an influencer, participate in the gig economy . . . just create something for you. *Your* story of *your* life.

It's a new era in the '20s. The old hard-and-fast rules are being debunked. Make your own rules, choose your own adventure, and most importantly, always be able to stand on your own two feet.

I am writing this for all of the people I've seen be abandoned by their partner and then forced to pick up the pieces of their life, often having to start from scratch. Keep something for yourself all along. Your story is too important to put into someone else's safekeeping.

Think of it as writing a happy ending into your narrative.

WRITE YOUR OWN STORY

Step 1: If your partner left today, are you in a position to move forward? Or would it cripple you financially?

Step 2: If it would cripple you, what commitments are you going to make to get something back for yourself? Think study, work, volunteering, gaining new skills, etc.

Step 3: What is the first commitment you're going to get cracking on?

Step 4: Are you telling yourself you're not good enough, not worthy, useless, more? Read **#Do you have voices in your head?** *(wisdom 4)* and get moving forward.

Notice the actions you take as you put this narrative into action.

Please, just don't leave yourself in a position to be stranded. It happens too often. Keep something for yourself, always.

#12

FROM JUDGMENT TO COMPASSION

SELF-AWARENESS

I GREW UP FEELING JUDGED BY OTHERS. Did you? Family are great for judgments, aren't they? I didn't like the feeling, and I don't think anyone does.

I also do not like to judge, because when I do, I leave no space for compassion. I'm not asking *how did this person get to this point? Why do they behave this way? What harm has been done to them to make them like this? And can I help them, or help them find someone who can?*

Sometimes, we have to work hard to see beyond the show people put on. The only way we can do that is through compassion. What is it like to be them? What are the reasons or pain behind their behavior?

For example, I read a story about a woman who had an issue with alcohol, as was commonly known around the town where she lived. One day she crashed her car into the school fence while collecting her three children from school. The article was extremely judgmental of the mother (mothers always get judged more harshly). The comments section was even worse.

I added my voice. I responded in the comments that this woman was clearly in pain and in trouble. Her problem was well known, so why didn't her community help her rather than attacking her after the fact? I could not see how judging and attacking a mother who was struggling to cope was going to help her move beyond her problems and their terrible consequences. Nor would it make her children safer, either.

Let she who is without sin cast the first stone, right? Tormentors often need understanding, too. Bullies and abusers leave so much human wreckage in their wake. Some have no idea what harm they've caused, for a capacity to inflict hurt often goes hand-in-hand with a lack of self-awareness, and the truth is, they are hurting too. They don't want to be alone in their pain, so they inflict it on others. (**#Lead with compassion**, *wisdom 58*)

Being compassionate towards our fellow humans doesn't justify bad behavior. It doesn't absolve people from accountability. It simply helps you adjust your perspective—away from judgment, which doesn't help anyone, and toward compassion, which creates the space for change, action, and evolution.

WHEN YOU JUDGE ANOTHER... YOU DO NOT DEFINE THEM... ...YOU DEFINE YOURSELF

WAYNE DYER

None of us are perfect. We can all look deeper and ask better questions. So, let's be more compassionate and help people out of challenges. Let's lift each other up and create a better world for all of us.

When we help our neighbors, everyone in a community thrives.

HAVE A THINK

Who around you do you find yourself judging? How can you look at them from a viewpoint of compassion instead?

What can you do to help foster compassion rather than judgement in your community?

#13

MY RECIPE FOR TRUE LOVE

SELF-EMPOWERMENT

DON'T BE SCARED OF LOVE. If you can let go of the fear of getting hurt, rejected, or ridiculed and give yourself permission to pour yourself fully into love, it's amazing when it happens. If you've ever seen a couple that embodies your idea of true love, you know it's possible, and it shouldn't be as rare as it is.

Of course, love doesn't always work out, but it's always worth it when you finally do find someone worth loving. The *love mistakes* along the way make you stronger, too.

I didn't make any big mistakes with love. Oh sure, I was rejected by people I thought were foxy. That stung for a while, but I was always capable of quickly moving on. I didn't get stuck in it. No bunny boiling moments for me.

But I always had this very firm idea in my mind, since I was young, of the qualities I wanted in my man, and I was uncompromising about them. I knew myself and I knew the type of person that would match me, so I had fun, but deeper commitment was rarely made. It was definitely lonely sometimes, but that always felt better than being in something that wasn't right.

Based on my experience, I definitely recommend putting your energy into determining the type of person and qualities you want. This keeps you focused, and focus is excellent to ensure you are relentless in seeking your perfect match, rather than jumping into something that is not quite right for you. And so many do. The pressure to *couple up* is too strong.

What I've learned from my own 50 + years of life and from those who have crossed my path is that love blossoms when you find someone who matches you, rather than being in opposition to you and your core values, because that's usually a disaster. It's stressful when you pull in different directions on every decision. You don't want that!

If you identify and anchor your coupledom in core values, relationships are easier and more harmonious. But be flexible, adaptive, and patient, too. Don't rush into it. Love, like life itself, is rarely a smooth road.

Just try not to be scared of it, no matter how badly burnt you may have been in the past. Believe in love. It doesn't always go the way you want it to, but love is worth *all the bumps in the road* when you finally find it. It's worth the heartache and disappointment too. There's nothing more magical than finding that special person and facing into the unknown side by side, as a team.

Believe it's possible for you.

MY JOURNEY

As a young woman, I had a lot of fun just being me. I travelled the world, lived in five different countries, loved my work, and met fabulous people everywhere I went. The whole time I was forever hopeful that, one day, I would meet my true love—because essentially, I'm a romantic at heart. Besides, life is a hell of a lot better when you've got someone to share it all with! For me, he just had to be the right one.

It took a while for someone who was capable of loving all of me to show up. When you've got a big personality with big dreams, you need someone who can say, "Awesome, I want to join that journey with you." (Needless to say, you must want to join their journey, too.) At the grand old age of 33, when I was really enjoying being me and certainly wasn't feeling needy in anyway, in walks Steve. It was a case of instant eye contact across a bar and blazing electricity sparking around the room, and well, that was it, really.

There he was, the love of my life and my perfect match at long last. We've been together nearly 18 years at the time of writing, and while the years have been rocky and stressful and pushed us both to our limits, we're bound firmly together, and he continues to be everything I hoped for and a lot more. I truly love him more and more every day.

When we fell in love, I realized that the idea opposites attract wasn't even remotely right—at least for us. He's pretty much a male version of me, as I am a female version of him. It was our similarities that really bound us together and continue to keep us strong, especially when it comes to our core values.

When I introduced Steve to my friends, one amazed pal said: "He is exactly what you've talked about for all these years, and you've actually found him."

That friend also said she'd spent her time thinking about what she didn't want and, guess what? She always attracted the same type of person—the not-nice ones. That got me thinking: was it my focus on what I wanted that helped find him?

We know that being deeply focused on what we want in life works. I figure why can't this be as true for love as for any other aspect of our lives? During my single years, I kept thinking about the man I wanted in my life. All through those lean times, the thoughts of what I wanted were always foremost in my mind. I did not spend any time thinking about what I didn't want, mainly because I hadn't spent any time with bad men anyway (I have excellent taste).

I absolutely believed that one day, he'd walk through my door, and this deep conviction kept me going through all those years of singleness.

YOUR RECIPE FOR LOVE

So here it is. Focus on what you want—all aspects of what you want—and keep this in your mind and heart every time you daydream about your future. Let your imagination soar and live this ideal relationship in your head and heart. You don't have to share it with anyone else. It's just yours to cherish.

Imagine how being with them will make you feel, the smile you'll have on your face, how much you are going to laugh, and all of the wonderful things you're going to do together. Live it and believe it.

Picture your ideal partner: emotionally, spiritually, and physically. (Hey—you've got to like looking at them, too! Being attracted is important whether people admit it or not. Chemistry is chemistry, and your attractive may not be my attractive. So, think about how they look—because it's part of the daydream you're creating anyway.)

Naturally, your logical side will kick in and tell you what a bunch of nonsense it is to daydream like this. Sometimes it's good to ignore logic and fantasize about what you want with no rules attached. That's the great thing about imagination—there are no rules.

Any time you start thinking of a negative man or woman you've encountered along the way, shut that thinking down immediately, and redirect it to your ideal partner. Remember how the law of energy works—if you allow yourself to focus on what you don't want, that's exactly what you'll get. Where the attention goes, the energy flows!

This is what it looked like for me when I put even more detail into my dream.

I needed someone with the same or similar core values (**#Integrity and values**, *wisdom 8*). I needed to know that even if something wasn't important to them, they'd respect when something was important to me, and vice versa.

I needed an adventurer, someone who wasn't scared of living life to the full. I needed someone who wasn't scared of love and was capable of giving his heart and soul in a relationship. Keeping my word is really important to me—when I give it, I don't break it. I can live with the fact that not everyone cares about this as much as I do, but I couldn't accept this in my partner.

He had to be true to his word, always. He had to be honest. Integrity had to be important to him. He had to be a hard worker, yet know how to strike a healthy balance between living, working, and loving. He needed to be able to laugh at the same stupid stuff as me. And last but not least, he had to relish in having a woman like me by his side. He couldn't be intimidated or scared of the sort of woman I was.

Even if you think these sorts of ideas are all nonsense (which is fine), focusing on what you want helps to make sure that you're not going to accept anything else. Through all the years, I never gave up, never settled for anything else. I truly believed that this person was out there, we just needed to find each other.

While you bide your time, don't let anyone tell you you're being too fussy. People said that to me all the time. If you've decided to be fussy about the person that's going to be by your side for life, that's nobody's business but your own! Love is worth daydreaming for, and it's definitely worth waiting for.

CAPTURE YOUR DREAM

What do they look like?

What's important to them?

What are the important values they must have?

How about work ethic or any preference for type of work? Free and wild, or serious and stable?

Want to have children, or want to live life adventuring?

How do you want them to feel about you?

These questions are just a start. Answers these or create your own. Write it down. Make a vision board.[7] Draw, write a poem, paint a picture—however you like to capture ideas.

---

7   For vision board ideas, take a look at https://www.developgoodhabits.com/vision-board-ideas/

Just spend some time thinking deeply about who you want by your side, then daydream about it every chance you get.

And if it works—if that vision turns into a reality—make sure you drop me a note on social media to tell me. I'll be so excited for you. Love is beautiful and worth focusing on to get the right match for you. Good luck and believe. You can be one of those inspiring couples who show the world that true love is real. xxxx

#14

FIND YOUR PURPOSE

SOCIAL LEADERSHIP

THE IDEA OF FINDING YOUR purpose is something that gets a lot of discussion these days. You might even be annoyed by the constant focus on the idea of purpose and the pressure it puts on you. But don't let that happen.

Purpose is as unique as each of us. Identifying it can transform your life. It has done so for me. My purpose is to unleash all of the amazing people in the world to own their voices and help transform our world. It's a big purpose and it gives me real drive every day. It helps me pick what I do, who I do it with, and where I focus.

For some of us, purpose means going out there and changing the world. For others, purpose is closer to home.

So, what is *your* purpose? Purpose is not a brain decision, it's a heart decision. It may be as simple as the action that drives you and makes you want to get out of bed in the morning, with a spring in your step and purpose beating from your soul. Or is it something bigger, more ambitious? Size it right for you.

Is it more than one thing? You're not required to laser-focus on just one purpose in life! I've certainly had a mishmash of purposes, and technology advances have helped broaden the possibilities too. Especially social media.

One way to work out your purpose is talk to your family and friends, the people you trust.

Remember to be careful, though; not everyone is well-positioned to advise you and it's really important you don't speak with people who will make you feel or think smaller. Always be very selective in your advisors.

After you ask around, ask yourself: what was I put on this planet to do?

As you get clearer in your answer to this, you may find yourself structuring your life around living it. Your purpose might be aligned with your work, or it might have nothing to do with how you earn money at all.

But what if your gut reaction is, "Why do I have to have a purpose?" If you're happy to cruise and life is good as is, that's cool too. I really believe some of us come into this life for a rest and some of us come for a challenge. Whatever the case, we're not here to put pressure on each other about purpose.

However, if you feel like you've got a purpose and you want to define it, take whatever time you need to do so. This comes easily for some people, but it's brutally hard for others. Either way, it's worth it.

The best part of defining your purpose is when you weave all the joyful threads together—your real passions, your true loves, the things that give you energy—and then step back. You'll realize how full of meaning life can actually be.

It's a joy to be driven this way, even if your purpose is challenging. You're doing it. That's a special life and a legacy to leave behind.

QUESTIONS TO PONDER

Are you open to your life having a purpose (or two or three)? Equally, is this life about a rest or a challenge? There is no wrong or right in this answer.

If you do want to define your purpose, who do you trust to explore this with? Who will expand you in this?

What are the things that are special about you? What excites you? What are the words that describe you and the things you care about?

What do you get really passionate about? Or even angry or outraged about? Hint, hint: this is always a sign of what is meaningful to you.

MIND YOUR JEALOUSY

SELF-AWARENESS

JEALOUSY IS A POISON that eats away at the soul. It can pop up when we see someone else achieve something remarkable, gain glory or fame, or simply getting the advantages in life that we wish we were born with.

Jealousy belittles us. It makes our worldview smaller and mean.

It is also a complete waste of energy and time: when we indulge in jealousy towards someone else, we are focusing our energy away from what it is we want to achieve and putting our finite energy into a useless, negative mindset.

Instead, we could be harnessing that valuable energy towards creating something beautiful we want for ourselves.

Let's support others and celebrate every achievement as though it were our own, and then stay focused on what we want to achieve and how we want to feel when we achieve it.

Keep your eyes on your feet, while you walk your path. Keep dreaming, keep working, and keep believing in the future you want for yourself.

#16

REJECTING THE UNATTAINABLE

SELF-EMPOWERMENT

WHEN I WAS A YOUNG TEENAGER, my sister, Phillipa, always brought home copies of *Dolly*, an iconic Australian teen-girl magazine. We devoured it cover to cover, wishing we could afford the clothes, suffering from the fact we didn't look like those girls, wanting the makeup, and just wishing our lives looked more like what we imagined theirs were like. There was an annual competition too, where anyone, even us, could submit photos of themselves and whoever won would get a lucrative one-year contract with *Dolly*. We dreamed and dreamed.

But of course I could never submit my photos. Of course I would never win one of these modeling competitions. Of course this was something completely beyond me. I wasn't born with a model's body. I was born with my body, and it didn't look anything like a *Dolly* model's body!

Gradually, I recognized I was subjecting myself to magazines that made me feel bad about my body. I was looking at images that devalued me and made me feel less significant. I was looking at the unattainable. Around that time, I took up bodybuilding. I was 14.

I also kicked the *Dolly* habit, and my new best friend became *Muscle & Fitness Magazine*. Interestingly, I didn't look like those ladies either, but it was up to me to get there. I was finally looking at something attainable.

My bodybuilding years were awesome. I LOVED my strength. The boys didn't think too much of it from a romantic point of view, but it was a life-changer for me. Bodybuilding helped me deal with a lot of the puberty attention—from boys my age who I wasn't interested in yet, as well as that from the older men in my community whose attention made me feel uncomfortable—it disappeared overnight. Double bonus. (**#Beg your pardon, Dolly Parton**, *wisdom 85* and **#From judgement to compassion**, *wisdom 12*)

In hindsight, this was another big milestone. When I got rid of *Dolly*, I was making the decision to no longer read or watch things that didn't make me feel good about myself.

There is nothing wrong with a classic model body type and there's nothing wrong with my body type. Models' bodies are great for hanging clothes off, mine isn't. We all come into this world with our unique genetic make-up. The problem is, from that day, we are marketed to in a way that makes us hate or despise ourselves. How did we ever let that happen?

These days we can change our looks with surgery, to an extent. Hey, we can do it with apps too! I don't judge anyone for wanting to make themselves look better. I know many people who have changed their bodies and gained self-confidence they'd never had before, much as I did when I transformed myself through bodybuilding. However, you do it, physical change can be powerfully transformative.

But not everyone can afford this surgery, and some shapes cannot be transformed through exercise or surgery. It's been a lifelong frustration that we celebrate so few shapes for women as "attractive" and anyone outside a narrow norm feels unbeautiful. The hugely damaging consequences can include depression, eating disorders, unnecessary surgery, and even suicide, which is on the rise.

I realized just how deep this runs in our society when I read of young teenage girls getting labioplasty because they think their vaginas are ugly.[8] Girls and women are told to despise how they look from an increasingly young age, trapping them in an endless cycle of self-loathing and "improvement." And this is starting to happen to boys and men too. The body-image crisis is widening its grip on us.

Have you got into a habit of paying too much attention to things that make you feel bad about yourself? If so, can you make a conscious effort to spend time doing things and taking onboard information that makes

---

8   https://www.independent.co.uk/news/world/americas/teen-labiaplasty-surgery-rise-adolescents-worry-about-appearance-and-symmetry-a7006081.html

you feel good about yourself? Find information that empowers you and reminds you that you're beautiful just the way you are.

The truth of the phrase *beauty is within* has resonated for me with more and more strength as the years go by. A woman with a mean, petty heart is not a beauty to be admired, no matter how artfully she's packaged. A woman with a heart full of kindness and integrity is beautiful to those who know her, no matter what she looks like. A beautiful heart glows brighter than the prettiest face—it always has, and no makeup can hide it.

Let's stop buying into advertising and marketing that makes us feel bad about ourselves. When we stop buying into it, they stop creating it. Let's do it for the boys and girls coming up behind us. They deserve for the cycle to be broken.

#17

FIND YOUR VOICE

SOCIAL LEADERSHIP

IF YOUR PURPOSE IS BIGGER than your immediate physical community, you have a wonderful opportunity to focus on finding your voice. Your voice is how you connect and communicate with others to inspire them to act in line with your purpose.

Many people are genuinely apprehensive about stepping out, speaking up, and being known in a bigger way. We often list public speaking as our number-one fear, but this is so much more than public speaking. We have much greater reach to be able to influence these days, after all!

When we are driven by purpose and from the heart, then owning our voice and unleashing it is a really important thing to do. It's a contribution we make to mankind.

It's also how we ensure the global conversation is not dominated by a negative minority of school yard bullies, noising up to scare the rest of us.

Finding your voice might mean refusing to conform to what you see happening in the world already, particularly when it doesn't feel right for *you*.

Finding your voice might mean taking a stand against that which is negative, destructive, or narcissistic. It's about stepping up to be a role model, if we don't like the role models we see around us. Our speaking out changes the way things are done, and such change is long overdue.

Finding your voice is about connecting to your authentic self. As you get clearer on this, it's easier to go out and become known for what you really care about—in other words, your purpose.

Your voice is the way you share your purpose and make it real.

Of course, many people say to me: "Why would anyone care what I've got to say?"

Simple: your unique perspective on the situations you care about is important. If you want to drive positive change in the world, then it is your voice that will help drive that change. Be brave and believe you can make a difference. Believing this is so important, and besides, you'll get stronger as you go.

If you're still struggling to know what you should say, look for clues by noticing what lights people up when you speak to them, or perhaps they lean into you when you speak on something you're passionate about. Body language from your listeners can be a sign that your message is landing in a powerful way. Pay attention to what it is you're speaking about in these moments. It's your special sauce.

See also **#Find your purpose** *(wisdom 14)* and **#The one-minute meditation** *(wisdom 28)*.

#18

EXUDE LOVE

SELF-EMPOWERMENT

THIS WISDOM IS LESS AN ACTION and more a state of being: exude
love in everything you do and in everything that you are. It's a life-
changer, I promise.

When we're in the energy of love, we are more at peace and more
forgiving. We are more compassionate, with our eyes wider open.

I've found that when I embrace this state of being, life frequently has a
touch of magic to it. It begins with trying to extend the feeling of love past
just those moments we're taught to feel it and progressively we integrate
it more fully into everyday life and everyday being.

I discovered this kind of active love when I met Mother Teresa in
Calcutta, India in 1995. This amazing lady exuded love, and I have never
felt such serene and loving energy emanate from another soul. It was truly
incredible.

Exude love. How can we do it? This is what I found that works for
me.

Close your eyes and focus on your heart energy. Visualize white light
coming into your heart and then push it through you, out of you, and
beyond you. Push it through your body, into your words, your thoughts,
your actions, so that love exists in your every expression. Let it flow out
from the depths of your being. This is not about a soft or romantic love.
It's a feeling of gentleness, acceptance, openness, and welcoming. It is a
beautiful state of being.

Let's be honest—when we are angry, frightened or frustrated, it's hard to exude love.

Sometimes life tips us upside down, and it's not easy to get back to that lovely white-light loving place. It might not be the right time to even try.

At the start, try this experiment in the morning, on a day when you wake up and feel a skip in your step, then do it then. Exude love, just for a minute, every day towards the people you love the most. Then next week, do it for a little longer. And then a bit more. Soon you'll be at an hour. Do it over breakfast with your loved ones, at work with your colleagues, or even when you're buying a cup of coffee from your favorite barista. Give them a blast of love. You'll make their day.

Start small. Practice small for big, lasting results.

PRACTICE

Step 1: Close your eyes, calm your breathing, and focus on your heart.

Step 2: Imagine beautiful white light sitting in and all around your heart.

Step 3: Once you can "see" that light, take hold of it and push it through your body. Feel it flowing through you, feel it living in you, and feel the peace it brings you.

Step 4: Practice holding onto that feeling in your body when you come out of this micro-meditation and for as long as you can, project it into how you speak and act and your attitude towards others.

Give it a try. To build your white-light love muscle, practice. Even what feels like a tiny flicker will make a difference.

#19

IT'S TIME TO HONOR MOTHER EARTH

CLIMATE COURAGE

EVEN FOR THOSE WHO MIGHT have been tempted to brush off the idea of a climate crisis and say all is OK with the planet, 2020 in its entirety showed us all is not well, not well at all. Between the global pandemic, record temperatures, rising seas, melting glaciers, and mega-fires in the north and southern hemispheres, it's clear something is very amiss.

And at some level, all of us are responsible for this.

It's a bigger question than politics, short-term security, and simple daily convenience. It's about what our lives will be like in a year, three years, or ten years, let alone in 2100!

When it comes to the climate crisis, it doesn't matter who you are, or where and how you live. This truly equal-opportunity crisis impacts everyone, one way or another. It affects you and I already, and our children will have to adapt in ways we can't even imagine yet.

Finding solutions will require courage and global commitment. It also requires simple individual steps, starting now.

Step 1 is to face it. We lucky few, in the comfortable developed world, have thoughtlessly gorged ourselves on this planet's resources. It's time to recognize our behavior for what it is—and stop. It's like choosing to get healthy. Change is achieved one day at a time, and it helps a lot to have a clear goal of how you'll look and feel once you get there.

Step 2 is to decide to get healthy by changing our lifestyles. Each of us can make small deliberate changes in our lifestyle that are healthy for Mother Earth. Many of these choices are great for our bodies and minds too! Examples include switching from beef to chicken, or even better, head towards a vegetarian or plant-based diet. One step at a time, we can do this.

Step 3 is to realize that each of us counts. Your actions count.

For more than a decade I've been deeply invested in learning about the climate crisis, and our lack of action terrifies me. Sometimes I want to close my eyes and ears to it all.

According to some predictions, humans could be extinct by 2050.[9] This is worst possible outcome, to which we're headed if we do nothing.

9   https://docs.wixstatic.com/ugd/148cb0_a1406e0143ac4c469196d3003bc1e687.pdf

Those collecting the data say the impact of climate change is likely to increase faster than what we think, because scientific information is being diluted to appease politicians, or is being discredited by businesses and the media who do not want change. I don't understand this kind of denial, based in a blend of ignorance and greed, but we all suffer if we don't face this crisis! The system is broken. Delivering shareholder value above all life on earth has got to be addressed. Companies, governments and the media all need to change, but so do investors and their expectations. It is beyond time.

When it comes to the climate crisis, the worst is not all set in stone—*yet*. Yes, we have passed many tipping points, but we can still stop the worst of it. I take hope from this.

And this is why I call out to you, as you read this, to choose to act with me in this. It's up to us now. Please keep reading.

HERE'S A SUMMARY OF WHERE WE ARE RIGHT NOW, AT THE START OF THE 2020 DECADE

The references for all the data quoted can be found online here.[10]

- The last decade was earth's hottest on record.
- Since 1970, we have lost 68% of the world population of mammals, birds, fish, amphibians, and reptiles.
- An ecosystem collapse is expected this decade, too. Which ecosystem will go? Will it be the ecosystem with sharks at the top? Or the bees? Let's hope it's not the bees. Any ecosystem collapse will result in starvation and misery. Any ecosystem collapse will result in millions, possibly billions, of climate refugees.
- Look at how well we're coping with refugees right now. More refugees are coming, and we're not ready. How did your government cope with COVID-19? Can you trust them to be ready for this?

---

10   https://andreatedwards.com/2020/11/environment-reference-materials-and-articles-from-2020-constantly-updating/

- We are on track for 1.5°C warming within the next five years. We're at 1°C now—and look at the impact. Now, what happens if global warming gets higher than 2°C? Tropical rainforests can't survive—directly impacting *all* life in this region of the world, and that impact will be far worse for those already at the bottom of society. We are already seeing early signs of this.
- Scientists are predicting the complete loss of Arctic sea ice by 2035. Yes 2035, not 2100. Glaciers are melting all over the world. We are holding funerals for dead glaciers! And today we have pink algae in the Alps, and as it absorbs more heat, it increases glacial melting.
- The South Pole is warming up, the Arctic is too. A town in Siberia recorded its highest ever temperature of 38°C in 2020, well over 20°C above normal! A hotter arctic means the permafrost melts. We've underestimated CO_2 emissions from melting permafrost by 14%.
- This awakens the methane dragon. Methane is approximately 30 times more potent as a heat-trapping gas than CO_2. *Just that should send a shiver down every spine.*
- We've seen out-of-control wildfires in the Arctic circle in 2020 that released more CO_2 in two months than was released in the whole year of 2019! We have acidified the entire ocean. Fish stocks are plummeting all over the world. We saw locust plagues across sub-Saharan Africa. We saw flooding of biblical proportions across India, Pakistan, and Sudan.
- In Indonesia, Malaysia, and the Amazon, deforestation increased during 2020. An Amazon expert has predicted that we've already passed the tipping point for this important treasure. What does that mean for global weather patterns when the Amazon becomes a savannah? And in 2020 the Amazon experienced the largest number of fires in 10 years, the majority of them started purposefully to clear land, of course (a head butt moment if there ever is one)!
- Another milestone for 2020 happened in Death Valley, which logged the hottest temperature ever recorded on earth at 54.4°C.
- We had apocalyptic fires in the Amazon, California, Australia, and Siberia in 2020. And in the US, fire tornadoes became a thing—yikes! Is the Age of Megafires the wake-up call we'll heed? Or have we already hit one too many climate tipping points?

And yet so many people don't believe in the climate crisis.

Surely they can see the rubbish choking our rivers, oceans and air? With the petroleum industry expected to triple its plastic production by 2040, we're drowning in plastic! We've all stood witness to birds and sea creatures dying with plastic in their stomachs.

Microplastics have been found in human organs for the first time, too. The World Wide Fund for Nature (WWF) and an Australian University proved we are all digesting a credit card worth of micro-plastics in our weekly food intake. And ladies, when we give birth today, our babies are born with plastic already in their bodies!

We are destroying the foundation of all life, including our own. Will we wake up? The time is now. This pandemic has stopped us in our tracks. This is the chance to rebuild our societies, in balance with all life on earth.

A great economic catastrophe was always a certainty with the climate crisis. We were never going to turn the economic engine off voluntarily; why would we, we had it too good.

So here we are, with a unique chance to avert the dire crisis facing us all, a golden opportunity, and we'd have to be insane not to take it. Vote, read the research, lobby your politicians, transform your business, educate your community!

I know it's not what anyone wants to hear.[11] I sure don't. But it's real. It is time to write a new future for all life on earth. We have the opportunity to do it right now.

11   https://www.ecopsychology.info/ecoanxiety

WHAT CAN WE DO?

- Understand the scale of the situation. I am sharing a Weekend Reads blog every week on andreatedwards.com, and it starts with climate news.

- Own your own contribution to the climate crisis. Change your lifestyle to reduce your footprint. Pick one area to address each month. In 12 months, your little bits add up to a lot!

- Share knowledge to awaken your community and help them see a course of action.

- If you work for a company, push for it to be emissions-neutral or negative within the shortest timeframe possible—by 2025 or 2030, for example. Later than this is simply too late.

- Vote for leaders who will do all they can to tackle the climate crisis.

- Show up—online to build momentum and in person for protests and action groups.

- Do not buy from companies continuing to abuse the environment. Name and shame the ones who are.

To stay current with Honoring Mother Earth

#20

TRUST YOUR OWN COUNSEL

CAREER THOUGHTS

NOT EVERYBODY IS IN A POSITION to give you meaningful advice. Why would they? Everyone comes at life from very different perspectives, experiences and expectations.

Which is why trusting your own counsel is a strength, not a weakness or an arrogance. You take input and advice from those around you and then you draw your own conclusions, based on your knowledge, your experience, and your insights.

You have your own perspective that the data of life has given you, while taking into account the viewpoints of people around you. Be focused and particular in choosing trusted people to ask. Make sure they are aligned to your values, to your level of courage, and to you as a human being.

When I was young, advice was freely provided by the adults in my life. Being very stubborn, I often followed my own plan anyway. What I found was that, flying in the face of the advice I was given, I would excel or I would fail—but both taught me valuable lessons that helped me to grow.

I started to understand that the advice was coming from their perspective, which wasn't always relevant to my own. I also remarked that people who were not capable of being courageous in their own lives regularly projected their fears onto me.

Taking other people's fears onboard is the number one thing that will hold you back and make you less courageous. Being sure in yourself and what you want in life is key if you want to get to the point of trusting your own counsel.

In my 30s I was offered coaching by a senior executive who wanted to help me reach the executive ranks of a global corporation.

I politely declined the offer. When I was younger, this would have been a dream for me, but by this point in my life, I realized that corporate politics and game-playing would never be my thing. I knew myself well enough to know that this was not my path. I had learned to trust my own counsel early.

Advice is only relevant when it comes from people in alignment with you. While we may and should go *outside* for advice, real strength comes from building the confidence to trust above all in your own counsel, your own wisdom within.

Here's an aside that will resonate with any woman who has ever been pregnant. When you are pregnant, *everyone* wants to give you advice whether you ask for it or not. Some of the unsolicited advice can be frightening and impact your ability to enjoy your pregnancy. Pro tip, if strangers ask you if it's your first pregnancy, tell them it's your tenth. No one will give you random advice then.

INTO ACTION

Am I strong in trusting my own counsel?

When have I taken advice that was not aligned with my own counsel?

Why did I listen to this advice? (Think deeply on that.)

Did I do something differently in life or work because I did listen?

Is it too late to change direction, back into alignment with my own counsel? (Hint, it's never too late.)

What kind of advice am I seeking right now?

Who is aligned to me and can help me on my way?

If I were a friend coming to me for advice, how would I advise myself?

#21

YOU'VE JUST GOT TO DO YOU

SELF-AWARENESS

HAVE YOU EVER BEEN TOLD you need to adjust who you are to attract love or work? I certainly have. I was told I was too strong, too opinionated, too much of lots of things.

The reality is, if you change who you are to please others, you can't please yourself or be happy with who you are. You can't attract the life you really want, or the people you want to be with.

When you tap into the true power of being yourself without trying to impress or seduce, you *do* attract the right things—friends, work opportunities, and, yes, romantic partners—who love you for you, on your terms. Life is richer when you do you.

Ignore external opinions. Work out for yourself how to do you—and be proud of what that means.

Back around the year 2000, I was walking down Venice Beach, Los Angeles with a friend. All along the beach there were fortune tellers. My friend decided to give it a go, and I hung around, though I wasn't in the mood for it that day. The clairvoyant finished up with my friend, turned to me, and said: "You know, you need to soften the edges. Get yourself a fluffy backpack. Feminize yourself more, and you might find the guy you're hoping to find!"

I did an absolute double take. What? Fluffy backpack? Me? Inside I said to myself, "You aren't a very good clairvoyant, are you?"

Now let me be clear, if you love fluffy backpacks, I have absolutely no issue with that. Each to their own on the fashion front.

But if, like me, you would never in a million years wear a fluffy backpack, for any reason, being told you should do it to attract a man is really quite bewildering.

What if I had taken her advice and softened my style to be fluffier and more feminine? Would it make any difference in the quality of man I attracted? If it did, surely that isn't a match you'd be placing bets on. Widening the net of attraction through a false show of fluffy femininity would not have changed the fact I'm a potty-mouthed, determined, and very stubborn gal with strong ideas about life, the universe, and everything in between! A good match for me is based on attraction to these things, not to a fluffy backpack.

The only goal in life is working out who you are and making sure you're happy with yourself. All external advice is completely irrelevant until you've worked out this bit.

No one else can do you, at your deepest level of authenticity. It's all about acceptance of who you are and allowing your full self to show up, in all its glory.

#22

WHAT YOU RESIST PERSISTS

SELF-AWARENESS

IT TOOK A LONG TIME for this principle to enter into my psyche as an essential truth. I'd read about it, heard about it, but it always felt a little *woo-woo* to me. I just struggled to really grasp what it meant. My husband Steve is still grappling with it.

For me, motherhood was the catalyzing moment when I started to grasp it as an essential truth. I finally understood that if I resisted something, it kept going for longer. This meant I was unhappy for longer.

Here's a very simple example to illustrate the concept. My son, Lex, was three years old. He wasn't really speaking at this point (that's another story, **#Don't lose yourself in challenging times**, *wisdom 64*), but he had a strong mind and he definitely knew what he wanted. One day, Lex decided he wanted to wear pajamas to preschool. I was surprised, but said, *OK mate, no worries—knock your socks off.*

My husband had a very different reaction, which totally surprised me. There was obviously some cultural meaning for Steve (he's British, I'm Australian), because Lex got: *No son of mine is going to wear pajamas in public!*

While Steve's response surprised me, I knew we weren't going to win the argument with Lex, either. He'd dug his heels in, for whatever reason, and I knew that if we resisted it, it would be a long, hard, annoying fight, and to be honest, I just didn't think it was worth it. (Pick your battles my friends, and pick them very carefully.)

So, after a lot of work with Steve, I convinced him to agree that we'd let Lex go for it. We stopped resisting, and guess what? Within a week it was all over. Lex had nothing to fight against, so he stopped fighting. This *resist persist* stuff is true!

If you're feeling stuck in what you're doing and unhappy with where you are, but you know where you want to be, work really hard not to wallow in the energy of hating where you are. That's resistance.

Instead, move into the energy of taking yourself where you want to go—in your mind and in the actions you take. Volunteer, freelance, work for a charity, read, research, plan. Do the things that will get you where you want to go—even if it will take a long time to get there because it involves something like completing a degree in order to move forward.

The path can be quick or it can be slow, and life may repeatedly disrupt you as you go, but you need to keep your chin up and your eyes on the prize as much as possible. Try not to sink into despair of where you are. Use your energy to focus on where you want to go.

I learned a lesson about this when I worked for Microsoft. Don't get me wrong, I loved my time working for that amazing company and the awesome people I got to work with. Deep down though, I didn't want to be there, because I wanted to do my own thing. There were many days I struggled, and some days I cried at the thought of going to work, because in my heart, I didn't want to be working for somebody else. I'd already evolved out of that stage of my life.

However, I was smart enough *most days* to know that, rather than sitting in a place of resistance, I had to keep reminding myself of what I was working towards: getting back on the entrepreneurial path *when the time was right!* Timing is everything.

Instead of despairing or throwing in the towel, I kept blogging, kept creating content, and kept building my reputation. It was my way of moving forward, and it was my way of not resisting, because I didn't want it to persist! I created my path out.

What it all comes down to is this: always be building towards what you want to achieve. Don't get stuck in the reality of where you are if it's not where you want to be. Focus your attention where you want the energy to flow.

I encourage you to really look at your life and work out what you're resisting. It can be absolutely anything. Wanting your child to be something that they're not is resistance. Wanting life to be different from what it is, is resistance. Being forced to postpone a special moment, like a wedding or a big trip overseas, is something we're all dealing with at the moment. Are you resisting it, which means you'll suffer more? I'm not saying you have to be happy about it, but resisting it makes it worse. Where is your resistance?

COVID-19 is a global case study of resistance. As we all went from shock to fear to acceptance—especially those of us living in Asia—we had an opportunity to stand witness as it rolled around the world, like a tsunami, often in shock at the resistance we were seeing to our new reality!

One thing that became apparent to me very early on was that if we all did the same thing at the same time for as long as was needed, we might have been able to deal with this faster and it would be over by now. Remember in March when the World Health Organization and other experts suggested the world should close shop for a couple of weeks, maybe a month, so we could see where it had spread? The response was instant: *we can't close the global economy!* Well, look where that got us.

The year 2021 is looking even worse because we allowed the virus to spread so far, giving rise to new mutations and variants. This was all avoidable if we just took it seriously from the start, and we almost certainly have a long way to go before we overcome this crisis. The impact is not just the massive death tolls around the world, but the immense suffering in developing countries, with 200 million people moving into extreme poverty. These are my neighbors, and it is devastating. (If you can afford to, please donate to the World Food Programme[12] and let's get through this crisis together.)

The resistance to the reality of this crisis has been staggering. As I've said over and over again from the beginning: until this is over everywhere, it's not over anywhere.

What are some simple ways to identify resistance? When you hear yourself saying words like: "Why me?" or, "This isn't fair!" or, "It wasn't meant to be this way!" When we attempt to control something that is out of our hands, it often extends our suffering. Resistance is a refusal to accepting what is right in front of our noses.

The truth is, we don't have to like it, but once we accept it—even without joy in our hearts—our suffering lessens or goes away. It also means we won't keep attracting more of what we don't want. Instead, we put that energy and our empowered selves into action for the change we want.

---

12   https://donatenow.wfp.org/wfp/~my-donation

What you resist, persists, because where the attention goes, the energy flows. This is an essential truth. Be very conscious of where you allow your energy to flow, because where you focus your energy is what you'll get in return.

HOMEWORK

Apply it to yourself:

What are you resisting in your life? Work, marriage, kids, anything? List it out, then ask yourself: can I give myself a week or a month off resisting any or all of this so I can test this idea out?

If you can't think of anything, consider anything that makes you miserable. Anything that doesn't bring you joy. Any relationship dynamic that has been constantly negative for some time, a behavior in someone else that you just can't tolerate? We all resist something, and when we let the resistance go—really go—it regularly disappears. We sometimes must give it more time, if it is a long-term issue.

Check in one week/month later. Did anything go away while you weren't resisting it?

#23

TRUST FIRST

SELF-EMPOWERMENT

IN MANY CULTURES, people are guarded against newcomers. As a global wanderer, you feel it intensely. It's why foreigners all over the world gather together in well-known haunts, always open to new friendships, because we are all seeking companionship as we wander or settle down in new places. The friends we make at first are rarely people originally from those countries we move to. Those friendships take much longer to establish.

When you live abroad and travel extensively for long periods of time, you learn to trust first. You have to—otherwise life can be very lonely. It's a switch you make once you *get on the road*, and it becomes a permanent change the longer you do it. You are always open to new people, receptive to connection and to a bigger, richer life.

For me, *trust first* was something I had to learn. What I discovered once I got out of my comfort zone (**#Get out of your life!**, *wisdom 1*) was this: making people pass a test to earn my trust closed me off to so much. Many people couldn't be bothered sitting the test anyway—why would they? Most of us have enough friends already!

Of course, you will find people who don't deserve trust. When intuition alerts you immediately that a person is not trustworthy—listen to it. Some people will lose your trust more gradually. When that happens, let them go. (**#Self-protection and the circle of trust**, *wisdom 68*)

Trust first might feel like a dramatic shift for you, but it's what we naturally did as kids. Give it a try when you're meeting somebody new. Go in with an open heart and you're likely to be met with the same in return.

Open that connection and see if it's something to build on. If it doesn't work out, move on—don't get stuck in it. We tend to spend a lot of time fretting in self-doubt about this sort of thing, but it's not about you, it's not about them. You're just not a match. That's OK!

We've all had bad experiences that could justifiably cause us to struggle with trust. But here's how I've learned to see it. By letting myself stay in feelings of betrayal and be overly cautious about trusting new people, I was taking something away from my own soul—the magic-making ability to trust first!

As I opened myself up to trusting first, I found magnificent people everywhere. And I found empathy for those that were reacting in distrust. I believe the onus is on all of us to try and help heal distrust. It's a wonderful gift to give, opening someone up to human possibility. And step-by-step, we heal the world.

A trust-first mentality is not foolishness or gullibility. It allows people to enter your life fully as themselves. When you drop your guard or stages to earning trust, you get to the core faster and build more amazing relationships faster too. Welcome strangers. The vast majority of them will be awesome.

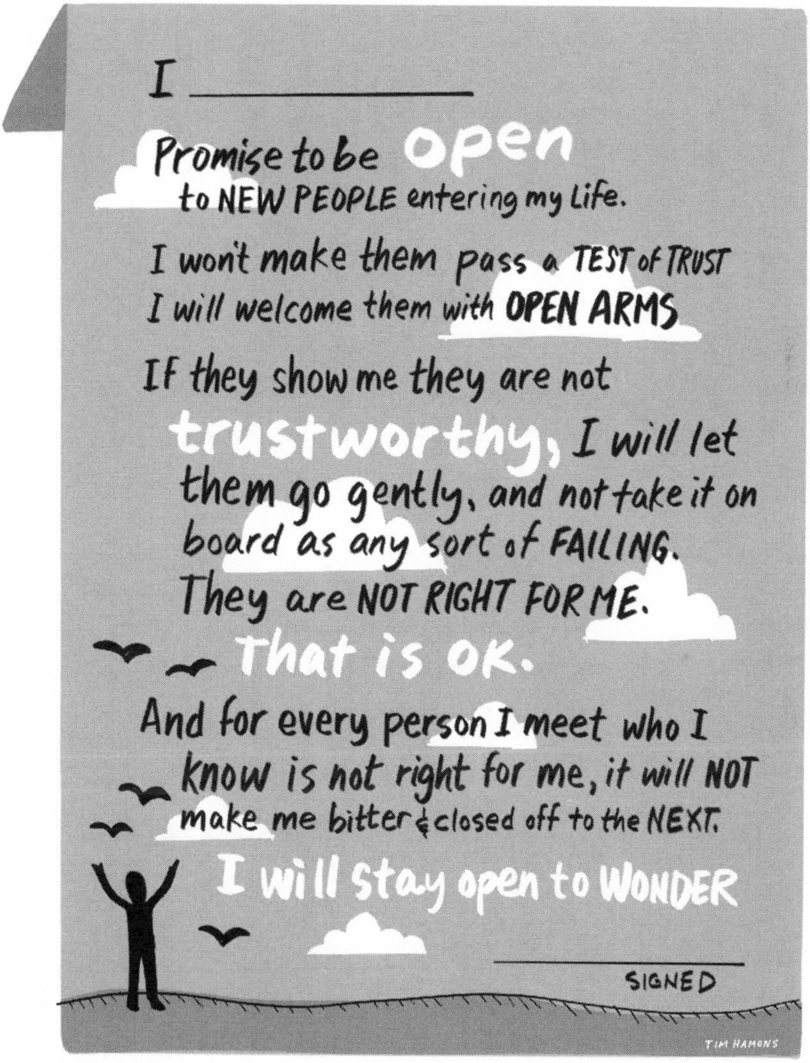

I _____

Promise to be **open**
to NEW PEOPLE entering my Life.

I won't make them pass a TEST of TRUST
I will welcome them with **OPEN ARMS**

If they show me they are not

trustworthy, I will let
them go gently, and not take it on
board as any sort of FAILING.
They are NOT RIGHT FOR ME.

That is OK.

And for every person I meet who I
know is not right for me, it will NOT
make me bitter & closed off to the NEXT.

I will stay open to WONDER

_____
SIGNED

TIM HAMONS

#24

BE AN
EXCITI-PANTS

EMPOWER OTHERS

WHAT IS AN *EXCITI-PANTS?* Exciti-pants embrace and celebrate the silly, lighthearted side of life. They show enthusiasm when others need it. By doing so, they bring joy into the world.

Exciti-pants counterbalance life's heaviness. They're excited for other people's crazy ideas and they buy into people's passion—no matter how outlandish that passion sounds. They're excited for weddings (including royal ones!), birthdays, and all meaningful moments—no matter how big or small.

They are like children as the seasons change, and they remind us of the joy of life. They make us reflect—why did we ever accept letting the simple joys go? The beautiful friends I've made in my life have definitely reminded me to keep loving life childishly. They remind me to be an exciti-pants.

Exciti-pants are life's cheerleaders. That's a gift we can give to each other. It may seem like small stuff, but it's all part of living a bigger, happier, and more hopeful life. Be an exciti-pants and cheer someone up today!

#25

IT'S OK TO WALK AWAY

SELF-EMPOWERMENT

HAVE YOU STUCK WITH a passion even after the passion has died? I did, and it was awful.

I began my music career at age seven. I played euphonium in the Wodonga Citizens Brass Band and then all the way through to the Australian Army Band as a professional soldier and musician. I loved my music for nearly 20 years and then one day, I just stopped loving it. It took a while to act on this, because my feelings of obligation to my musical family went deep.

However, the day came and I left. Something central to my life was over. I made a clear decision and moved on from something that was no longer making me happy. This is not to say I am not nostalgic, but nostalgia is about the past. And I'm all about the present and the future.

It's the same for all passions in life, including human relationships. If it's no longer serving you and bringing you joy, it is time to fix it or move on. You don't need anybody's permission but your own.

The time is here and it's about taking the leap of faith. Sometimes you have to take that leap with big, bold decisions and not look back. It's a simple rule for life: if it doesn't bring you joy, it is time to stop doing it.

Obviously, there are no easy answers to this question, especially when it comes to affairs of the heart. Let's walk through how you might approach such decisions in various areas of your life.

Activity—Whether you consider an activity to be a hobby or passion, when you start recognizing your deep feelings of dissatisfaction, consider talking to someone you trust about it. Tell them how you are feeling. Ask for their feedback. Really think about why you feel the need to continue (a sense of obligation?) and ask yourself if you are ready to hang up your hat. When it comes to community activities, there can be a lot of pressure, but if you need to move on, it is important to listen to and trust those feelings.

My music days came to an end slowly. In the final months, I would sit outside the band hall for a long time, just not wanting to go in anymore. It was a clear sign I needed to let it go, no matter the heartache it was causing me. I was 25 years old and music had been a core pillar of my life until that point. Jumping on a plane and leaving Australia gave me a definite end date. When I arrived in the UK, there was pressure to join a band in London, too. I stood firm. I no longer wanted to play.

Relationships (non-romantic)—If you have a relationship with someone and it's not serving you in a positive and wholesome way, it might be time to close that door. It can be very challenging to do this, as feelings will be hurt, but this is your life, and you have a right to happiness. Look around at the relationships in your life. Who fits this category for you? Who have you been enduring? This can be family, too.

If you don't want to make it a sudden severing, do it slowly, bit by bit. You can keep them in your life, but reduce the amount of time you are with them, as well as the influence they have on you, which is reducing the circle (**#Self-protection and the circle of trust**, *wisdom 68*). If you feel you can speak with them, go for it. Honesty is always the best policy, but soothe your words with love and gentleness. Keep in mind that this can be painful for the person on the receiving end.

Another option I've had, moving countries eight times as I have, was to let the relationship gently die out with the natural distance created between us. That always felt gentler for me. I didn't hate these people, I just knew our time was over.

Love—The hardest relationships to walk away from are love relationships. If you are married, especially with children, there is massive guilt thrown into the mix as well, not to mention cultural or religious pressure. If you know your relationship is starting to break down, which is always obvious to those around you, the first job is to get professional help if you want to save it. Do everything you can to help the relationship succeed.

Open communication is critical in this; far too many separated spouses spend years in shock afterward—they had no idea it was coming.

I have witnessed many relationships fall apart because one party chooses to have an affair, and when it's found out, the real fireworks start. I think the worst part of affairs is the deep shame and embarrassment the abandoned party feels. It can be life-destroying. I know it sounds judgmental, but honestly, affairs always feel like cowardice to me. Sure, it creates the path to an end (because it always gets found out) but there are much more gentle and honest ways to end a relationship.

What I have seen is that affairs start *after* the dissatisfaction with the relationship. A person truly in love is never looking around. (Of course, there are exceptions. Some people are just driven this way and will always have affairs. Maybe give them a miss on the marriage or relationship front, because they will always let you down!)

I believe a lot of people get so unhappy in their relationships, they can't see straight. They often feel trapped or guilty, and because of that, they make decisions that leave everyone around them unhappy, angry and devastated. I grew up a child of this experience, and I have seen it far too many times in my community as an adult, too. After witnessing my parents' divorce, I remember pondering the question: *how can we ever have world peace, when we can be so brutal to those we once loved and shared a bed with?* It doesn't have to be so bad. Keep talking to each other and recognize when the damage is done. Try not to hold onto a broken relationship for anyone else's sake—even children—because that extends the damage.

If you are considering an affair, stop and think—why? What is driving you to it? Is it because you are really unhappy in your marriage/partnership? Is it fixable? Or is it done? Have you been speaking with this other person about your marriage problems and felt a growing attraction towards them? Shouldn't you instead be having that conversation with your spouse? Can you pull the breaks on an affair and tell your spouse you are unhappy? Tell them why you feel the way you do, and then perhaps commit to a course of action.

Perhaps you've both recognized the time is over. Have this conversation *before* taking that next step, and so much carnage and heartbreak can be avoided. If your relationship is dead in the water, open communication is the most dignified way out for both of you—and the least painful way for your children, if you have any. Give your partner the opportunity to leave the marriage with their head held high, instead of feeling shamed in the eyes of their community. You loved them once, so give them that final consideration and respect. Your love-life future will be nicer and more peaceful too.

REFLECTION

Where in your life might there be something you need to walk away from?

An activity?

A friendship or business relationship?

A romantic relationship?

Which is it? Any?

What is stopping you from walking away?

What action will you take that respects you, those involved and your future?

#26

EPIPHANIES ON ANGER

SELF-AWARENESS

ONE OF THE GREATEST LESSONS I've learned in life is about letting go of anger. When I was a young person, certain people around me were very free with their anger. I could have copied their style, but I took a different path. This does not mean I don't get angry—it means anger doesn't control me.

Neale Donald Walsch once said, *"Anger expressed is never about the person it's directed towards. It's always about the person who is angry."* I heard this wise man's words at the right time; they went in deep and forced me to reflect.

Since then, any time I find myself moving into a place of anger towards someone, instead I ask myself whether I was really angry at that person or simply projecting my own frustrations or angst onto them.

I'd ask myself, for example, "Am I angry with my children, or deflecting my frustration of mothering onto them? Am I angry with my husband, or directing all of my pent-up angst about everything onto him?"

Catching and questioning yourself when you feel angry needs to be a continual and conscious practice. It will help you dig deep into your self-awareness and understand where the anger is really coming from. And it will improve and make more joyous your relationships with the people you tend to project that anger onto.

If you've got a bigger problem with your anger than the occasional frustration-driven flare-up, maybe you've got some deeper issues that you could try to get to the bottom of. There are some amazing professionals out there who can help with that kind of work. Whatever its source, your anger is toxic to you, your life, and your relationships. Face it. Sort it out.

For the average person, when you feel your anger rising, ask yourself if it is really about someone else and their actions, or if it may be a frustration deep inside of you being projected onto them? If you're completely honest, you'll find that the vast majority of the time, your anger comes from your own feelings of frustration misdirected towards someone else.

Now I'm still human, so yes—anger impacts me too. I get angry when I see unkindness or injustice directed toward people who are helpless, downtrodden, or not in a position to stand up for themselves, socially or economically. That definitely gets me going. But this is not the kind of anger that leaves me feeling poisoned, and it has no consequences for my relationships.

I will also defend myself and the people closest to me, but I've always found this can be done without losing dignity or resorting to anger for anger's sake. Standing up for yourself or someone else is absolutely important, but again, I don't hold onto it. It is released quickly and easily.

My husband often gets frustrated that I don't get angry or stay angry. But he also knows I just don't want it in my body—it doesn't serve me. However, when someone does make me really mad, and I actually feel that way for a week or two, Steve feels relieved. He tells me it makes me more human. Personally, I detest feeling that way and can't wait to get rid of it.

The important thing is, any time you feel anger, go inside and ask: is it them? Or is it me? The latter will be your answer most of the time, if you can be fully honest with yourself. Acknowledging this changed my life and I hope it changes yours.

REFLECTION

What are your frustrations with someone or something in your life? Think deep and list it down, all of it. Be completely honest with yourself—what's getting your goat?

Take a minute or two to go within and work out what it is that you are projecting onto others in your life.

Every time you can, when you feel anger rise in you, stop, think, reflect and ask yourself: am I angry towards them, or is it something deeper? This is a wonderful muscle to develop.

#27

USE TIME WELL, ESPECIALLY DURING A CRISIS

SELF-EMPOWERMENT

THE WORLD IS IN CRISIS and that will probably be the case for some time to come. There is little certainty right now. How we live is changing. Humanity is undergoing a fundamental transformation—and whether that's for better or for worse is on us, all of us. If we choose to rise to the occasion, when future generations talk about this moment, they may well tell a story of innovation and creation.

In the meantime, there's a simple solution to avoid getting anxious, fearful, or slipping into depression: *just do stuff.*

Use this time to do stuff. It doesn't really even matter what. Get your house in order or plant that garden. Direct your energy in any direction where you feel the urge to get active: write, draw, paint, launch a podcast, start something. Just do stuff.

If you can embrace this opportunity and create something worth paying attention to, you will find the stuff you've spent this "downtime" doing will open doors faster and create opportunities you didn't even know existed! Be active and you will become the story of this time—innovation and creativity at its best.

#28

THE ONE-MINUTE MEDITATION

SOCIAL LEADERSHIP

DEVELOPED THIS ONE-MINUTE meditation for my executive clients at IBM, BNP Paribas Securities Services, DHL, Microsoft, and beyond. I use it to help clients define their core focus as social leaders.

One thing I've observed when working with executive teams is that they're often so busy in their minds they can't connect easily with the wisdom in their hearts. I put this meditation together as a fast way to tap into the subconscious mind. For anyone who feels this all sounds a bit *woo-woo*, you should let the fact that it has worked spectacularly well with business executives alleviate any reluctance you might have towards giving it a go. It won't harm you, I promise! And it might just do you a world of good.

Over the years, I've seen it be a very powerful tool for thousands of executives, sales leaders, and other businesspeople, and it works to help them find their focus as social leaders. I've also seen it lead directly to $40 million of business for one client, as well as $140 million in the business pipeline. Why? People buy from people they trust. Owning your voice, with integrity and a mindset of service is what matters in business and in life.

While the one-minute meditation was designed to uncover focus for social media, it is relevant more broadly. I find this an excellent exercise to do anytime I am asking myself what I should do with my life.

Be open. Give it a go and see what comes up.

CONTEXT

To gain clarity on your focus or life goals, it is important to reflect and consider what you want to be known for, or what you want to do with your life.

Reflection helps you arrive at a strong, defined, and powerful voice for your professional social media channels. It can offer a clear direction for the journey ahead of you. You may discover you already know the answer to whatever question you have, but it is buried in your subconscious mind and you can't quite grasp it.

Coming up with answers to these questions can be a challenging process. Some of us keep the answers buried deep, quite simply because we are nervous about facing them. The reality is, when we accept our truth and our voice, it means it's time to find the courage to step more fully into our future. That can be frightening for a lot of us. I speak from experience: I've been working on this for years and I've yet to reach my full voice and role in the world. I'm getting there step by step, though. This book is part of that journey.

There is no denying it—owning your voice is an act of courage. I encourage you to support those you see doing so, for while it is a powerful path, it is not an easy path to take.

Ask yourself what you want to be known for. Look at this as a challenge to identify your own special talent(s) or message. We often take for granted what comes easily to us. In fact, coming easily is a sign of what makes us special (*and* that thing we have this natural talent for), but often we don't value it because it's easy. This is one of life's crazy contradictions, and it can make this process really hard.

The following meditation will hopefully help you overcome that challenge, if you approach it with an open mind and look at it as a starting point for the journey to becoming your whole, best, beautiful self.

THE INSTRUCTIONS

1. Sit down with paper and pen, your phone, or a computer—or simply use the space below in this book. The important thing is to have everything you need to write ready in front of you before you start. Clear away unnecessary clutter.

2. Read the questions below. Select one that speaks to you *right now*. All of these questions are relevant. You can go back and do the others separately later.

3. Get comfortable in a quiet place where you won't be disturbed. Uncross your arms and legs and set your timer for one minute plus 10 seconds. (Those extra 10 seconds will give you time to relax.)

4. Start your timer, close your eyes, take some deep breaths, and relax.

5. When you're ready, silently ask yourself the question you chose— over and over again—until the alarm goes off. Push away any other thoughts that attempt to break in while you're doing this exercise. Just keep asking your question over and over again, meditating on it for one minute.

6. When the timer goes off, open your eyes and start writing. Write whatever comes up, and if nothing comes up, doodle or scribble. Do not judge what is coming out, just write for as long as you need to write and capture the messages that emerge from your subconscious.

In front of you will be words, sentences, paragraphs, or maybe even patterns. Consider your words. Do you have your answers there? Are you surprised by what you see? Or are these the words you knew would come?

If you are struggling or apprehensive about doing this, invite a good friend or colleague to do this exercise with you. When you get your results, you can discuss it together. Regardless, the answer to your question is here. Be open to seeing it.

MEDITATION QUESTIONS

Reminder: all questions are equal, so select the one that speaks to you today.

- What do I want to do with my life?

- What do I want to be known for?

- What makes me stand out in a crowd?

- When I light people up, what is it I am talking about?

- What is my expertise?

- What am I unique at?

- What are my core values?

- What comes easily to me?

- What do I read about until the early hours of the morning?

- What gets me out of bed eagerly?

- What gives me energy?

- What feeds my spirit?

- What do people compliment me on?

- What makes me amazing?

NOTES AND INSIGHTS

Now spend some time defining your message and make a plan to contribute your voice to the world. And for insights on how you can be a social leader, follow my blogs on **andreatedwards.com**.

#29

UNLEASH YOUR VOICE FOR EQUALITY

CAREER THOUGHTS

WHEN WOMEN SPEAK UP, they become beacons and role models of courage for all of us, regardless of gender identity.

When women speak their truth, out of belief in a cause and regardless of potential consequences in a world where they often face deeper criticism and scrutiny than their male counterparts, they become our heroines.

I do what I do in solidarity with such amazing ladies. I am committed to driving positive change in the world, and I truly believe I can make the world a better place by using my voice. We all can. Because if I don't speak up, if you don't speak up—well, who will?

This is our chance. This is our time. And to be honest, the only thing stopping any of us *is us*. Time to be brave, ladies!

Yes, being a woman with a voice can attract negativity BUT when enough of us speak up, there'll be too many of us to deal with. They can't keep us silent.

Equality is one of our most important global goals, because equality is good for everyone.[13] Equal education opportunities for girls tackles so many of the economic and social issues that we face today, the world over. Educated girls have fewer children and are better able to manage

---

13   https://www.un.org/ruleoflaw/thematic-areas/human-rights/equality-and-non-discrimination/

their family finances.[14] They achieve more, and they go out and live more impactful and fulfilling lives. When companies have more women in leadership roles, companies are more profitable.[15] When countries make equality a priority for their country, their GDP skyrockets.[16]

Equality benefits everyone across the board. When both men and women have more opportunities to live their best lives, men get more choices outside traditional roles.

So, ladies, it's time to stand up and speak your truth. Don't be scared, don't wait to be asked, don't wait to be perfect, and don't ask permission.

Be a role model and a beacon for your own generation of women, for the next generation, and even for women older than yourselves.

And men, join your voice to this. Be a **#Manbassador!** *(wisdom 31).* We need to stand side by side, shoulder to shoulder, men and women together as humans.

Anyone fighting against equality holds *all* of us back from advancing and evolving.

14 http://www.ungei.org/
15 https://www.mckinsey.com/mgi/overview/in-the-news/power-with-purpose
16 https://www.mckinsey.com/featured-insights/employment-and-growth/how-advancing-womens-equality-can-add-12-trillion-to-global-growth

#30

DON'T BE A MAYBE

EMPOWER OTHERS

REMEMBER THE DAYS when your RSVP to an event or a party meant a simple *yes or no*? There were two possible responses. You committed, one way or the other.

These days, we've moved into a world where there's a third box: *maybe*. Heck, you can even just tick *interested* now!

When our lives are operating as normal, we live in a commitment-optional world, running around in circles, busy *all the time*, but we're not committing to the stuff that matters.

I understand that obligations come up sometimes—but I'm not talking about sometimes. We've moved toward being very indecisive creatures, with too many distractions making it hard to focus on making a commitment.

But *maybe* has consequences. It can lead to unclear communication, inconvenience, and hurt feelings. Yes, that lack of commitment can hurt someone as surely as sticks and stones.

You've probably heard a host lamenting the people who said they were going to come to her party but haven't shown up. For the host, it sucks. And if it's a professional situation, the embarrassment can hurt careers.

If you've experienced this let-down yourself and, like me, you wish that more people could have the decency to be clear and honest, join me in making a change.

Let's do better for each other. Make the commitment and stick with it. Be an unapologetic homebody or a social butterfly, but don't put yourself in the limbo category. Be a yes, and if you can't be a yes, do the host a favor and be an affirmed *no*. Let's stop doing *maybe*.

The only time a *maybe* response could be appropriate is when you really want to attend an event but there's a real possibility that extenuating circumstances might prevent you from doing so. Make *maybe* the rarity it deserves to be in our interactions with each other.

SIGN THE PLEDGE

I promise not to be a *maybe*.

I promise to honor the people organizing events and social gatherings. I'll be clear on my *yes* and my *no* and show up when I've promised to.*

_ _

Signed

_ _

Dated

*This is powerful wisdom that applies well beyond your social life.

#31

MANBASSADORS

EMPOWER OTHERS

WHAT'S A MANBASSADOR? They are men with a particularly powerful attitude and a whole lot of integrity. But first, some context on what they stand for.

The #MeToo movement gave women an opportunity to express and share a negative part of the female experience. While not a pleasant issue, it has opened up a positive conversation, an enlightening and empowering one. It has made us look around and say: *wait, it is time for us to say no, we no longer accept this behavior.* It has been a time for all of us to grow—together.

#MeToo is not about hating men.

And it has inadvertently created a situation where some men, concerned that their behavior could be misinterpreted, have become overly cautious around women, especially in the workplace. This is not a good thing, if taken too far—when even something as straightforward as having lunch with a female colleague becomes fraught with uncertainty and unintended meaning.

The truth is, both sexes have power players and manipulators in their ranks. Our challenge, as men and women, is to make sure they don't continue to drive the global conversation! They define our global societies and I don't know about you, but I've had enough of that. We can't allow the minority to continue to define our lives.

The majority of men and women are great. Most men and women are reasonable. And most men and women know the difference between appropriate and completely inappropriate behavior.

The creep who targets vulnerable women is known by the observant people around him. It is not a secret. And this is not about trying to put up rules about the natural and comfortable chemistry between two people. It's about uncomfortable behavior that disempowers one party.

Instead of pretending it's not happening—as we have for too long—let's bring this behavior to the surface, identify those power players and manipulators, call them out, and make sure they can't keep perpetrating their abuse.

All the great men I've known and met throughout my life never feel so inadequate that they needed to dominate women in any way—especially sexually.

In his discussion of the 25 Characteristics of an Alpha Male, Chad Howse really nailed it:

> **"The alpha male doesn't try to be an alpha male. That's where so many fail. He is interested in life, in living. He's fascinated by the world around him, in becoming the best man he can possibly become. He genuinely cares about people."[17]**

That, to me, is what makes a man an alpha male. He's a #manbassador.

The men who think domination is what it means to be a man are not alpha males. They'd struggle to be considered a beta male! A man who seeks to dominate, sexually harass women, encourage hatred of others, or create division in society . . . That's not a man. The vast majority of humanity has evolved beyond those animalistic traits, but unfortunately, some men around the world haven't moved forward with us. Those men should never be given a place of authority, especially not as leaders of our countries!

There are many great men who are supportive of women—who applaud them and see them as equals, capable colleagues and leaders.

A manbassador isn't frightened of women or other men, because he doesn't need to manipulate or put people down to feel powerful. These men are role models in business and in life. They are examples to other men of what it means to be a great man.

A manbassador is comfortable in his own skin and comfortable in the role he takes on in his life—even if it is not a traditional male role. He steps in for boys and younger men lacking a role model of what it means to be a man today. He shows them how to respect themselves, others, and the world. Manbassadors are a beautiful gift in any community, an incredibly important and valuable member of society.

If you are a manbassador, speak up, show up, raise your voice, set the example, step in when needed to help raise the next generation of men, and let's overcome the growing divide in today's world.

---

17 http://chadhowsefitness.com/2012/11/25-characteristics-of-an-alpha-male. Readers interested in alpha male theory might also enjoy Tricia Christensen's essay for WiseGeek, in which she puts this leadership idea in its zoological perspective: https://www.wisegeek.com/what-is-an-alpha-male.htm#didyouknowout

Honor the manbassadors in your life. Help them understand the role they could play in having a bigger impact in the world. Let's put the voice of manbassadors on a bigger platform. An example to look at is The Try Guys—I love them. Dwayne "The Rock" Johnson, is also a personal favorite.

Those "pussy grabbing" macho males have been getting all the limelight, and we see how much damage that has done. Time to drown them out with the glorious voices of the manbassadors. Are you up for the task?

And fellas, what do you reckon, shall we stop allowing a minority to hijack us all? Join the conversation and help take it in a positive #WeToo direction. The world needs to move forward, united, with grace, love, and integrity at the center.

SEIZE YOUR MOMENTS

SELF-EMPOWERMENT

ALL THROUGHOUT OUR LIVES, we are given moments to shine. If we seize them and excel, doors open up to more of what we want in life. We find our feet on unexpected paths.

Seizing our moments is something we see and celebrate in certain people—Olympic athletes, musicians, artists, writers, authors, influencers, business leaders, and more. We admire people who reach the top of their profession, listening intently to stories of their journey to success.

But we can have that, too. It's about seizing the moments when they appear, which earns us respect in the eyes of others, and more importantly it gives us confidence and belief in ourselves that we can do more, achieve more, be more. Letting them pass us by shrinks us and dulls our shine.

Have you seized your moments?

Or did you panic and fail? Were you too nervous, too unprepared, too unappreciative of the moment you had been given? Maybe it just wasn't your day to be in top form? Whatever the case, did you go back again or was that the end of it?

The secret to achieving what we really want is about seizing these moments when they arise throughout the course of our lives. There will be many of them.

Recognizing them is the key, and then having the courage to step up and rise to the challenge we've set for ourselves. Should we fail, we keep at it, again and again and again, learning a bit each time until we succeed.

HERE ARE SOME EXAMPLES OF MOMENTS WE MAY HAVE OR NOT SEIZED—CAN YOU IDENTIFY WITH ANY?

- Moving to a new city or country for work
- Giving a speech in front of your colleagues
- Applying for a job you don't feel qualified for
- Standing up for yourself or others
- Taking a chance without knowing the real outcome
- Stepping into your voice as a social leader
- Claiming your space in the fight for humanity's future
- Singing on stage or in front of others
- Speaking to that gorgeous person across the room
- Saying yes to an interview

Here are two wonderful examples of people seizing their moments in recent times, which are fodder for inspiration.

Captain Sir Thomas Moore or Captain Tom, raising money for the UK National Health Service (NHS) for his 100th birthday. RIP Captain Tom. We salute you!

And of course, youth poet laureate Amanda Gorman at the US Inauguration. "The Hill We Climb" was celebrated around the world, and for me, she is a beacon of what seizing your moment means.

Remember her words:

> "If only we're brave enough to see it
> If only we're brave enough to be it"

HOME-PLAY

What were the moments I seized?

What were the moments I didn't seize?

What were the reasons I didn't seize my moment/s?

What can I do right now to seize the future I want for myself? Where can I step it up?

Who around me has amazing potential that needs support to seize *their* moment?

WATCH OUT FOR NEGATIVE NELLIES

EXTERNAL INFLUENCE

IS THERE ANYTHING MORE DRAINING than spending time with people who are constantly negative? They never have anything nice to say about anyone or anything, always looping back to a well-worn thread of misery.

Now, I get it that crap stuff happens in life. But my life experiment has taught me this: wallowing in negativity consumes your soul. It makes your spirit stingy. It drains the person being negative, and it also drains everyone around them.

It is so easy to get caught up in negativity. Many of us are lonely, especially in the age of social distancing. When we see people on social media sharing perfect-looking lives, it's easy enough to fall into the slump of seeing our own lives as rather crap, right? On top of it all, complaining or telling a sad story can get us an awful lot of attention. We learned that as children, but today we can have much greater reach for our sob stories.

When we peddle in negativity for decades, it becomes a tragedy that defines us. Bit by bit, the negativity builds as we age. Most of us don't even recognize when we are being negative, so we don't see the acceleration of this downward spiral. We think we are simply expressing what happened, and we don't see ourselves as being consumed.

We all know that older person so fully immersed in a negative mind-set, no one wants to be around them anymore.

It's a chicken and egg situation, because if they weren't so negative and miserable, people would want to be around them, but they need people around them to find their positive mojo again. As human creatures we naturally crave attention, reassurance, and love.

So, watching out for the negative Nellies is really about watching out for this habit in ourselves, too—the habit of holding onto something negative to get attention. It's a habit you can break if you see it in yourself.

It requires a mindset shift grounded in action. That action is a daily check-in to keep any negative tendencies down. When you feel the urge to complain or to say negative things, *even if those negative things are hilarious and will garner laughs and likes on social media*, check yourself and ask whether it would honestly change anything for the better? Nine times out of ten, the answer will be no.

When you can flip to kindness and generosity of spirit, things change fast. The more kindness and positivity you give off, the more these tendencies will become habit, and the more positive energy you will receive. Remember, it may require more sophisticated communications skills, but kindness, generosity, and positivity can be funny, too—and will never feel like cheap shots.

When you do your daily check-in, focus on the increase in the positive things you see and experience.

And as for those people in your life who wallow in negativity, you can help them too, and break the cycle by giving them positive support. (**#Breath in love, breath out hate**, *wisdom 47*)

HELPING OTHERS

If you know someone who is a negative Nellie and it's becoming harder and harder to spend time with them, but you still care about them, try one or all of these:

1. Speak to them about their negativity and how it makes you feel when you're around them.

2. Take them on an adventure—somewhere quirky, with life in abundance—and ask them to share the most amazing experiences they're having as they're having it, as well as the craziest stuff they're seeing. Make it a day for taking the best photograph and share those together at the end (and on social media if that's where they do most of their negative wallowing). Check in on them a few days afterwards. See if they're still buzzing from the experience together, and put another outing on the calendar. Keep the momentum up and give them something to look forward to.

3. Take them to a place where life is really hard and show them your compassion in action for the people you meet. Ask those people to tell you their stories.

4. Help them understand how to watch their thoughts and flip them when negative reactions arise.

5. Write in permanent ink, on their bathroom mirror, how awesome they are.

6. Leave them loving notes, send small gifts to make them smile, show them they are thought of and loved. If social media is where they do their negative wallowing, engage with them positively there. This can take an amazing amount of negative wind out of their sails!

#34

BE A QUEEN

CAREER THOUGHTS

ONE DAY WHEN I WAS FOUR, my dad put me in front of the TV and said, "Watch this." It was "Bohemian Rhapsody," and that was the start of my love affair with Queen and Freddie Mercury.

From that day, **Freddie became my idol.** The celebrity, the superstar, the enormous character, the showman, the performer, the legend . . . yes, Freddie has always been my personal role model. Brilliant, amazing, wondrous, unique, Freddie. I adored him, I mourned him. I'm sure if I was born male or with dark hair, I would've worked really hard to mimic him. Instead, as a blond, I could only mimic ABBA and Billy Idol (that was fun too).

I've learned a lot from Freddie.

Freddie broke ALL the rules. I admire that he gave the finger to all the rules. Just because it had always been done that way, wasn't a reason for him to keep doing it. He mixed musical genres with abandon, dressed however the hell he wanted, and got braver and braver as his journey evolved.

(To paraphrase one of my favorite Seth Godin quotes: if we follow the data, all we get is more of the Kardashians. Same goes for rules.)

I believe rules are nothing but guidelines that need to be carefully considered and then tossed away if they don't serve us. I mean, who wrote the rules anyway? Today, more than ever, we've got to break the rules, every chance we get, no matter the cynicism around us.

Freddie had an unbreakable belief in himself! Self-belief can be a big struggle. It holds back the greatest people I've ever met. There are so many reasons why we don't believe in ourselves, but if we could all be a little bit more Freddie in our self-belief, imagine what we could achieve?

We all need to embrace our inner magic and go out there and own it. We might face criticism, scorn, judgment, and more.

> **PRO TIP:** when you realize that those comments often come from people struggling with their own self-belief, you stop taking them to heart.

If you can embrace your inner magic and your inner weirdness, as Freddie did, you'll attract more magnificent people to you. Self-belief is a huge gift to give to ourselves—in many, many ways.

Freddie's self-belief had no limits. He was aiming for the stars and he got there! Repeat after me: *I refuse to play small!* A new mantra for us all.

Freddie owned his genius. Ok, his geniuses. He owned them all. Not just as a musician, an artist and a performer, but as a visionary. He changed the field of popular music, pushing it to new heights. He took his art where no other rock god had taken it before.

I mean, the man sang opera with Montserrat Caballé! Rock stars weren't singing opera in those days. He never stopped working to refine and improve. He was constantly transforming. This why so many artists put him on their list of greatest inspirations to this day.

Freddie wasn't looking for shortcuts to success, because he knew they don't exist. Genius requires commitment, dedication, and constantly pushing yourself. It's about sacrifice. Actually, it's about choice. To be the best, you can never stop! For me, this was always reflected in his art—even the art considered failures by the market . . . whatever that means in the long run. I loved it all.

Freddie embraced his showmanship. And what a showman! He owned the stage, moved the crowd with his magic, and was simply marvelous to watch. I still feel a thrill watching his performances, no matter how many times I've seen them. Even when I'm watching an actor playing Freddie, I'm still thrilled!

While our costumes might be a little less dramatic, putting on a show is a gift we give to any audience—even an audience of one. The *show* reflects how much we care about them. Let's all make that effort to delight our community.

Freddie understood his audience. How do you drive an audience to care? To really listen? In the business world, putting yourself into the shoes of the customer is the centerpiece of success (whoever that customer is for you).

But here's some insight. The vast majority of people have no idea how to see the world from their customers' point of view. It's a rare talent, so if you have it, celebrate it. Freddie understood his audience beautifully! When he entertained a crowd, he brought them in and they became part of his music. He was brilliant at it.

QUEENLY REFLECTIONS

Who's your hero and why?

What qualities do they have that you admire?

Which of those qualities could you focus on developing?

What rules do you play by that need to be broken?

#35

BEWARE THE VICTIM MINDSET

SELF-AWARENESS

(Note: this wisdom is not about abusive relationships. That is a more complex conversation best had with a mediator or mental health professional. This wisdom is about taking responsibility for our own lives or owning our own shit!)

WHEN THINGS AREN'T going well in your life, you have a right to moan, because it's not your fault, right? However, if it's *always* someone else's fault, you give yourself permission to never take responsibility for the path of your life. That's what we mean when we talk about a *victim mindset*, which seldom has to do with any trauma.

When things aren't going well, it's easy to blame the company you're working for or the people in your life. In a relationship, it's very easy to blame the rough times on your partner. If you can't get on top of everything as a parent, it's easy to blame the children.

But in reality, the only way we can ever overcome challenges is to face into them and take responsibility for them ourselves. Recognizing and reversing a victim mindset requires a deep level of self-awareness.

I was well into my 30s before I heard of this concept, and once I knew about it, I had to train myself to catch my victim mindset when I was blaming somebody or something else for my circumstances. I trained myself to really pounce on these thoughts and replace them with: "That's not someone else's fault, that's my responsibility, so what am I going to do about it?"

The words you use are a good sign of having a victim mindset. Fill in the blanks . . .

"Well, I'd like to do that, but . . ."

"Why does everyone else get to . . ."

"Well, I could achieve that if . . ."

"I would've liked to have the choice to do that, but . . ."

"People like me don't get those sorts of opportunities to . . ."

"Why is it always me that has to . . ."

Whatever we put in the blanks . . . is a touch of the victim mindset.

Getting out of a victim mindset is critical to putting yourself in control of how your life turns out. When you stop being a victim, it empowers you. Focus on the words you use. Focus on how they disempower you, not excuse you from being and achieving what you wish in life.

Step 1 is to assume responsibility for having a victim mindset.

Step 2 is to pounce on those thoughts immediately. This can be hard (*see* **#Do you have voices in your head?**, *wisdom 4*).

Step 3 is to look at where there is a problem in your life, a problem where you are the common denominator. Reflect on your role and on what you need to take ownership of and what you can change.

Personal responsibility is well within your reach—and it's powerful.

PUT IT INTO ACTION

Do I have a victim mindset? (If you're not sure, run through the questions in the text above to see if any of them sound like something you say, either to yourself or out loud.)

Is it just sometimes, or am I really bad?

What are the challenges that keep showing up in my life that I haven't been taking responsibility for?

What am I going to do about changing them? List three commitments!

1.

2.

3.

#36

GIVERS AND TAKERS

EXTERNAL INFLUENCE

WHEN YOU'RE NOT NATURALLY a taker, it can be confusing to encounter those who just don't understand that life is as much about the give as the take—especially if you want to have a fulfilling and beautiful experience in this world. And if you are constantly giving to someone who always puts themselves first and always takes, it can definitely be exhausting.

Can you help a taker change their ways? Yes, sometimes, and slowly. Showing them the better path through your example is a good strategy, but you may also need to tell them how you feel. Gentle, honest conversations can help. Many takers are completely unaware of their behavior, after all, and its impact on others. But do beware, some of them will never see this. They are completely oblivious.

However, if they are willing to change after your talk, do you have the spare energy to be that wise, patient friend for this person? This is an honest question you *must* ask yourself, especially if you've already given them a lot of your energy and time. It's a worthwhile path, but you have to love them and believe in them enough to make the commitment. And you have to make sure to take care of yourself while you're at it.

We are all different; some people are further evolved while some have a long way to go. Connecting to the core truth of who you are will help you not to be tarnished or changed by those who take too much. The worst they can do is change who you are and turn you into a person who can no longer give, because you're tired of the takers. Please don't let them do that to you.

When a taker takes too much, and you've already given all you have to give, step away graciously, gently to get on with doing you. Protect yourself, move forward, and be careful about welcoming more takers into your life. Be generous but not at your own expense. (**#Self-protection and the circle of trust**, *wisdom 68*)

If a taker asks you why you stopped giving, keep in mind that tough love is a favor you may choose to give them, but sometimes it can make the situation worse.

You have to make a decision based on who you know this person to be.

But the critical lesson I've learned for ensuring you don't diminish your own light (and beauty) is to not let takers change your generous spirit. Even if you can't change them, do not let them change you.

COLLECT YOUR THOUGHTS

Who are the takers in my life? Can I help them? Do I have the energy to spare for that?

What about my role in this? What am I giving to someone who always takes? Why do I do it? What is in me that feels the need to give to someone who always leaves me a little let down? Is it time to address this within myself? Am I seeking some form of validation from them?

If I agree to help the takers, what three things will I do for them?

1.

2.

3.

HAVE YOU MET YOUR SOUL YET?

SELF-EMPOWERMENT

I HAVE A CLASSIC MONKEY MIND. It bounces around and it's always on. It's curious and it'll try anything. It is open to everything.

So, when it was suggested that I try a guided meditation, I didn't think much would come of it. A monkey mind and meditation had never been a great match for me, but I was game to try.

My guide, the brilliant Australian Peter Hoddle, talked me through this experience. He has a lovely voice . . .

Peter suggested I walk through a natural environment and there I was, walking through a beautiful field of flowers, and then I walked up a small mountain. At the very top of the mountain, he asked me to look out for a wooden hut. Yes, I saw it. He asked me to go inside the hut. "What can you see?"

I described a huge room with beautiful red velvet couches and candelabras. It was dark, expansive and stunning. It was like walking into a Tardis—the inside looked completely different to the outside. After looking around at this majestic space, Peter told me to walk towards the center of the room. There was a door at the other end opening now, with somebody coming out: a woman with long white hair in a beautiful purple dress was walking towards me, but she didn't have a face. Where her face should be was a clear space. Pure white light I suppose. This disturbed me for a long time afterwards.

This graceful, faceless woman greeted me warmly and hugged me. We sat down on one of the beautiful red velvet couches and started talking to each other about *everything*. And I mean everything. It was beautiful, loving, and calming, and it became an opportunity to reassess myself and my life, top to bottom.

Peter told me that in that moment, I met my highest possible self. My best possible self, the beautiful, gentle, good me that is and always has been deep inside. And why would this self have a face? It took me a long time to understand this. A soul does not have a face. What we look like is central to our identity in the physical world, but when we meet our soul, that true identity is so much deeper than how we look on the surface.

Knowing she's *there*, within, me, helps me believe that I can become more like her. Maybe it will happen in this lifetime, or maybe it will take thousands of lifetimes to get to her level. But she is in me and that has given me direction in terms of where I can go, who I might become, and how I can be in this world.

I'm a kinder, gentler, more loving person knowing she's in there. She showed me who I essentially am, if I can let go of all ego. I call on her often. It's not easy to stay connected to her in this mad world in which we live, but meeting her has changed my life.

Since then, I have meditated many times. In my version, I go to a beach, and a boat pulls up to shore. I take the boat to a small island and sit on a bench. Every time a me from a former life comes to speak to me. They tell me what they learned in their lifetime.

Nature is abundant in these meditations: dragons, a white rhinoceros, and crystal-clear waters full of life as I cross to the island. I can speak to all of the animals in these meditations, too.

I always come out of these meditations feeling amazing. Is it true? Is it real? Is it my imagination? Who knows? One thing I do know is its positive impact on me. I also know its transformative power, and that is everything if it makes me a better me. I want to be like her, which is me, pure, beautiful, loving. She is my goal in life.

Have you met your soul yet?

SOUL EXPLORATION

Sit back and relax. Imagine or meditate if you can. What is the highest version of you? What qualities and values do you have in this version of you? Try the hut meditation if you can. I find guided meditation—even self-guided—unbelievably powerful.

Some people find drawing to be a useful tool to tap into this part of who they are. What symbols would represent this highest version of yourself?

FORGIVENESS IS FOR YOU

SELF-EMPOWERMENT

IF YOU'VE LIVED, you have likely been wronged. You may still be in pain from it. You may even feel anger or hatred towards those who did that wrong to you. It may have been intentional, or simply the result of thoughtlessness.

My life has not been all roses, let me assure you. I've taken many dents along the way, some of them very deep. However, as I learnt to deal with my own **#Epiphanies on anger** *(wisdom 26)*, I learned something else: forgiving someone who's done you harm is not about them, it's about you.

This is a lesson Nelson Mandela gave us all. We grew up hearing about him and how he endured life imprisonment for voicing and fighting for a vision of equality. As punishment, they took most of his life from him and attacked his name and his vision. Yet even when he was released from prison, he was able to forgive the people who took so much away from him. They took so much of his life! We admire him for this, because it is admirable.

When we don't forgive, we allow those who've wronged us to live and linger in our bodies, minds, and hearts—poisoning us, sickening us, and worsening our lives. When the wrong was unintentional, which it often is, they often have no idea we even feel that way. However serious the wound, it's our story, not theirs, and in order to heal we need to be conscious of the fact that we control that story.

When you forgive, you let go of this story and release its toxins. If you don't, it eats away at you. If you allow yourself to continually suffer because of another person's actions, it is joy-crippling and, ultimately, life-crippling. Why would we ever let somebody else's actions take our joy away?

Screw that!

Forgive others, not for them, but for yourself. Let go of your hate and move on from that story, because it's time for the next chapter of your life to commence.

So, what are the practical steps to take toward forgiveness, which is definitely something easier said than done? This is what I do. No matter what they've done, anytime I feel negative feelings towards someone who I think has done me wrong, I send them *the bolt of forgiveness.*

It works like this: close your eyes and picture a huge ball of clean, love-based light, sitting in your heart. Then use all of your energy to throw this bolt of white light from your heart and aim it straight at the heart of the person you're angry with.

Do this anytime a negative, sad, or angry thought comes up. It will bring you incredible peace. Give it a go. It doesn't cost you anything but a few seconds with your eyes closed, and you'll be astonished how good it feels.

Contemporary spiritual thought and quantum science suggest that our energy can change the world in measurable ways. If we take this to be true, why not expand the bolt of forgiveness to bigger world issues?

When you're feeling angry and powerless about what's going on in the world and the decisions world leaders are making, it's time to throw your white bolt of light into the hearts of those leaders.

While you're at it, hurl white bolts of light at the CEOs of companies whose modus operandi is to make money at the expense of the planet. Just as in our personal lives we can forgive someone without allowing them to continue to hurt us. Although this forgiveness for leaders is not the same as letting them off the hook for their accountability toward us all.

What kind of energy and impact could it create if we all come together, focused our positive intentions, and sent bolts of beautiful and loving white light into all the hearts of world leaders? That's our powerful collective consciousness in action. I'm in if you are. It will certainly feel good.

In the meantime, keep it closer to home and send it to those who have done you harm. Don't do it for them. Do it for you. *Forgiveness is always for you and your own good.*

MY COMMITMENT: PLEDGE 3

I will send daily bolts of white light to:

#39

CONSEQUENCES

SELF-AWARENESS

A FRIEND ONCE TOLD ME he was having an affair with a married woman and asked for my opinion on it. I told him it wasn't my place to offer an opinion on his decisions, but I did ask him if he was prepared to accept the consequences of his actions. To me, that's the most important thing. Are you willing to face what comes with an act or decision that is almost certain to have negative consequences?

If the possible or likely consequences of your actions are something you don't want to face, then is it the right decision to make in the first place? If you stand by the decision and accept the consequences that's fine, but don't moan about it after the fact.

My friend did have to face the wrath of the husband. He didn't like it very much and I had no sympathy at all. We teach our kids about consequences, but we seem to forget about them when it comes to ourselves. Curious, that!

On the other side, there are physical consequences in life too. And we need to get stuff sorted out, or we will really suffer the consequences.

Put your neck out? Back hurting? Aches and pains limiting your daily movement? Get those sorted out and don't stop until you get the result you want.

Living with chronic pain has a serious negative impact on quality of life. It's not good for your spirit. The systemic stress and inactivity pain leads to can result in other health problems, too.

Don't wait to address the causes and symptoms that will eventually lead to chronic pain. Don't put off the benefits of getting pain sorted and feeling well. Get on it.

My physio is my fourth favorite person, after my husband and my boys! Ask around, do some research, find an expert practitioner you trust, and make the investment in your wellbeing. I speak from experience: I didn't address my back issues for 20 years. *Don't be an Andrea in this.* The consequences are awful.

#40

WHAT IS SUFFERING FOR?

SELF-AWARENESS

WHEN I WAS A CHILD, the main painting in our living room was one painted by my dad of Jesus dying on the cross in excruciating agony. In our family, it was never something we thought about. It was just there.

But when my husband saw it for the first time, decades later, he was physically repulsed and had to leave the room. He found it that confrontational, graphic, and violent.

I was amazed. I'd never seen the painting through fresh eyes before. And he was right. It *was* a horrible picture in the middle of a family living space, but we just couldn't see it. It simply had always been part of our family home, and we knew no better.

Here it is!

Long before this moment with my husband, I had moved away from my Catholic upbringing as a young teenager. There were so many reasons, but central to them all was the concept of suffering. Everything seemed to be about suffering and negative emotions—guilt, shame, sin, and pain. From my experience, there was no joy, no hope, just misery and torment. It took a long time to get Catholicism out of my system too.

I've often wondered since then, if Jesus did walk amongst us right now, what would He think of what was created in His name?

And yes, I do believe the man we call Jesus existed. From all I've read, he was a good man and a prophet for his time. However, my issue has always been with the church built in His name. That's what I couldn't accept anymore. (And please note, my intention here is not to question anyone else's faith, for which I have great respect, but to share my experience with as much sincerity as I can.)

When I struggle with understanding, I read. I actually started reading the Bible because it was my way of entertaining myself in boring religion classes at school. Since then, I've read hundreds of religious books covering various faiths going back to the beginning of mankind—from our earliest civilizations all the way through to now: Christianity, Judaism, Buddhism, Islam, Hinduism, Druzism, Sikhism, and more.

In these reading years, I was seeking to understand the role of religion in human development so I could understand the deeper impact it continues to have on all societies to this day. While I didn't find the answer to the BIG question, there was one consistent thread across all of my reading—the idea of suffering.

When it comes to faith, suffering appears essential to living a blessed life, and as a young person, that just did not resonate with me.

What irked me was the idea that to be worthy of a heavenly reward, we must suffer. I challenged this idea because it seemed to justify misery by equating it with worthiness and righteousness. Thus, from my perspective, misery became an energy we tolerated and even celebrated as something that makes you closer to God. To be faithful, we must accept suffering without questioning it.

To me, this idea has oppressed generations of people, across the world, and held them down for centuries. So I questioned it. I questioned it a lot.

People suffering develop a mindset of suffering that does not end when the traumatic incident or period might come to an end, for the human body encodes trauma into its tissue. Suffering becomes integrated into our lives. Can you imagine the millions of refugees currently on the move, especially the children, ever being able to shake the suffering of that nightmare off and just getting on with life? It's buried deep in their souls.

My own wandering around the world helped me to look at suffering through a lens that went beyond religion and to reconsider the role it plays in our lives. After all, everyone you ever meet has suffered in some way or another. And the extremes of suffering in this world are wide and varied.

I've learned to look at suffering in terms of what we can gain or learn through it. It can teach us strength, passion, purpose, and beauty. That is where we've really gotten the concept of suffering wrong. It is a gift of growth, and a challenge to be overcome, but it is not a place to reside, a state of being to accept as an inevitable test of faith.

When it consumes us and prevents our joy, that's when it's time to stop accepting suffering, time to buck against it. This is true on a personal level and at the level of society.

We need to help the people who are suffering the most around the world right now. This is our challenge and our collective obligation to our fellow humans. If we want a better future for humanity, it's how we ensure strength, passion, purpose, and beauty in our lives, our communities, and our world.

And for each of us personally, when we suffer—as we have all suffered during this pandemic—can we emerge from it kinder, more beautiful, more community-minded? Or will we stay stuck in suffering for the rest of our lives, and continue to allow this to be part of the human story?

PRACTICE

Ask yourself: am I suffering?

Have you uncovered any growth, learning, or opportunities through our collective suffering in this pandemic experience?

Do you believe you have the right to claim suffering, when so many others are suffering more? Many of us struggle with this, the notion that our own pain is not worthy of being called suffering. However, when we do not fully acknowledge and validate our own feelings, we cannot address them and move forward.

Are there any small steps that you can take to overcome this challenge? Some actions you can take right now which will reduce your current suffering? Whatever your answer, remember that it's OK to be in this moment with tears and pain. In order to move past our pain, we must first feel it.

More broadly, what can we do to help alleviate collective suffering? Who can you see around you that might be suffering, and is there something immediate and tangible you can do?

Note: one of my dreams with this book is that some of you, dear readers, have the wisdom to take action for the millions of people suffering right now. What a gift it would be if we could make it happen. Let's come together and solve the world's biggest problems. No one should suffer starvation, desperation, and lack of dignity in a world of plenty.

#41

TAKE TIME OFF AND THINK

CAREER THOUGHTS

I'VE NEVER BEEN GOOD AT chilling out or switching off. I worked hard to build a business long before the day came to actually launch the business. This meant I've worked seven days a week for as long as I can remember. I can't see it changing either, because I love what I do.

However, in launching my business I had a couple of goals that go beyond the business. One is to live where and how I want to, and another is to take two big chunks of time off every year.

During the Christmas/New Year period I take a month off, and again in July, when my children are on school holidays, I take another whole month. It's a big goal for an entrepreneur and a huge amount of time. For the last few years, I have been able to do it—even during the pandemic.

What does this kind of down-time bring? One benefit is I get to finish conversations with my husband. Imagine this—really having the time to have a conversation with someone you love, not to mention, actually finishing those conversations. It gives us both time to think and to connect.

It also means time to be with my children while they're still young enough to want to be with me. I get to show my two beautiful sons my love of the world, adventure, archaeology, nature, people and more. They see me taking risks, being spontaneous, loving the quirkiness of the world, talking to random strangers, being generous to those in need, and more. I can see how these experiences affect them too. When we took them to Disney World, they were unimpressed—manufactured fun is not their cup of tea! On the other hand, on a random adventure in an ancient city, they're like me in that they can't wait to see what may be around every corner. I love that!

As I travel, even with two boys—or three if you count Steve—it's my quiet time, my thinking time. I use this time to go on adventures around this amazing world, which is pure soul food. But it's time I spend in my head, too, and it feeds my mind, my creativity and my spirit. It allows me to put so many ideas into context with the larger world. My life and decisions can never be focused egocentrically when I live in this wider world.

Ideas are constantly trickling through my brain. Some float in and go straight out the other side. Others hang around for a while, morphing, changing, marinating. The really good ideas get a little more attention, a note for later reference. An opportunity to talk them through live, as they appear, with my husband.

Travel provides me with this time to dig within, and I have learned that the answers to our deepest questions are always best answered from within. Other people's opinions are definitely valuable depending on who they come from (**#Trust your own counsel**, *wisdom 20*), but when we take external inputs and meld them with our own insights, better insights come.

The challenge is, we're just not giving ourselves the time for this melding of internal and external stimuli. In our busy daily world, we only hear the external, and that's a huge miss. Time for your own thoughts is too important not to rank at the top of your priorities.

Silence is a gift that will give you so much in return. Take it. Don't let life be a state of constant overwhelm or noise. Give yourself the time you need as you go through the process of a life redesign. There really has never been a better time.

MAKE A COMMITMENT

Your commitment to time off: what is it? When, where, how often, how long? Alone, with family, with spouse, with . . . ?

Determine one place to capture ideas—a notebook, app, etc. Put every idea in the same place.

Ideas you will marinate during your next time away: list ones that have been hanging around, unresolved for a while. Come back to this if the epiphanies don't strike immediately, but do make an effort to actively capture the thoughts when they arise.

1.

2.

3.

4.

5.

6.

7.

8.

9.

10.

PRO TIP: for a beautiful shortcut to capture ideas, download Otter.ai. Speak into the app and it will transcribe your thoughts.

#42

FOCUS ON THE BEST IN PEOPLE

EMPOWER OTHERS

TO BE A POSITIVE CONTRIBUTOR in the world and your community, focus on the best in the people around you, not their worst. I have found that people grow into the best version of themselves when you show it to them and help them have confidence in its beauty.

But you have to mean it. If you're pretending or being blasé, they will know.

Why does it work? Because people know what their best self looks like, even if they have been keeping it under wraps. They are often just waiting for someone else to see it, which helps them believe it more deeply and it then gives them permission to fully step into that more beautiful version of themselves. It's beautiful and real.

So, when you see something praiseworthy in others, tell them! And keep telling them until they believe it, because once is not always enough. This is such a gift to give another person.

And as always, what we give is what we receive. Expect to have the best version of yourself reflected back when you make the conscious effort to help the people around you see themselves in a more beautiful way.

The friend in my life who really helped me embrace this wisdom is Lorna Pringle. My friend since we were young teenagers, she is glorious in bringing the best out in others and I have seen so many people come to life because of her loving focus. She helped me to see the true power in giving this gift to others. Try it. It will make your heart soar.

THE BEAUTY OF ABUNDANT THINKING

SELF-EMPOWERMENT

INTUITIVELY, MANY OF US UNDERSTAND that what we think defines and shapes our lives. For example, if you're negative all the time, life will probably feel negative. If you're positive, life will resonate. When I understood the idea of what an *abundance mindset* really meant, I decided to throw myself into an experiment at a time we were on our knees, financially. When the chips were down, I decided to put abundant thinking to the test.

The idea of abundant thinking resonates very differently with different people around the world. It was made famous by Rhonda Byrne's 2006 film *The Secret* and subsequent book, both of which were international sensations. However, they were also mocked and criticized by many. I found *The Secret* to be weak and foolish in its focus. It was all about material gains and silly things, like getting a car park if you *believed* hard enough.

But there was an underlying message beyond mere selfish acquisitions that spoke to me more, and that is what perked my interest.

At the same time, I was paying more attention to how people speak abundantly or from a place of lack. I've travelled and worked across many cultures around the world, and regardless of where I've gone, the majority of people I talk to speak about money from a place of lack. "We can't afford this." Or, "Prices are going up." Or, "Everything is so expensive these days!" Today, in the middle of a serious economic crisis, we hear such talk everywhere around us.

However, when you think about how our thoughts control our reality, then surely, when we speak about money only with words of *lack*, that's going to lead to more lack. Furthermore, why should abundant thinking only apply to financial outcomes?

All of this was going on in the background as I fully threw myself into my abundance experiment on every level.

No lack thinking was allowed in my life. I was vigilant about my mindset, my family, my work, my contribution to my colleagues, and how I made other people in my community feel.

What I found was that the more I leaned into the abundance experiment, the more energy I allowed to flow *through me*—energy of plenty, peace and hope—the more I received in return, in terms of financial success, community, love.

Abundant thinking is recognizing that there's enough and that you're OK as you are. When you are OK as you are, you don't crave more because you are already abundant.

From a logical level, this is a really hard concept to embrace. You have to completely surrender to the idea. If you can fully surrender and live *in* an abundance mindset, your life will transform. Really, there will be enough. And remember, I did this when there was nothing for us. We were counting our coins and the debts were mounting.

When you're fully present in this mindset, it's a giving energy. You don't suck energy in and constrain it, as you do with a mindset based in lack. You push loving energy out. My experiment showed me that embracing an abundance mindset makes me feel alive, happier, and more positive. And yes, our finances changed too, but my mindset changed first.

When you have this mindset, the people around you feel it and they too feel energized by your vibe. They want to be part of it. They want in. It's beautiful. Embrace it.

GETTING ABUNDANT

Can you identify one area in your life that feels constrained or lacking?

Try to think about it from a "there is enough" mindset and surrender to it.

As an example, let's say you hate your job. Rather than hating it, start thinking "it is enough" and do your best to believe it fully. This example will help you feel differently towards your job, and while it doesn't mean you shouldn't change jobs, your change of attitude toward the job will not only make you feel better right now, but it might also open up other, more wonderful opportunities.

Say you're not getting enough recognition. Change it to "I have enough recognition" and see how you change. Because it's always about you, not the external environment. This, for me, is what an abundance mindset is about.

Once you surrender (and you really have to be 100% in this), be open to what happens. Who knows where it will take you? That's the beauty, but one thing for sure, it will take you to a better place, not worse.

And yes, you can repeat this more than once on the same area before moving to another area of your life.

Right now, with the whole world locked in struggle, it is a great time to try the experiment. What have you got to lose? And the good news about abundance is that it's abundant!

#44

JOIN THE GIVING ECONOMY

SOCIAL LEADERSHIP

SOCIAL MEDIA HAS A REPUTATION for narcissism and self-absorption. Some of this reputation is definitely well deserved, for in many ways, social media is an example of the taking economy.

But if you flip it, social media is also about collaboration, discussion, participation, service, and giving.

When you choose to use social media to serve your audience and give to your community, you'll see it's a pretty magnificent thing indeed. This is the giving economy.

The giving economy values generosity ahead of money. It helps each of us be more for each other, as communities and as friends, it's so much more than a dollar sign.

On social media, the giving economy is actually easy. Comment on and share other's ideas. Be a champion for your community.

It's a double good. You feel good for helping. And the person whose post you've commented on or shared gets a dopamine hit every time someone in your network comments, likes, or shares their content. It's what happens for you when someone shares yours, so why not flip that around and do someone the favor of giving them a dopamine hit? That's neuro-chemistry in action. It's real, and you might as well put this aspect of social media to work for the greater good.

Is someone you admire running a workshop or a public event? Share it. If you love creative people—musicians, artists, performers—go out of your way to support and promote what they do. Do you have friends fighting for the environment or social justice? Be their biggest cheerleader and you'll be contributing to those movements, too.

We fall over ourselves to interact with and *like* famous people online. Let's do the same for those people closest to us. They need it. Participation and engagement in your immediate network will make it stronger and more vibrant for everyone.

TIM HAMONS

Your generosity to the people around you, through the giving economy, will enhance your life in so many ways. What you get back will be magnified by a thousand. The karmic energy it creates is the best.

Participate generously and help the people in your community be stars. There are no losers in a giving economy. You grow by helping other people grow.

#45
HOLD YOUR CYNICISM

SELF-AWARENESS

TALKING ABOUT CYNICISM REQUIRES deeper reflection, because yes, I can be cynical with the best of them. If we're honest, there's nothing better than having a snigger with someone who laughs at the world in the same way as you do. A little sarcasm is an opportunity for release and relief through expressing the worst possible scenarios in a humorous way with those we trust, and we need that. A touch of cynicism is like salt adding flavor to an otherwise bland dish.

But we know how unhealthy it is to over-season our food. Cynicism, when it takes over our outlook, harms more than it helps us.

People who are cynical to the bone have lost hope. They have given up on humanity and on the idea that we can overcome our challenges. While they may be intelligent, in this mode they can be depressing and a non-constructive influence on our communities.

Being a realist is important. Seeing the truth is important. But cynicism shouldn't be mistaken for realism; it's as warped a perspective as only being nice and pretending all is fine. Once we sink into cynicism full time, it's hard to get back out.

Back in ancient Greece, a Cynic was someone who lived a virtuous life, someone in alignment with nature. But the tables have turned on the meaning of that term, and today it's about a lack of faith in humanity and a lack of trust in the people around us.

Trust is a HUGE issue around the world, to the point that regardless of how worthy a spokesperson or initiative is, it will be met with cynicism in many camps.

I think of Bill Gates when I say this. Regardless of what he does or says, a certain sector of naysayers will be cynical about his intentions—remember, he's trying to get microchips in us! Many people cannot believe he is a worthy human, contributing as much as he humanly can to the greater good of the world. If you believe he is inherently bad, I don't want an argument, I just encourage you to really look into the story more deeply.

To resist cynicism is not about ignoring reality—it is about understanding the challenges and working out ways to overcome them. It's also about believing no matter how big the challenge, we CAN do it. Humans are incredibly innovative and resourceful when we have to be. It's about believing in the possibility that we can succeed if we work together, and even believing that humanity is capable of working together is too much for many, but we can do it! It doesn't mean it's easy, but what can we expect when we don't even give it a chance?

A cynic gives up on trying to understand people or provide any additional thoughts or ideas to get us out of the challenges we face. Cynicism is inherently defeatist. It doesn't serve us or make any positive difference in the world. It can be healthy in very small doses, but don't ever let it consume you whole, or you will be lost to us.

#46

HOW'S YOUR BRAND RAGE?

CLIMATE COURAGE

WHEN I SEE EXXONMOBIL advertising plant and algae fuel, I feel incandescent rage. Why? They are doing good, right? And yet for more than 50 years they've known exactly what emissions would do to our planet.[18] Now they want to pose as our savior, when the damage done is so immense? Not to mention that theirs doesn't even look like a promising solution.[19] This is hardly a surprise, when more has been spent on marketing than actual research![20]

I feel this "brand rage" a lot these days. Not just about the energy industry but toward large consumer brands like Coca Cola, PepsiCo, Nestle, to name a few—the worst plastic polluters in the world.[21] They know it, and nothing has changed. Literally nothing.

I feel it when I'm sitting in the cinema or watching TV, seeing car brand after car brand advertise cars as the next desirable purchase for the consumer. I feel it all the more when it's sold as a status symbol. In many

18 Exxon knew of climate change in 1981, email says – but it funded deniers for 27 more years | Climate change | The Guardian
19 https://theconversation.com/algal-biofuel-production-is-neither-environmentally-nor-commercially-sustainable-82095?fbclid=IwAR3spqpGfO9j6p8xffZsiziqhJpoR1q6M1Dp-twa5hVq1QnEL_vvOTomOis
20 https://www.eenews.net/stories/1063717527?fbclid=IwAR1WXQLsu9aEFC4RkZqCNqSf6V-L3bYvR6x73HPajgWFryUKK9ci56FLgE4
21 Coca-Cola, PepsiCo, Nestlé Are Worst Plastic Polluters of 2020, Have Made 'Zero Progress,' New Report Finds

developing countries, once you move from a motorbike to a car, well, you've "made it" without a doubt.

However, if everyone *makes it* and we have two billion more cars on the road . . . what does that look like for the environment?

GM and Ford have known about climate change for 50 years, too![22] These advertisements are what zero responsibility to anyone besides their shareholders looks like. We can't keep feeding this beast.

I feel anger toward big brands and small. I feel it toward alcohol brands dressing bottles up in useless plastic gimmicks to sell more. It's time to say no to those gimmicks, and to freebies of all sorts. Everyone loves freebies, but they are always cheaply made and completely unsustainable and they never last. All of the above are fodder for landfill, nothing more.

I've felt this anger every time I walk into a supermarket for years now, and nothing has changed. It's all just getting worse. Aisle after aisle filled with unsustainable products, "disposable," yet expected to last in the environment for 100 to 1,000 years.

Everything we buy is wrapped in plastic: toilet paper, diapers, sanitary pads, washing detergent, shampoo, bread, fruit, and veg, all wrapped—so much waste. And not one of those brands takes responsibility for reducing waste or cleaning it up. Where are the mainstream alternatives that are good for the environment? These brands know the damage being done. We all do.

We've known about it for a very long time. Many of us feel guilty buying products that create waste. But when we need essential items and no one is making them sustainably, what choice do we have?

In my own life, I've made the choice to go alternative wherever I can. I bought bamboo toothbrushes for the whole family to kick off 2020 and I bought them from a sustainable company, too. However, after nearly nine months of swollen gums because the brushes are just too hard, I knew I had to buy a sustainable brush from a company with a long history of making toothbrushes—and it was Colgate, finally offering a bamboo toothbrush option. Colgate's bamboo option is only a tiny percentage of what they sell where I live—it's still a wall of plastic toothbrushes, but maybe a tiny, long-overdue acknowledgement. I hate supporting Colgate,

22   https://www.eenews.net/stories/1063717035?for-guid=643e3cb0-ce92-11ea-84ca-fa0752a64f84&utm_source=usatoday-Climate%20Point&utm_medium=email&utm_campaign=narrative&utm_term=article_body&fbclid=IwAR3F5hWVvIU6E3UBPTU1ijn2X04I5w1v7lnYkRVZhqocwDMG-W9LIObEP-4

but I had to find a compromise between environmental sustainability and my own health.

If Colgate were serious, they would have ditched plastic years ago. I have such rage towards all brands who have changed nothing, leaving consumers with no choice. All of the big consumer brands have known about the plastic problem they've created for years and continue to do nothing about it. They may say they care. But such lip service is not the same thing as implementing real change.

They are greenwashing, and we are left with rivers and oceans full of plastic. We eat this plastic. We breath this plastic. We drink this plastic. Our babies are born with this plastic inside their bodies, and our children may never know pristine waterways.

Every brand that contributes to the production of products that end up in our oceans, rivers, land, and air should be made responsible for the global cleanup. They took in the profits, now it's time to take on the responsibility. Sorry shareholders, you can wait.

Tech companies must take responsibility for e-waste, too.[23] E-waste is expected to double by 2050.[24] Clean it up. Make sustainable products that last longer! And cease and desist with aspirational marketing. We need to stop wanting the latest and greatest and learn to use what we have for longer, and tech companies need to take a leadership role in that. Also, no more sneaky operating system updates that make your older model run slower or more inefficiently.

When are we going to wake up? When are brands going to do what they need to do, so that the consumer at least has a choice, if not a chance?

If we don't manage to turn the tide, it might be worth working out where you will be moving your family in a warmer world,[25] if in fact, this option is open to you. I can move mine up north or way down south, due to my passport and that of my husband. If you don't have that privilege, what is the future going to be for you and your family?

23 http://ewastemonitor.info/?fbclid=IwAR32W-LL5hA5SfQ5iAP4C7YsaSHH6zgBmUHIaMYbS9kqAkvef7Au6
    tSkE4o
24 https://sdg.iisd.org/news/un-report-highlights-possible-future-scenarios-to-address-e-
    waste/?fbclid=IwAR3Xb85bJ854oceD-CUhJXTNREZUZceH1e8Rto5Gv7URS-jMWgeZ1I7PX2A
25 https://www.propublica.org/series/the-great-climate-migration?fbclid=IwAR3W12wuI8Rxgi5s9hZe
    mbEojrlELrQtY1grWgeDyPKkOg5HAUHN3dG411c

According to Roger Hallam, the head of Extinction Rebellion, if you are 60 or under, you will experience severe climate catastrophe in your lifetime.[26] We're not talking 2100, my friends.

We can all do what's in our power as individuals, but if the big brand polluters continue, we cannot avert that catastrophe. Demand change and accountability from the brands you support.

If the brands you love don't change, stop buying their products. If enough of us take this stand, they will have no choice.

26 https://www.youtube.com/watch?v=0Zo2DWW_fhc

#47

BREATH IN LOVE, BREATH OUT HATE

SELF-EMPOWERMENT

IF YOU'VE EVER DONE MEDITATION, mindfulness, yoga or anything similar, there's a strong chance you've been asked to breath in love and breath out hate—or a variation on this—as part of the practice. Recently this particular meditation entered my body in a new and deeply powerful way.

It happened when a very old friend asked to spend some time with me. We hadn't seen much of each other in recent years, mainly because this person had become so angry with life that I found it challenging to be around them. While we had not lost touch, there was a growing distance between us.

This friend came to a point of recognizing that they were sick of being angry, and asked me if I'd be willing to spend time with them and be open with them. They were determined to become a better version of themselves. Now, I am not a mental health professional, but we'd always been close. I dearly love this person and was impressed by their willingness to face themselves—which is the bravest thing anyone can do.

So, I said yes. I didn't know if I could make any difference, but we booked the time in and got going.

This kind of work on yourself is frustrating and hard. It can be a brutal thing to face your own history and the actions that caused your anger to rise. It's equally hard to walk through another's pain with them. However, sometimes that's what people need—someone to stand witness.

As the one accompanying someone through this work, I found the whole experience life-changing for me, too. I listened attentively to my friend's account of their pain, where I heard so much anger that had been kept inside, brewing and poisoning their body for decades.

The one thought that kept coming up in my mind was *breath in love, breath out hate, breath in love, breath out hate.*

Those words sound so simple, but until then, I'd never really felt them as powerfully as I did during this experience.

I shared this surprisingly effective exercise with my friend, just as I'm sharing it with you now, and they found it to be a helpful part of the process of self-exploration and healing. Anytime you feel deep anger, just do this exercise for a few seconds and see if you can let it go. It's worth getting past the first bit of discomfort to feel these words deeply, powerfully.

Breath in love, breath out hate. Breath in love, breath out hate.
Breath in love, breath out hate. Breath in love, breath out hate.

ACTION

Do this for a minute . . . for yourself. *Breath in love, breath out hate.*

And if you know of someone who needs it . . . plant some karma points and do this exercise while thinking of them. Share it with them if you think they'd be open.

If you are feeling a general sense of unease, sadness, frustration, loneliness, or whatever else may be happening for you right now, just do this a couple of times a day. One minute each time. It will help you feel better, promise.

#48

LISTEN TO THE QUIET ONES

EMPOWER OTHERS

THERE IS WISDOM EVERYWHERE when we open ourselves to hearing it. But it's not always going to come from the loudest voices or the expected sources. I say this as a talker—a loud talker. However, through my career I've been at the table with people who seldom say a word, and I've learned they are at the table for good reason.

I think fast, make decisions fast, read fast, and take everything on board fast. That's my style, and it's only one style.

Quieter people tend to be more thoughtful. Their ideas develop and emerge over time, but when they are given the space to share their ideas at *their* speed, everyone at the table benefits from their long maturation and revision.

Introspective, deeply reflective, and refined thinking is the kind of thinking we need today. Be sure to listen to the quiet ones. Let's give them the space to be heard and ourselves the space to listen.

#49

IT'S TIME TO SPEAK UP

SOCIAL LEADERSHIP

ARE YOU READY TO STAND UP for what you believe in? Yes? Then now is the time to put your big girl/big boy pants on and do it. If you believe it is time to change the path for humanity and all life on earth, now is our chance to make it happen. If you want to see a kinder, more generous, more loving and equal world, now is the time to claim it.

Yes now, right now.

You want to see change? Speak up! Speak up loud and strong.

You want a different future for humanity? Then speak up.

You want the climate crisis intelligently discussed and acted on? Then speak up.

You want to help people without hope? Then speak up.

You want dignity to be a central priority for every human on this planet? Then speak up.

You want a better, kinder world for your children if not for yourself? Then speak up.

Speak up my friends, speak up! Support those in your community who are speaking out, too.

Every single one of us can be an agent of change. The only thing stopping us is our misguided belief that what we do makes no difference.

I speak with people all over the world. I can hear it in their voices: their throats are constricted in fear of releasing their words—fear of reprisal, criticism, rejection, or simply looking stupid.

Here's the problem with that. All around the world, a small percentage of people are dominating the landscape—both the traditional physical landscape and the landscape of social media. Their influence in the information world is particularly outsized compared to their physical numbers. Those dominant voices do not represent all of us.

Which means the rest of us need to raise our voices and speak up for how we want life to be.

We need this so very badly, because the extreme voices are becoming more and more dominant on digital platforms, and it's doing great damage to all of us. We can't let it continue.

Before you bite, I'm not talking about Conservatives, Republicans, or Tories, or Democrats, Labor or Socialists —I'm referring to the stuff happening outside these traditional schools of thought. I'm talking about the extremists: QAnon, anti-vaxxers, trolls, haters, dividers, and other purveyors of conspiracy theories. They are organized, united, and in recruitment mode. They are embracing every opportunity to make noise, and they sound strong because they are speaking up for their beliefs. I believe they have a right to do it too, but that doesn't mean I'm going to sit back and accept the status quo. No, I want to change it.

Those of us with less extremist positions need to speak up about our beliefs, too. When we do this, we see how many of us there really are. There are far more of us than them.

When we speak up, we drive the global conversation back into alignment with how the majority of us are feeling, because it continues to be out of balance. Balance is critical right now! We cannot allow the negative and depressing narrative to continue to consume us. We can't stop extremists speaking up. But we are bigger, and we can take responsibility by showing up.

199

HOW DO YOU SHOW UP EFFECTIVELY?

Step 1: You define the message you want to be known for. (**#Find your voice**, wisdom 17)

Step 2: Then you connect deeply to your own intentions. You sit in the energy of purpose to envision the change you're seeking to drive, the awareness you're seeking to build. If you can connect on that deepest level, it's incredibly fortifying. (**#The one-minute meditation**, wisdom 28)

Step 3: From this position, grow your voice, your influence, and your power to create a better future for humanity and all life on earth. Anchor your presence deeply in your intentions and go!

If you want to polish up your social presence online, there is plenty of help out there. For starters, check out my website where I blog on this topic extensively.

GET OUTSIDE YOUR SUCCESS ECHO CHAMBER

CAREER THOUGHTS

HAVE YOU EVER BEEN TOLD to only spend time with people you admire and aspire to be like, to ensure you are successful like them? I certainly have.

Rich and powerful people are the ones we tend to look up to. But I believe they represent too small a base of influence to help you live your best life and become the best version of yourself. What qualities do you really want to aspire to, and therefore, who do you really need to be around?

When I think of the influences I want in my life, I think about complex, brilliant, simple, wise, quiet, or understated people. Or crazy generous people who love to have a party. Wallflowers. People who are practical. Every possible variation of humanity, across all dimensions of life. Catholics, Christians, Muslims, Hindus, Buddhists, shamans, people with black skin, people with tea-colored skin, people with pink, freckled skin, and everything in between. Believers, non-believers, spiritual seekers.

If you want to be successful, hang out with successful people for sure, but first answer the question: what does *success* mean to you? And when you've defined success, find the people who model it for you, but also find the people who define success differently, especially in your society or culture.

For example, hang out with people who failed and succeeded when they tried again later on. Or study up on people we recognize as successful but whose path or vision is unconventional. Is the Dalai Lama successful? Yes—that's what I mean.

There are so many different dimensions to being human, and so many lessons to be found in every kind of experience. What is success? Isn't that the bigger question?

When I was younger, I wanted to be the CEO of a company. I didn't know which company, but I always had my eyes on the top job. Then, with years of working in large companies and traveling the world and meeting every variation of human, I realized I didn't want to be the CEO at all. Well, only the CEO of my own company.

I also no longer desired the trappings of success. I didn't want to live my life the way I saw leaders of business living their lives. I didn't want to be part of human politics either. I saw the success I dreamed of as a child in real-life, and it didn't look like a life worth living to me anymore.

The important thing is to watch and reflect on what *you* want—not what others want for you. The best way to do this is to get outside the limits imposed on us by the echo chamber of society's idea of what success is.

With all of humanity to learn from, cast your net wide and be in dialogue with people whose ideas or ways of thinking are fundamentally different to yours. In so doing myself, I've learned ways of thinking that I did not fully comprehend in my younger years. Growth lies in remaining open.

HOME-PLAY

List the people you are going to speak to about their definition of success:

List the various experiences and backgrounds you will seek to learn from—through your reading, writing, watching, etc.

#51

THERE IS ENOUGH TO GO AROUND

SELF-EMPOWERMENT

ONE OF THE THINGS I LEARNED in devoting myself to a truly abundant mindset was that judgment, envy, and cynicism cannot co-exist with abundance. Let's just say the chemical reaction between the three of them forms an abundance-blocking compound in us.

A person with an abundant mindset has made a commitment to the idea that there is enough of everything to go around, especially success, and because of that, they are capable of genuinely celebrating other people's achievements, big and small—even things they would love to have achieved for themselves.

You can't envy and celebrate fully at the same time. The envy holds a part of you away from celebration.

You can't judge and celebrate fully either, because judging is about seeing others as small or insignificant. In reality, judgment diminishes you more than the people you're judging.

Cynicism can be the hardest one to shake, but I believe we can be clear-eyed about the world and the people around us while still having an abundant mindset. Cynicism is a cop-out; it is not courageous, and it does not make anything better. (**#Hold your cynicism**, *wisdom 45*)

Identify where you express—in thoughts or words—judgment, envy, and/or cynicism. Be honest with yourself. Can you let it go? Can you release yourself from these negative thought patterns?

When you do, it's really easy to sink into the true energy of abundance. From there, you can watch your life become bigger, more beautiful, and yes, more abundant. Even in hard times, you can do this. I know you can, because I've been there, too.

CHECK-IN

Have any of your thoughts or actions in the last day come from judgment, envy, and cynicism? List it out!

It is incredibly easy to sink into these negative mindsets, especially at moments when life is particularly tough. The important thing is to watch your thoughts carefully, and if something negative comes up, pull yourself up instantly and halt it. Then put that attention toward a constructive view of the world that fits your values.

Even simpler: if you have a moment of jealousy over someone else's achievement, catch yourself and switch to thinking (or saying), "Good on you mate, that's just fantastic!" Then get back to focusing on what you want to achieve, and keep working towards it, regardless. This mindset means you won't allow yourself to be distracted and pulled down by the energy that jealousy takes from you.

Build the muscle to stop yourself from doing this. It takes constant thought monitoring. Be vigilant if you want to stop doing it.

#52

POSITIVITY AIN'T ALL IT'S CRACKED UP TO BE

SELF-AWARENESS

WHILE NEGATIVITY AND CYNICISM are a poor foundation on which to build anything permanent, uncritical positivity is not the answer, either.

The rise of a new "positive thinking" movement in 19th-century North America created social acceptance of the idea that our thoughts determine our reality. However, this idea is anything but new.

For example, first-century Greek Stoic philosopher Epictetus taught that the thing that upsets people is not so much what happens, but what they think about what happens.

As the idea of positive thinking became more mainstream this century, backlash started to rise against it.[27]

The backlash claims, in essence, that if it means we fail to see the truth before our eyes, the emphasis on positive thinking *only* can be harmful. To achieve balance, we must acknowledge the negative aspects of life as much as we celebrate the positive.

Spiritual guru Osho is someone whose teachings I've always appreciated, and he belongs to the school of thought that holds the positive thinking movement is doing more harm than good. Why? Because it means we're denying reality and being dishonest with ourselves.

27 See this article 'The ethics of positive thinking in healthcare' (nih.gov)

Essentially, I interpret this idea that when we believe we must only be positive, we do not allow ourselves to get to the source of our discontent to address it with self-awareness.

The challenge we create for ourselves by making constant positivity our goal is that we can manufacture a sense of failure for ourselves if we don't get there. We can also cut ourselves off from the full range of human experience and emotions—the negative ones have their place, too.

We push back on negative emotions as though we're afraid we'll get stuck there. I've learned that when we let negative emotions wash over us and really allow ourselves to feel them and sink into them, we come out faster on the other side—and stronger!

Our emotional weather system is a bit like seasons—we can't always expect summer! A bit of winter is not only natural, but necessary in the cycle of life, right? Then again, I live in the tropics, so it's pretty much summer all the time for me!

Developing and sustaining a predominantly positive mindset is a huge challenge. It's something I've worked on for decades. I think I've come a long way too, sitting around the 70–80% mark on being positive. But there are too many factors in life that make it extremely challenging to maintain it all the time—like home schooling during a pandemic. It's hard insisting on being positive when you're having a really bad day with your kids.

And besides, is it really positivity we're chasing anyway? Or is it a deeper contentment and acceptance of life, as it is? That feels more in alignment with the journey I'm on—the path towards my soul's highest potential. (**#Have you met your soul yet?**, *wisdom 37)*

I will continue to move forward on this path towards deeper happiness and contentment, but there are so many external influences at play, regularly knocking me off. Every time it happens, it forces me to stop, reflect, ponder and when I'm ready, move to a place of acceptance before I can return to the path. Can you see how that's not positivity? I am too *of the world* to be separate from the world, and I don't mind that. It can be a pretty dark place sometimes, this world, but I'm still here for all of it because balance means embracing the gamut, accepting the darkness with the light.

And the truth is, my "negative" emotions are where I build my self-awareness muscles. I dig into them, I pick apart why I feel them, and then I release them.

Being positive is awesome but sometimes, being unflappable even when things are terrible is even more awesome. It's about getting the balance right between the two, and it's about not being scared to face our negative emotions. We can't turn our eyes away from ourselves and what's around us.

As a species, we're very good at denying our own role in what is wrong in the world. At this level, the time for acknowledgement and deeper self-awareness is long overdue.

Let's get better at understanding our emotions and our response to them, and at engaging constructively with the bad emotions rather than resisting them (**#What you resist persists**, *wisdom 22*). This is how we grow.

PRACTICE

Ask yourself: what's my balance between negative feelings and happy ones? On a scale of 0% (completely miserable and angry all the time) to 100% (a radiant saint), how would you rate yourself?

When something negative comes up in me, can I simply be OK with it while it plays itself out? Or do I fight it?

Do I accept that my negative emotions are something within me, or do I project them onto others? How are my self-awareness muscles when it comes to facing up to my own negative emotions?

When I am angry, do I hold onto it for days, weeks, months or even years? Or am I able to release it quickly, after sinking into it? Spend a week trying to release anger quickly. You cannot release it if you continue to project it onto someone else, telling yourself it's their fault you feel this way. You can only release it when you accept it as your own emotion.

Blaming others and projecting is a HUGE part of the problem we all struggle with. Think about why these negative emotions rise. What is it within yourself that you need to see? Frustration with yourself or your life, regrets, more?

Breath in and experience it, then breath it out. Biologically, many emotions last only up to 12 minutes—which is not so long!

#53

LET'S TALK ABOUT FEMININITY

EXTERNAL INFLUENCE

AS A WOMAN, when you start to move into what's thought of as marriageable age, it's highly likely you'll encounter all sorts of opinions on what you should do, how you should behave and dress, the education path and career you should aim for, how you should style your hair, how you should speak, your ideal weight, and the list goes on. All of this, of course, is to attract a desirable mate before the clock runs out.

Men get plenty of nonsense opinions on how they should be, too. Many of these ideas cripple their possibilities. As traditionally defined, masculinity and femininity are both very narrow options that limit possibilities of abundant living for both sexes. I've obviously experienced the female side of this more, which is why I am focusing on femininity. Masculinity could be its own chapter, but I'll leave it to you fellas to sort that out. ☺

We ladies are raised from a young age to diminish ourselves, to make ourselves smaller, softer, and more feminine to attract a man. Now, I have no issue with femininity, as long as it's expressed in a way that really reflects how you feel inside. (**#You've just got to do you**, *wisdom 21*)

However, I think femininity deserves an updated definition, and one with a whole lot more variation. For example, I did bodybuilding as a teenager and *loved* it! My greatest feminine role models at that age were female bodybuilders. I thought they were the most divine women on the planet. I didn't care if I met with disapproval for not being girly enough. I loved my muscles and I loved being strong.

The point is, it shouldn't matter what other people think and we shouldn't let such limitations be put on us! We need space for all forms and shapes to emerge and be loved. We need to focus on becoming the best version of ourselves—our true selves—and we need to learn to really love ourselves, regardless of what others think. It's the secret to life!

Warren Buffet, the world's best investor, said the most important decision in your life is the person you marry at whatever age you choose to. If you choose to! I completely agree with him. If you are going to marry or settle down with someone, choose well—it's everything.

This is particularly true if you're a strong woman. If you want to be supported in taking your place in this world, find someone who is proud of who you are and what you're doing, and gives you the space to achieve whatever you're capable of achieving. Your partner should be there to support you in reaching for your greatest potential.

Don't settle for someone who encourages you to play smaller, to match some limiting ideal about what it is to be a woman. Run away and don't look back. We women always lose when we allow ourselves to be defined and constrained that way.

Guys, this goes for you too. Look for someone who lifts you, encourages you, and gives you space to be your best and biggest self. You'll attract the best to you if you accept the best in yourself, right?

Oh, I know none of this is easy, and even more so when the world is full of people telling us what we should do. The only *should* you should pay attention to is about doing you!

#54

REFUSE TO PLAY SMALL

SELF-AWARENESS

HEY, YOU—YEAH, YOU. Are you playing small in your life? Scared to put your head up for fear it will get chopped off? Worried what others will think of you? Anxious about losing the community around you? Scared of feeling foolish or ignored, of getting mocked, shamed, or laughed at?

You are not alone.

I have played small. Most people who know me wouldn't think I have, but in my heart, I know there are moments I could be braver, bolder, and do more. This book is an example of not playing small. Will it be well-received, or will it be a disaster? My head has been full of doubts as I put this together, but I really don't want to play small, so I will publish it, doubts and all.

It's common to feel scared when we play a bigger game. But when we play small, we diminish our own potential, the gift we can give to the world. We diminish ourselves, constricting our voices and our legacy.

When we do this, we slip into a downward spiral in our lives, which often sees us moving into our older years bitter and dissatisfied. We risk feeling like we didn't claim our life the way we wanted to. We risk regret, which is an ugly thing.

HAVE A THINK

Where are you playing small?

What have you always wanted to do but haven't?

What's held you back? Be honest and list it out.

What are you going to do now to play a bigger game?

What are your heart and mind calling you to do?

What first step will you take to get started?

#55

HOW TO DEAL WITH ECO-ANXIETY

CLIMATE COURAGE

Note: This particular wisdom is not offered from the standpoint of a mental health professional. I'm offering it as someone who's felt overwhelmed by and then dealt with eco-anxiety. I found a way to move through it.

I AM HEARTBROKEN WHEN I go to a beach, knowing my children (and yours) may never know the pleasure of walking on a clean beach or swimming in a clean ocean. It is devastating to me that we have made such a huge mess of the world and it's well beyond time we cleaned up our act.

In 2018 the IPCC released its damning report. However, it featured tempered language to satisfy political entities across the world, which—when you read between the lines—makes it even more alarming. We are facing a crisis the likes of which we've never experienced in human history. In a nutshell, all life as we know it on planet Earth is at risk.

After reading this report and delving into the science and commentary more widely than I ever had before, I crashed. I went into the dark pit of what I now know is called eco-anxiety.

When you decide to fully face and try to grasp the scale of the climate crisis, you're almost certain to pass through a period of despair. It's a frightful thing to face.

And when you see it so clearly, the thing that's hardest is the fact that most people are not seeing it at all. They are not understanding how urgently we need to drive massive change across the globe. It becomes painful and upsetting to witness continued abuse of the Earth and climate-change denial by those around us: our country, our community, our business colleagues, our friends, and sometimes even our families.

There's a word for how this feels. According to Wikipedia, *solastalgia* is "a form of emotional or existential distress caused by environmental change." When I discovered this word I understood it instinctively, because it really is the most painful hurt I have ever felt.

It pushes at me deep inside. How can I leave this world the way it is for my boys? I still struggle to understand how others don't feel it, as we destroy the very foundation of our ability to live!

No question, the facts of the crisis are hard to face. Denial has its comfort and convenience. Powerlessness is not a good feeling. Looking it square in the eye is not easy. The amount of misinformation and intentional fake news around the issue is also incredibly challenging. But if you stick with the science, the truth is there.

Why do you even want to go there? Into the depth of the data and the despair of climate anxiety? I found the only way to get past it was to go through it. Ignoring it won't make it go away. Climate change keeps tapping. It's knocking *very hard* at the door.

So what are the stages of eco-anxiety? Recognizing them can be helpful. I'll share what I've learned in my journey through to the other side.

When you dip into eco-anxiety, hope is the first thing to go. This hopeless stage is a hard one. Your job, therefore, is to allow yourself to sink into a stage of overwhelm or even despair, *and* to be kind to yourself, acknowledging how it feels. Yes, it's hard. But if you resist this stage, it will last longer. Sink into it and feel it.

After a while, you'll find you are ready to come out. You'll hit a point of *enough, let's do something about it*. This is when you are ready come back fighting. Fighting means showing up. Contributing to creating awareness. Getting engaged by engaging with your community. A great place is to start at home, and then look to contribute on a bigger scale. Help others through their environmental awakening journey, too.

SOME ACTIONS YOU CAN TAKE

Start with yourself and your family. Look honestly at your lifestyle. Get ready to face up to the horror of how much you personally contribute to the mess. There are apps to help you calculate how much pollution you contribute, how much energy you use, and the impact of your flights. Take a look at the amount of plastic central to your lifestyle.

Inventory your life top to bottom and pick some areas you will change. Maybe you'll buy less stuff (like clothes) or go the extra mile for sustainable solutions. Look for alternatives to the wasteful packaging and high carbon footprint of many supermarket products. Maybe you'll start composting, maybe you'll eat less meat. You may choose to use your mobile phone for longer instead of adding to the e-waste mountain. Maybe you'll choose to focus on making sure that everything that comes into your home is more efficient.

It's really about switching mindsets to create less waste in all aspects of life!

If it goes into the trash within minutes of buying it or getting it as a freebie, then it should never exist in the first place!

Once you clean up your act, the next step is help promote awareness and get other people engaged.

However, speaking out has to be done carefully, with empathy and sensitivity to others. Being aggressive or sounding judgmental doesn't work. Even when you're being gently suggestive, something along the lines of, "Hey, you know, maybe you don't need that plastic bag," there's still a level of embarrassment and shame for the people to whom you say it, and they may resent you. It's a tricky position, which is why it's always great to start close to home.

If you want to see fewer plastic bags, go to the shop supplying the bags and get them to stop! Getting closer to the source of the problem is always the best strategy.

Each of us taking action in different ways adds up. We're all connected to different communities. You can speak up in the company you work for, or be at the coalface on the front line. You can be a spokesperson for your own community or nation, wherever you feel comfortable standing up.

It's really important not to let eco-anxiety swallow you whole—which it can do. Think about it: if we lose everyone to despair, how are we going to achieve anything to make sure the worst does not happen?

There is no time to lose. Joining us in the fight is a powerful way to deal with eco-anxiety.

WHERE ARE YOU ON THE ECO-ANXIETY SCALE?

ASK YOURSELF

How can I move to the next stage—beyond overwhelm and eco-anxiety—while being kind to myself? What is my first action to move past despair?

What's one commitment I can make this week that helps me become more climate positive?

Who is one person in my community I can speak with and encourage to join me on my climate positive journey?

#56

THE HABIT
OF COURAGE

SELF-EMPOWERMENT

I HAVE A REPUTATION FOR BEING COURAGEOUS. It's something I've worked at. As the wonderful Brené Brown said, courage is a habit cultivated over time. The more we practice courage, the more courageous we get.

The fast path to building courage is to be brave in our decisions. When there are two paths, take the one that scares you more! It's not about taking the hard path just to stubbornly pick the hard way. Ask yourself if that path will stretch you and help you grow? If so, that's the path to take.

In 1995 I had $25,000 in the bank, which was enough (at the time) to pay cash for a brand-new red convertible Mazda MX5. I love convertibles—I love the way they feel and the joy of driving one. There's nothing quite like it. I could do it, I could . . .

Or I could jump on a plane with a one-way ticket and start exploring the world, with no job at the other end. I had no idea what would happen. I could have been hurt, raped, or killed, or I could have gotten extremely sick. There was no certainty in the decision to leave, other than the glorious experiences and personal growth I suspected awaited me. I chose the travel path and I've always been grateful I was courageous enough to make that choice.

(And I've still never gotten that red convertible. I care about life, memories and expanding my mind every day more.)

A decision like the one I made is a critical part of the courage journey and is often the difference between a life of frustration or a life of success, however you define success.

People often tell me, "I can't afford it." And that may technically be true right now. But if you look at it differently, you may see another way forward. Once you make a decision and commit to it—regardless of your current circumstances—you will dedicate your energy and finances towards the path you've chosen, and you will make it happen. But you've got to make the decision first, and that can take some courage. Once you're committed, you *will* find the way. Believe it.

Another courage-killer can be those from whom you seek advice (*see* **#Trust your own counsel**, *wisdom 20*). If you need input, take it only from courageous people—people who you know have taken the harder, braver path. Remember, don't pay attention to criticism from people who are simply projecting their fears onto you.

My son Lex was a world-class, super athletic climber from the age of 10 months old. Anytime we were out, people would freak out at what he was doing. To be honest, I wasn't always comfortable watching my tiny Lexy do what he did, but I knew his conviction.

My thinking was: "He needs to do this, and I'm glad he's not afraid to test his own limits." So, instead of holding him back, I'd ask myself: what can I do to support him? The answer was clearly to put myself in a position to catch him if he fell, and always remember to trust him! It's the weirdest thing watching your baby make a decision to test their skills way up in the air. But he knew his limits. He was amazing. I could see his decision making in his face. He trusted his decisions and I had to trust them too.

The people freaking out were projecting their fears onto him. Those fears were about them, not him. Lex's climbing period gave me a few gray hairs for sure, but I was proud of how courageous he was, and proud of myself for not getting influenced into a position of fear.

Courage can, and should, be nurtured from the cradle!

I really believe that courage is about decisions. The most effective way to build courage as a habit is by recognizing small steps toward a big goal and making the decisions step by step. Don't be scared to aim for what you want, even if it seems out of reach, because courage is knowing that the next step isn't out of reach.

Decide what you really want to do, make the first decision to move in that direction, stay focused on what it is you want regardless of external opinions and distractions, and step by step by step you'll get where you want to go. Don't give up.

Remember, courage is when we choose to confront the things that scare us, despite the fear inside. Start small and build your courage muscle.

WHY BE SO HARD ON YOURSELF?

SELF-AWARENESS

I WAS A CHAMPION AT putting myself down for a lot of my early life. An absolute champion! I had nothing nice to say about myself, ever! It was a form of self-loathing, self-hatred even, and to this day, I don't know where that came from.

It actually became a rather ugly habit, and I could see it shake people up when they met me. What I said about myself didn't make sense to them, because it wasn't how they saw me. I eventually realized that it was a self-defense mechanism. I was getting the criticism in *before* anyone else could. My husband, Steve Johnson, was really the person who helped me see this, which meant I was already in my mid-30s before I addressed it. Crazy huh? A complete waste of time and energy.

If you are in the habit of putting yourself down or even hating yourself, stop it now. Write a line in permanent ink on your bathroom mirror so you see it every morning. *I am awesome, I am clever, I am beautiful, I am magnificent*—whatever speaks to you. Read it every day. Let it go into your subconscious and if you didn't before, you'll start to believe it.

Anytime you catch yourself putting yourself down, say those words instead.

Seriously, it is time to love *you* in all of your unique and fabulous gloriousness. Get rid of any idea of what you should be like and instead, just work on being awesome, exactly as you are.

There is no value in putting yourself down when the most magnificent version of you is waiting in the wings for a chance to shine. It's time to shine. The world needs your sparkle.

#58

LEAD WITH COMPASSION

SELF-AWARENESS

IF YOU'VE COMMITTED TO BECOMING the best and kindest version of yourself, a critical aspect of the journey is discovering a deep well of compassion—towards others and yourself.

This compassion extends to those who've done you harm, because you can see, in the story of their pain, what has made them capable of hurting you. It doesn't excuse the harm; but the understanding that comes when you embrace compassion can help mend what is broken in those around us and thus in the broader communities of which we are part.

It's important for society that we extend this compassion to people we don't even know. How else will we move forward?

To ensure we're all on the same page, compassion is awareness of another's suffering and a desire to alleviate it.[28] We don't just observe the suffering—compassion means taking action to do something to change the situation.

According to Compassion.com, *the component of action is what separates compassion from empathy, sympathy, pity, concern, condolence, sensitivity, tenderness, commiseration or any other compassion synonym.*

---

28 https://blog.mindvalley.com/what-is-compassion/

Compassion gets involved. When others keep their distance from those who are suffering, compassion prompts us to act on their behalf.[29]

One definition of compassion I find particularly useful is "to suffer together."[30]

Compassion is not a weakness. In fact, it takes enormous courage and strength, especially if it is toward someone who hurt you. Compassion may not come naturally, but it's definitely something we can learn, a muscle we can exercise.

Compassion requires commitment. Soothing words are not enough. It requires action. And that's the hard part—committing to taking action. It's easy to feel sad about another's life, but much more complicated to do something about it.

However, hats off around the world, as we are witnessing many compassionate humans during this pandemic. They see pain and they want to help, so they are taking action that matters. Compassion is beautiful.

When it comes to social breakdowns and the burden of people forgotten, ignored, or left behind, the challenge we continue to face is more focus on punishment than compassion, when people really lose their way. This emphasis on punishment is a logical end point when institutions like jails have become private commercial concerns. What this creates is a social system where we never acknowledge it's time to fix what is broken. Instead, we punish those who get lost in a broken system.

We don't accept the permanence of the punishment approach, either. When a young person breaks the law and they are thrown into prison, it almost guarantees a long life of crime and more incarceration, because it is now the only career they will ever know. They never stand a chance, because the legal system is unfair to those at the bottom of the social hierarchy all over the world.

What if we ask why, instead of just meting out punishment? What made them do this? What was the family situation they came from? How can we help them overcome their pain so they can become a positive contributor to society? What social programs do we have that can help them move forward and grow? Restitution has its place, but so does redemption.

29 https://www.compassion.com/child-development/meaning-of-compassion/
30 https://greatergood.berkeley.edu/topic/compassion/definition

Reinforcing the cycle of violence and pain isn't working for us. We can all see it's failing.

Of course, not everyone who has done harm is from a broken home or a painful past. Some have, quite simply, been raised to feel privileged and dominant towards others. They believe they are completely right in their thinking too. Even then, we can step in and show them they are misguided and on a path that will bring no joy to their lives.

Here's an example of where it can all go wrong. Ruby Bridges was six years old when she walked into William Frantz Elementary School in the US in 1960.[31] This small, beautiful, black child changed history for America, but to be the example back then . . . well I can't even imagine how frightening that experience was for such a little lady. In 2020, new film footage emerged of this moment in history, and the thing that struck me the most was this.

Raging adults, faces distorted in their anger and hatred, towards this tiny tot of a girl. It's really quite upsetting to see. But it wasn't the adults I was looking at. It was the small children looking up to their parents, and turning around, mimicking their anger. I would love to speak to those children now. I want to know if they grew into believing these same ideas, or if they rejected their parents' racism. This is where many of our society's problems start. It's also why we need compassion, to understand what happened in these formative years, and then work out how to help people move past limiting beliefs and move forward.

If we can help people move past their restrictive thinking—because it only makes their own lives worse, as well as the lives of the people they target—we will move the world forward.

When it comes to men who feel entitled and superior over women, how can the **#manbassadors** *(wisdom 31)* of the world step in and show them a more soulful way? How can parents guide our boys to become men? How can our communities make sure none are left behind? As for the ones who are already lost, are they beyond help? If not, how do we move them towards balance and joy?

The common response toward groups of people who are angry and hateful (men, women, or a specific race or religion) is "sort yourself out."

---

31 https://www.msn.com/en-us/news/us/ruby-bridges-was-6-when-she-walked-into-a-segregated-school-now-she-teaches-children-to-get-past-racial-differences/ar-BB17RwB3

But so many of these communities are not sorting themselves out, and their anger has very dangerous outcomes too, such as violence toward people in real life, especially with online communities riling each other up. Yes, adults must take responsibility for themselves. The media and governments have their role to play too—but more broadly, what can we do within our societies to help people already lost down rabbit holes?

Big ask? Absolutely! But nothing worthwhile is ever easy.

There are many examples of those we can feel compassion for. Those who fear losing something they hold dear or even sacred, who fear being forgotten and left behind or being perceived as weak, useless, a burden, or broken. Those with feelings of anger or righteousness or disdain. Those who are hateful toward someone or a group of people they don't even know, yet they've been told to hate them (**#Were you taught to hate someone you've never met?**, *wisdom 100*). There are those who are incapable of trusting in people or institutions, who live in fear despite tough exteriors, such as QAnon conspiracy theory believers and the anti-vaxxers pushing dangerous misinformation and deepening distrust. The list goes on.

There are so many confused and in pain. Laughing at them and their fears, diminishing or ridiculing them, jailing them, or executing them adds to the abuse and the negative cycle, which only hurts us all.

Is it any wonder there is more of that pain emerging around the world? We don't like to make excuses, but so many people causing harm in the world survived horrendous childhoods and bear the scars of that suffering, and many are suffering from personality disorders. We have little support in place for dealing with crime and violence at their roots instead of punishing after the fact. We really do need to address childhood suffering worldwide—in all its forms and outcomes—so we can ensure more whole adults operating in society.

Pain and failure may have occurred in adulthood, too—with society changing so fast around them, many people run out of opportunities to hold their heads up high. Shame is a vicious master. Loss of self-respect is a cruel blow, and we must be compassionate towards those who've lost, rather than having a *stuff you* attitude. People are being left behind. There is a cost to that, and we all pay that cost. Besides, who says we won't be left behind? Do we really want to live in a society that has no compassion for us when it's our turn?

When we stake out a position of compassion in our thoughts, speech, and actions, we're on the path towards healing the world and improving life for all.

Let's commit to the action required to be truly compassionate. All over the world, let's focus on what we can do in our communities to heal the pain. Let's fix those who have been broken by life. Let's create safe spaces for those who have been too damaged by life *before* they commit a crime and do something unthinkable, like we saw with Lisa Montgomery, who was executed in the US in early 2021.[32]

Isn't it time we addressed the underlying challenges in the foundations of our societies that causes all of the above and more? Let's change our societies from within and leave no one behind. We can do it, we just need the collective will.

When one suffers, we all suffer. We must remember to help those who are in need right now. Help them. Hold them up. Give them safety. One day you might find yourself in the position of needing that support and compassion, too, so start by giving it. And remember, compassion becomes a real force, not an imaginary one, when we join it to action.

PRACTICE

Is there someone in your life or community who has done you/yours great harm?

Who are they? What did they do?

---

32   https://www.bbc.com/news/world-us-canada-55642177

What is their story? Early life, adult life? What happened to them? Who hurt them? When was the hurt?

Are they lost? Or do they have an opportunity for redemption? Are you capable of helping, or is there someone else who should do it?

What communities and community support do you see available for those needing this kind of attention right now? If there isn't any, can you find other compassionate citizens and start building a community to help those in need?

SOME THOUGHTS ON CONSPIRACY THEORIES AND FAKE INFORMATION

People who contribute to their spread often believe 100% in the conspiracy theories they share, and yes, it's alarming, because many of these people are intelligent. There is always some element or kernel of truth in these ideas too, which is why so many people get drawn in. One clear way to identify a false conspiracy is inconsistency in the information. Note, someone convinced of the truth is incapable of seeing these inconsistencies. If you believe you can help them:

- Ask them if they'd be willing to speak with you about their beliefs and promise to have an open mind. Do your research beforehand.

- Let them share their truth openly—let them feel heard.

- Then delicately discuss the theories and gently show them the inconsistencies.

- This will take time, but gentle, loving, educated attention will help them.

- Please don't laugh at them. It's a frightening place to be (many conspiracy theories are based in fear) and being mocked for their beliefs never changed anyone's beliefs.

- Keep sharing the truth in your social communities. We all have a network of people online we can influence. Be a voice of measured calm and insight within your communities.

#59

DON'T BE SO OVERAWED BY POWER

EXTERNAL INFLUENCE

MY CAREER HAS TAKEN ME all over the world and I've been in rooms with some of the richest and most powerful people in the world. Hey, I even played "The Star-Spangled Banner" for President Bush (Senior) when I was a musician in the Australian Army. Later, I worked with some of the world's most powerful tech icons. Through all of this, I've observed two sorts of power.

Some powerful leaders are passionate about elevating humanity to take us to the next level of what's possible. Some of these people attract valid criticism, but the truth is, from what I witnessed, many of them are good, decent humans with amazing brains and they want to leave a positive legacy for humanity.

When I see the way society, governments and the media treat these people, is it any wonder us *normal* people don't want to raise our heads above the parapet? Please give the benefit of the doubt to people seeking to do good in the world. I don't know why so many want to rip them down or question their motives. We are not very trusting of each other, are we?

On the other end of the spectrum, some of the powerful people I've encountered are very average, uninspiring, and even mean. The only thing they care about is their own ego and being number one against their competition. They have no real interests beyond themselves. They're often so distant from reality, it's mind-boggling. They have no desire to create positive change—and in some cases they are active forces of destruction—yet no one doubts them at all. They often get praised for contributing exactly nothing to the world. Humans are strange creatures, aren't we?

How do you recognize a *real* leader, someone whose power is truly earned? I'll give you a clue: look at the culture of the company they have created. If it is jam-packed with inspiring people who believe in the mission of the company and are excited to be contributing to the future of business and humanity, that comes from the top. If it's a machismo culture, a bro culture that's competitive, aggressive, unjust, and does not bring joy to employees' hearts in a meaningful way, that comes from the top, too! That's how you really know a leader.

Given all of this, when you see or meet someone in power, respect them, but don't fear them. Let go of the intimidation feeling. Yes, it can be daunting meeting the richest person in the world, but they are still just another human on their life journey. Don't accord them more deference or power than they genuinely deserve. Pay attention when you are with them too, because when you are close enough to listen to them, you will easily know the truth of who they are, and you can decide where in the spectrum above they reside, and how much you want to admire them.

We are all human. Remember that. Hold your head high, regardless of who is in the room. That goes up and it goes down too. People *below* deserve respect too.

#60

WHAT DO YOU REALLY WANT FROM YOUR CAREER?

CAREER THOUGHTS

WE SPEND SO MUCH TIME WORKING. Wouldn't it be great if we also loved what we did and how it makes us feel?

One of my great professional privileges is that I am regularly asked for advice on career next-steps. I like to tell people that the most important question to ask yourself about your work is, how do you want to feel?

People often tell me about the pain they've suffered because of corporate politics in the company they're leaving—a very common form of professional unhappiness—yet they are ready to move to another big corporation, which will likely be more of the same in terms of politics.

I ask them, why would you be willing to accept that? Does being in that sort of environment make you happy? Don't get me wrong, some love it and flourish in it. They genuinely get a kick out of playing the game. But if you've had enough of it, stressful workplace politics can become quite hazardous to your mental and physical health. We don't seem to think we have an option, though. We tell ourselves we must grin and bear it.

For success and satisfaction moving forward, you've got to start asking yourself deeper questions on the professional future you want. If you find yourself job-hunting (or even just to make sure you shouldn't be looking for a change), try these questions:

1. When you wake up and get dressed to go to work every day, how do you want to feel about that? A job impacts our emotions in and out of work. How would you like to feel emotionally every day?

2. What does work look like to you?

3. How do you want to speak about your work?

4. How do you want your family to feel about your work?

The idea here is to get clear about the impact your work has on you and the people around you—especially your family.

The more time we spend thinking through this side of work (how we feel when we're doing it), the better we align ourselves to what we really want. Then our job-seeking path is more proactive and focused—we're not just waiting to see what drops.

If we're lucky, we've each had one job that was a complete delight. Mine was working for Aerospace Technologies of Australia. My husband has a joyful memory too—he was so happy in a certain role, he would run across the carpark to get to work. I hope you've had a good work experience as well. Wouldn't it be great if we all had more than one? It's still so rare.

Determine what you want first, then look for the job. You'll be surprised at how much control over this you really have.

GIVE YOURSELF PERMISSION TO DREAM

SELF-EMPOWERMENT

IT'S SO EASY TO GET SIDETRACKED from our dreams, whether due to social expectations, cultural pushback, or just too many people telling us why we can't do something. What's hard is to keep in mind that they are expressing their own ideas and fears, and that those ideas and fears have absolutely nothing to do with us. (**#Trust your own counsel**, *wisdom 20*)

And for many of us, we're also tackling that little voice in our head, the one relentlessly telling us why we can't achieve something. Shutting that voice off takes work, but you can do it. (**#Do you have voices in your head?**, *wisdom 4*)

The most damage to our dreams is done by the limits we place on ourselves, because we listened to other people or to that little voice in our heads. We convince ourselves: "I could never achieve *that*, so I'll pare it down and dream towards *this*."

Some of our doubts come from the social expectations of us—like what we are capable of as a woman or as a man. Self-doubt can also spring from Imposter Syndrome, our upbringing, or a perceived lack of education.

We look at the people who have become superstars in their fields without seeing what they've done as possible for us. Why not? In telling ourselves, every hour of every day, a story about how we are not good enough, we let our inner dialogue drown our dreams and guarantee they won't come to light. In asking, "Why would anyone want what I'm offering?" with that negative inner voice—you know, the one that gets to say things we'd not accept from anyone else—we take ourselves out of the running.

I know what it's like to be full of fear, self-doubt and anxiety.

When I launched my business for the second time, I had to tackle that voice. The first time I'd launched my business, I "failed." One thing I learned from that first effort was timing. If you're too early, it can be challenging to succeed, but it doesn't mean you're wrong to try again.

I decided not to look at my first try as a failure, but rather as a learning opportunity. Giving it this new status in my head helped me overcome my inner negative voice and dream of starting my business again, this time armed with more wisdom.

So, my friends, why not dream to be a superstar in your field if that's what you really, *really* want, deep down in your heart? Particularly if you're yearning for it daily.

Why not listen to the whisper of your soul instead of your negative voices, identify the truth of your dreams, and then go out there and chase them with every fiber of your being?

Why not admit it to yourself that this is what you really want and keep at it until you get there?

You don't even have to tell anyone about your dream, just believe it deeply for yourself. I know it's not easy. I know it takes time. But no one can stop you if you really believe it's possible.

Of course, if you just can't sing and want to be bigger than Lady Gaga; that might take something more than focus, commitment, and hard work. Some dreams may be a wee bit delusional. But there's a difference between being honest with yourself and being overly hard on yourself.

To achieve your dreams, you need to work like you've never worked, believe like you've never believed, and most of all, drown out the voice that's coming from fear and doesn't serve you.

I'm cheering you on as you reach for the stars, as my friend Kerrie Phipps likes to say. Give yourself permission to dream, and you've already taken the first step toward success.

GET DREAMING

If those negative voices are still in your head, push them out for a bit (see **#Worry is a waste of time**, wisdom 5 and **#Do you have voices in your head?**, wisdom 4).

Get comfortable. Go to your happy place or for a walk out in nature. Listen to your heart.

What is your heart dreaming of?

What is your plan to start acting on that dream?

1.

2.

3.

4.

5.

The best way to move forward is to take that first step. Go and do it today. And if that voice in your head gives you an excuse, tell it to get lost and get going anyway.

#62

PLEASE DON'T DISENGAGE

SOCIAL LEADERSHIP

THERE IS SO MUCH GOING ON in the world that is horrible, truly horrible. We are at an inflection point in history—the doomsday clock is ticking closer towards annihilation, and we're heading blindly, even apathetically, towards repeating the worst atrocities of the past as we lack preparation for a challenging future.

The word unprecedented has been used an unprecedented number of times. There's considerable uncertainty around the future and the changing role of work. Add to that the economic fallout of the pandemic, and it's natural to feel scared for the future.

There's no disputing it, COVID-19 is tough, but so is the climate crisis we have to deal with at the same time as the pandemic.

And yet people are stepping away, stepping out of public discourse, saying it's all gotten too horrible. Politics have become so negative and polarizing that some people say there's no point participating in the conversation at all.

I'm here to tell you that stepping away is the same as copping out.

When we thought leaders and influencers step away and disengage, we are missing the point of our real role in society. We're here to shift people to embrace new ideas and ways of doing or thinking about things. How can we show any integrity if we duck out from the most urgent issues and questions of our day?

Now is the moment when we all must step up and say enough of this divisiveness, enough of massive profits at the expense of the planet, enough of the increasing divide between the haves and the have-nots worldwide. Enough.

But you can't speak compellingly from a stance of disengagement. You have no credibility.

We need you to be engaged.

Engagement means keeping up with the important issues through trusted, reputable sources. Engagement means asking, OK, what can I do now? How can I help? What action can I take? What volunteer groups can I be part of?

When you do this, you'll start to feel and see you're making a difference, which is a great way to overcome the overwhelm we're all facing. Your children will see your engagement and feel less fearful for the future. Your community and industry will see it, too. Some of them will follow your lead. Engagement breeds more engagement. (**#The ripple effect**, *wisdom 96*)

Yes, the news *is* overwhelming, but please, we need you. Stay engaged, pay attention to what's going on. You've got to stay informed and influence the conversation if you want to have any say in creating the future. Speak up to make the world a better place. Speak up for equal rights for all so all achieve their potential, whatever it is. Speak up to give your children the opportunities they deserve.

#63

BREAK THE RULES

EXTERNAL INFLUENCE

WE LOVE OUR RULES, DON'T WE? We have so many rules, like the time of year you can wear linen, or dressing your age. Who decides who's too old—or young—for something? Some rules are simply silly. It's your life.

Social media is full of silly rules, too. For one thing, rules about how long your content should be—written or video. (Apparently, we don't have attention spans anymore.)

Come on. Surely quality is the only rule worth following, and surely it's exactly these sort of rules that got the world into the chaotic place it is right now!

One of the best rules I ever heard went something along the lines of:

Have a great time, but don't mess with anyone else's great time.[33]

---

33 I encountered this rule in New Orleans. If you have never been there for Mardi Gras, put it on your bucket list. There is nothing like it in the world. However ladies, a quick heads up. I have never been a gal who shows my boobs in public and I didn't in New Orleans, either. I saw many get carried away in the moment and give the crowd a flash. When I went in 2000, social media and camera phones were not a thing. They are now. If you don't want your assets spread across social media, perhaps keep them covered. Nothing is off limits these days.

Here's another one I like to live by (enjoy the irony of a rule about rules): give yourself permission to break rules when you can't see any point to them.

Just make sure you're not breaking an actual law or harming or inconveniencing anyone else!

#64

DON'T LOSE YOURSELF IN CHALLENGING TIMES

EXTERNAL FACTORS

ONE AREA OF LIFE that has been anything but easy for Steve and me is parenting. It's taught me a lot about dealing with challenges, my own and those faced by the people I love. While I'd learned to handle myself and my life, learning to show up as who I really am and be a good parent taught me a whole lot more.

Whether or not you have kids, keep reading anyway, because the two stories I'm going to share with you here are also a way of discussing a way of facing challenges without getting lost in them.

I wanted to share this complicated and painful story to demonstrate that you can go through life's hardest journeys and still not lose yourself. It's about not getting stuck in a negative experience, even if you don't fully recover from it. If you know someone stuck in past pain, do everything you can to help bring them out of it and move forward.

HELPING OUR SON FIND HIS VOICE WITHOUT PUTTING HIM IN A BOX

My son Lex was diagnosed as speech delayed at three and a half, and even today he still struggles with the order or selection of some words (he is 14 at the time of writing). However, the major issue we're trying to overcome these days is reading and writing. Otherwise, our hard-working champion is getting there.

A huge factor in his success was our move to Phuket, Thailand in 2017, where Lex and his brother Jax attend the Arrowsmith Program, which is run by United World College Thailand.[34] Arrowsmith was the solution we were always looking for, and we finally found it. It's not going to help every child, but it is a game-changer for the children (and adults) it has been designed for.

But let me take you back to the beginning of a very painful journey. We have consistently stood by the fact that Lex is not autistic, he does not have Asperger's, and he is not ADHD. He is speech delayed as a result of his tonsils and adenoids growing so quickly that they compressed his ear canals, and his ability to hear was significantly reduced. To give you an idea of how that plays out, if you cup your hands together and speak into your hands, you'll have an idea of how Lex heard the world for his first four years.

Unfortunately, when he was a baby and toddler, we didn't know when his hearing problems started or how long they went on for, and we didn't know what he missed developmentally, because a speech-delayed child isn't completely deaf. Their hearing is muffled. It's also not something very young children can communicate with you about. My second son Jax had the same issues at six. At least we knew what to look for, and so it affected him less.

I took Lex to an ear, nose, and throat (ENT) specialist when we were still in Australia in 2009, because when he started really trying to speak, as opposed to his sing-song speech—at around three years, six months—his tongue was coming out of his mouth, not dissimilar to what I have seen in hearing-impaired people. Until this point, I wasn't worried about Lex's speech delay because I knew he was exceptionally intelligent and he was communicating with me all the time, just not with words.

The other problem then was that we were nomadic. The global financial crisis hit us hard, and we went from Singapore to Thailand to different parts of Australia, then eventually Singapore again, and now back to Thailand. This meant we did not have a consistent community around us, so while we could understand our son, we weren't as aware as we might have been that other people couldn't.

The ENT who diagnosed Lex's compressed ear canals also asked about his behavior, which was quite wild. That's when we learned that this, too, is typical of a child with his condition. He then asked if Lex snored,

34 These are awesome. For more on the school: https://uwcthailand.ac.th/. For more on the program: https://arrowsmithschool.org/

to which we replied that he had snored since he was born. The doctor informed us that no child should snore. (Pro tip: NO CHILD SHOULD SNORE—PASS IT ON!)

When Lex was finally diagnosed, we rushed him to hospital to have his tonsils and adenoids removed, with grommets inserted in his ear canals. That was September 2009. After the operation, we couldn't get appointments with speech specialists who could help him in Australia. None were available. Years later we were told a speech therapist specialized in the hearing impaired should have been assigned to Lex immediately. Sigh.

Less than one year later, with minimal progress for Lex, we moved back to Singapore and he went straight into speech therapy and other forms of therapy. We definitely saw progress, but we also faced Lex's frustration stemming from his inability to communicate and be understood. This often resulted in behavior different to that of other children his age—especially at school.

The whole school journey has been intense. We started him in a brand-new mainstream school back then, but the teachers were not equipped to deal with him. They were not motivated either, especially once they filled all the classes and had a waiting list. At this point, all the "challenging" children were asked to leave the school. This was a very disappointing experience in its own right. After that, he was in special-needs schools (because we had no other options), and while we saw some progress, it was never good enough.

We have always said Lex has a special need right now, but the world seems to have two categories: mainstream, or "normal," and special needs, which means forever. There isn't an in-between and there very much needs to be. We always knew Lex would catch up. Over the years, we've seen that what he needs most, aside from patience and love, is for educators and specialists in his life to be more open and curious about the solutions that would help him overcome *his* challenges. Such curiosity was very rare indeed.

Lex needed professionals to never stop working out what *he* needed to help him move back towards mainstream. Instead, schools pegged him permanently as a special-needs kid, which was backed up by medical professionals, and no one seemed to have any motivation to do the work necessary to help him move forward. There was a total lack of curiosity.

A huge parenting challenge was that too many people—especially those closest to us—were also pitching in, constantly pushing us to have him diagnosed with something else, too. These people were not specialists—in fact, they often had absolutely no idea what they were talking about. Some made observations gently, trying not to offend, but many people were downright rude in their assumptions. Yes, some of Lex's behavior was not dissimilar to that of an autistic child, but he is not autistic. He is speech delayed. The problem is that while a lot of information is circulating around autism, Asperger's and ADHD, there was and still is a lack of information on speech delay and associated behavior.

Based on my understanding (as a mother, not a specialist) a speech-delayed child goes two ways—quiet or loud. Lex went loud, and his behavior was reflective of that. The good thing about him being loud is that everyone knew there was an issue that needed to be addressed, whereas the quiet kids get lost in the system.

Lex didn't get lost (thankfully), but his going loud was definitely a double-edged sword. Very young speech-delayed children often present with "difficult behaviors," and if you're not paying attention, this behavior is usually interpreted as attention-seeking, or a problem that needs diagnosis.

In the early years, we worked very hard to identify what happened before Lex "changed." Diet was one of the first things we made sure to rule out. We didn't always know what he was experiencing, but we did know that certain changes in Lex indicated that something had happened and that he was not happy about it: being with an adult with whom he wasn't comfortable, too much noise and chaos (especially high-pitched noise from other children, so schools were a nightmare for him), people interfering with him by physically guiding him in a direction he didn't want to go and ignoring his protests, and so on.

He was always good at expressing his unhappiness—which is not a bad thing! As his speech started to develop, he was able to tell us these things, and that was a huge relief, I can tell you. Besides, I like the fact that he stood up for himself. He still does.

A speech-delayed child typically acts up because something happened before the "naughty" behavior, and the important thing is identifying what happened.

This is the only piece of information we received back in 2010. A speech therapist gave us this, a photocopy of a page in a book, attributed to Liz Elks and Henrietta McLachlan.[35] They gave the following advice:

---

35   Used with permission of the authors. You can discover more from here https://www.elklan.co.uk/about

What is the child communicating?

Be aware that the child is probably trying to communicate through his behavior and look for what he is "saying."

Use positive statements. For example, "Walk in the corridor" is preferable to "Don't run."

Be aware of your own behavior.

How you respond to the child's behavior may be aggravating the situation. Are you reinforcing the behavior? Are you part of the problem or part of the solution?

Consider the antecedents (causes) of the behavior.

Does he understand the task?

Always check the child has understood what he has been asked to do and ensure that your language is appropriate to the child's level of understanding.

Use structure.

Reassess the structure being used. Does the child understand it? Is it being used?

Stress aggravates!

Remember that for most verbal people, communication is harder when they are emotional. This is also true of children with speech delay. The more upset they are, the harder they will find it to use appropriate language and communication, and so the more likely they are to resort to communicating through their behavior.

Strategies based on pleasing others may not work. Children with speech delays are not often motivated by making others happy, and so behavior strategies dependent on this are not effective.

This was the first time I ever read ANYTHING that helped explain my son's behavior. Just that little snippet! It makes me wonder how many children out there are speech delayed and either getting lost in the system because they are quiet, or worse, being diagnosed as something else, when what they need is to develop their speech?

As our ENT specialist predicted, helping Lex overcome a challenge like this has not been a quick process. Making decisions for special needs children can be a very confusing state of affairs. If you're facing a similar situation, make sure you only listen to specialists that you trust and who really know what they're talking about. We met many specialists who did not earn this trust.

The intense pressure of trying to work out how we could help our child impacted every aspect of our lives, including our marriage. We were dealing with something extremely challenging and there was practically no information available to help us understand and work out what to do. But the hardest part was having people pressuring us into a diagnosis for the sake of diagnosis—Lex must be put in a box that could be ticked.

For example, after his surgery we visited a pediatric doctor on the insistence of his school, which let us know that if we didn't get a diagnosis, there was a high chance Lex would no longer be welcome back at school. So, we went along, only to have to wait nearly two hours for the doctor, in a tiny waiting room with our busy little man, and when the doctor finally showed up, he asked us how many words Lex used. Was it 50, 60?

Yes, maybe. We'd never paid attention or been asked before.

"Aha, that's far too low," said the doctor, nodding his head gravely.

Is it? Maybe it's more. We've never paid attention.

After that he asked whether Lex was left or right-handed. We said it wasn't clear yet, he hadn't decided on a preference. That got an *aha* too.

I replied, "I'm ambidextrous, so perhaps Lex is too? Could it be one of those genetic things."

He then measured Lex's and said, "Aha, big head." Steve and I looked at each other. We knew by now his *ahas* were for confirmations of what he already believed about our son.

Steve offered, "I'm one of the largest sizes for male heads and Andrea is one of largest sizes for female heads. Could that have something to do with it?"

He responded that we were obviously unconvinced that there was an issue to be diagnosed, and we said, "We know what's wrong. He's speech delayed due to enlarged tonsils and adenoids. What do we do to help him move forward now that we've fixed the problem causing it?"

This specialist had zero interest in taking the conversation where it needed to go. Lex was kicked out of school.

This was 2010. We were still trying to find answers in 2017, when we somehow managed to get an appointment with the eminent pediatric specialist in Asia. We signed up for a brain MRI, hearing tests, vision test, blood tests, assessments, and numerous intense appointments. After eight weeks and $32,000, we got the result: a 28-page report that repeated back to us exactly what we had shared with the doctor, concluding they had no idea what was wrong with Lex, but provided a list of drugs they recommended we put him on.

When Steve followed up and asked why, regarding the drugs, they said: *to make your life easier.* Well hell—if we wanted an easy life, we would have done that years ago!

We've fully accepted the reality that Lex may be quirky for life, regardless of what we've done to help him catch up—partly because we just couldn't find the right specialists when he was young enough to really get things sorted out. Moving fast in the right direction is critical, especially when they're little.

However, if we'd moved too fast and allowed Lex to be diagnosed when he was three years old, do you know who would have benefited from it? The school or preschool, because they would get funding for a free teacher subsidized by the government. But a wrong diagnosis (for life) and a free teacher wouldn't benefit Lex.

If we'd allowed him to be wrongly diagnosed in Singapore, he could be kicked out of any international school lacking a philosophy of support for anything other than "normal" kids, despite what they say about inclusivity in the brochure.

Regardless of all the pressure and the huge impact it had on us, Steve and I were united in our determination to proceed with utmost caution as we sought a diagnosis. If we'd gotten it wrong and allowed Lex to be defined by a faulty diagnosis, that's it—he would think of himself as different for the rest of his life and he would never be able to reach his full potential. That is why getting it right was the only thing that mattered to us.

THIS IS HARD WORK PARENTING

What no one seems to pay attention to is the huge challenge this desire to get it right presents for the parents as they fumble around, trying to work out the best thing for their child. We're not experts, just parents, but at the same time, we're not deluded. We know there is a challenge to be overcome.

No one seemed to know anything about speech delay and the behaviors associated with it. No one seemed capable of stopping and taking the time needed to understand a child who is communicating every day, just not with their voice.

No one seemed to appreciate how exhausting it is to work with a child who has unusual challenges, trying to help them be their best. No one seemed to understand that the external pressure to get your child diagnosed is really not helpful and can make the situation worse.

No one seemed to have the patience and love to help a child with special challenges get through childhood without judgement and stigma. And no one understood how painful it is for the parents of a child when the system decides they are too hard and gives up on them.

In those younger years, we had to make dramatic decisions to ensure our children were OK, decisions most people would never make in their lives. But we have both worked hard in our professions to be able to do what was necessary—like packing up the family and moving to Thailand *again* in 2017 for the boys to attend UWCT and Arrowsmith. We would have done anything for our Lexy, because we have always believed in our little man and his potential.

We believe in him more than anyone else. No one can make us doubt him. We're very strong, stubbornly so, and Lex is stubborn too. While that might not be a good thing all the time, I believe it helps my son stand up for himself. Lex has had to go through an extraordinary amount of change in his life, and if people just had a little bit more patience, they could have seen that he was progressing slowly but surely, and that continuing to work out what we needed to do next was all that ever mattered.

We insisted the system give us the time we needed to get our child through the entire process with speech therapists, occupational therapists, and behavioral therapists as the first priority. We had a confirmed physical issue with a physical impact. We fixed the issue, so the next obvious step is help him overcome the consequences of it, before adding another label, which would have been completely unhelpful.

If you are a parent going through something similar, please know you're not alone. Also know that your confidence in your child is valid. And if your child has a reason for difficult behaviors or disabilities and you've dealt with the reason, all you can do is provide the therapy and education *they* need and insist that everyone gives your child love, patience, and the time necessary to help them catch up. Leave no stone unturned. We refused to give up, no matter how hard it got.

And to parents struggling, I know how hard this is, but please, be very wary of anyone, even a specialist, trying to convince you to change your path. The wrong education or therapy will not benefit your child. In fact, the best advice I ever got was from an eye specialist. He said if you don't see any dramatic difference within your child in three months, then it is not the right therapy.

You know your child best. Try and resist the pressure people put on you—even when they think they are doing the right thing.

With this said, following this path means you may suffer as we have, with Lex being rejected from schools because we wouldn't get him diagnosed with anything other than speech delay. If it helps at all, just know that there are two parents sitting in Asia who really know your pain.

Steve and I lay together on our bed so many times through these years, holding hands and crying, not knowing what to do next. But once we'd let the emotions flow, we hardened up and got ready to fight for our little dude once again. We didn't always agree on the approach on that journey either, but we made it, together. Sometimes one of us wobbled, but the other stayed strong. It evens out.

Parenting is hard under normal circumstances, but it's intensely challenging when your child has a developmental challenge the world doesn't want to recognize. And if you add to that the overwhelm of everyone around you thinking they are an expert about your child, well then it can be downright despair-inducing.

It really helps to find a community facing similar challenges. And even though the pressure can be so intense it almost breaks you, hold on for your child. The most important thing is they get what *they* need, not what is easiest for the system to provide. As a parent, we are with you.

The journey is ongoing, but we will never give up on Lex.

A CONCURRENT CRISIS IN THE EARLY YEARS

We were coming to terms with what was going on with Lex and how we could help him, and the boys seemed happy at their new preschool, which felt so much better than the one before. And then—BAM, we got some news that shook our world.

We learned that for the first six months of the year following his operation, Lex was being physically and verbally abused by his teacher at his preschool in Australia. As far as we know, the abuse included hitting, kicking, throwing shoes at him, putting tape over his mouth, making him sleep outside in the sun, and kicking sand at him.

We never got to the bottom of what actually happened, because everyone zipped up in a bureaucratic effort to protect themselves. The school was in the process of being sold, so everyone was "gagged" and threatened with losing their jobs if the sale got screwed up. A staff member who recorded the abuse on video was told to hand over their phone, and the video was destroyed.

The government department responsible for certifying childcare establishments ran a shadowy investigation that we could not access and for which we couldn't see the results. Even the police were not allowed to tell us what happened, because it wasn't sexual abuse. The staff member (the adorable Amanda Robbins) who was brave enough to report the abuse went through a ton of shit for doing so and lost her job. As far as we know, the government department responsible did nothing, the police thought it was no big deal, and the abusive teacher still has children in her care.

It was all very perplexing and upsetting, and we went through a lot of shock as we tried to come to terms with what had happened. As the primary school drop-offer during the period when the abuse happened, I beat myself up for a long time because I didn't see any resistance from Lex going into school. Did I miss something?

Then I wondered, is it because he thinks that's how things are and that's how you get treated in the world? That the world is a mean place? It was a confusing, heart-breaking, and very tough time for all of us to get through. I know people deal with a lot worse, but it was a rock-bottom moment for us. Our beautiful little lad had been hurt by someone in a place where he should have been safe. We didn't catch it, and once we knew about it, we were powerless to do anything.

My husband was keen to explore taking legal action. But I said no, mainly because I believe that taking this to court would screw us up more than anything else. It's ugly and no one wins in the end. I also felt we couldn't rely on the witnesses, many of whom had witnessed this abuse towards other children for seven years before Lex joined without saying anything, so why would they stand up and speak now? My trust in that community was long gone.

I was also constantly running into people involved in that preschool when I went into town. I am not a judgmental person—but looking into the faces of people who thought their jobs were more important than the safety of children in their care? Well, I couldn't hide my contempt for them. And I *really* don't like feeling contempt towards anyone.

After this all came to light, a child psychiatrist told us Lex's main challenge would be an inability to trust outside the home, and that this might manifest itself in bad behavior. In the early years back in Singapore, we could see he was still struggling with it. His teacher said to us when he was five, "It's like he's constantly pushing us, testing us, asking us to prove to him that we do love and care about him. It's like he hasn't got any self-worth."

Our biggest priority in raising our kids has always been ensuring they are confident, respectful, and contented in themselves. To know that during a pivotal time in his life, when he couldn't hear properly or speak, our lad felt unsafe outside his family unit and was struggling with his own self-worth well . . . it was heartbreaking. What has mattered most all along is doing everything we can to help Lex fully love and value himself, as well as to find his voice. And boy, has he found his voice. He never shuts up. He has a mind full of ideas and he never stops sharing them either.

Deciding we were done with Australia and heading back to Singapore really gave us a chance to move on from that time. It was also a decision to move on and focus on giving Lex the best life we could. We wanted to show him that the world is a gentle place and that he is loved beyond measure. We work hard to reassure him every day, but we often wonder if we ever can do enough.

THE DEEPER LESSON OF THESE EXPERIENCES

If you take anything from what I've shared about our journey as parents, let it be this: even when you go through a horrendous time, with multiple "bad" things going on simultaneously (we were also in extreme debt, financially destroyed, work wasn't happening, relationships were fraying, and so much more), keep looking forward.

Focus on the good. In our case, this meant helping our son get his confidence and self-worth back and letting go of the small people who were roadblocks or did something that was downright wrong. Steve still struggles with this experience to this day. That time hangs very heavily on his soul, for so many reasons. We still talk about it a lot.

For me, I decided I would not let what happened shape me into a negative version of myself. If I had stayed in that place of anger, I would have diminished myself as a person. This would have impacted Steve and my boys, potentially changing who they were, too. That, for me, has been one of life's biggest lessons—painful for sure, but I never lost hold of who I was on the hard journeys, and I encourage you to not let life take you there, either.

Hold onto the most beautiful version of yourself, regardless of external influences. This is how I move beyond challenging times, intact and still kind. It's about looking forward. You learn from the past, but you don't hold onto it. You don't allow yourself to get stuck in it. That's when life gets diminished. Please don't let it happen.

#65

UNLEASH THE YEARNERS

EMPOWER OTHERS

DO YOU YEARN? Do you *allow* yourself to yearn? I can't remember not being a yearner. I don't yearn for stuff, I yearn for experiences—life, knowledge, fun, excitement, incredible connections, travel, and more! When I leave this world, it's my lofty goal to go out completely and utterly spent, because I've reveled in the magnificence of living my life.

I see yearning in three parts:

1. It is the starting point that creates desire

2. Desire turns into passion and determination

3. Determination gives you the wings and confidence to believe you can do anything!

Yearning is longing and it can be wistful or sad, or a strong desire to make a difference in the world. It is a deep and powerful energy.

Part of yearning is expressing yourself in action towards that yearning, and so when it is unfulfilled it is a terrible burden to bear. The first part of fulfilling yearning is actually being able to express yourself fully.

I wasn't born into wealth or privilege, but I am white and heterosexual, which is privilege enough. The true wealth in my upbringing, however, was creativity—music, fantasy, unusual sporting passions, nature, and curiosity. I had space to chase everything I ever yearned for. I did not ask for permission. Comparatively speaking, I didn't need to break down many barriers either, because I didn't feel I had them. And I wouldn't have respected them if I did!

That's the privilege of where I grew up and the family I was born into. In fact, the only thing that could ever stop me was me.

I can earn as much money as I want if I put my head down, work hard, believe in myself, and refuse to take no for an answer.

I can travel as much as I want, because I've lived my life in countries with economies that gave me enough money to afford travel.

I gained my tertiary education in Australia at the time where if you could get into university, you could afford to attend without incurring burdensome debt.

Being female never held me back either. Sure, there are things that probably would have gone differently if I was a man, but let me assure you: being a woman has never and will never stop me.

I'm free to yearn, and then I'm free to act.

When I think of the many people all over the world who are stuck in yearning but aren't free to act, I realize how lucky I've been. One example that comes to mind is LGBTIQA people in countries that will kill them for their sexual or gender identity. But even in countries that are relatively free-thinking and liberal, the LGBTIQA community continues to suffer discrimination and prejudice. This prejudice holds them back from showing up as their full selves. If they can't be who they were born to be, how can they ever fully contribute what they were born to give?

Women in countries who are not allowed to follow their dreams simply because they are women are another example of yearners suppressed. Every country around the world, holds women back in big ways and small—think of the number of women who cannot chase that for which they yearn, simply because of their sex?

When we accept that so many are held back from fully expressing themselves, we all lose, the world over.

I wonder what we could create if we gave each person with whom we share this world the space to be who they were born to be, with the space to yearn and to chase those dreams deeply held in their hearts? Do you think about this too?

Let's unleash all the yearners. The world is missing their beautiful contribution.

YEARNING IN ACTION

What do you yearn for?

Now give yourself permission to yearn and act! What will you do next?

Could you also take a moment or two to really feel for those who can never full express it? What is it like for them? Is it fair that we continue building societies that suppress so many?

Then join the conversation to create real change around the world—a world of acceptance for all to be as they are. Are you in?

#66

STUFF ISN'T IMPORTANT, PEOPLE ARE

SELF-AWARENESS

MY MUM HAD A LOVE AFFAIR WITH POTTERY. It never made any sense to me, but it was one of her passions. I remember the day my mum brought home *the pottery lady*. It was an ugly thing in my eyes, but Mum was excited about it and thrilled to finally be able to afford it. We were not a wealthy family at all, and finances were always a stress. It was a special and unusual extravagance for my mother.

On the momentous day she was finally able to bring this figurine home, Mum dropped it as she was walking from the car through the back door. Bits broke off and essentially, it was destroyed.

My mum sat down on the doorstep, where she cried and cried and cried.

I was six or seven at the time. Rather than feeling sad, I thought it was a ridiculous thing to be crying about. It was just an object.

Before you judge me for being harsh, consider the fact that at such a young age, our understanding of our emotions isn't well developed, and I was just being real and honest in that moment.

When reflecting back, the one thing I knew in that moment—even as a tiny lass—is that stuff isn't important. It's not worth crying over.

Back then, I would have appreciated some of that emotion and care coming *my* way when I was sad or hurt or broken. I didn't get what the pottery lady got. It just wasn't in my mum's character. She is an amazing mum on so many levels, but this was not her strong suit. Still isn't. Sorry mum, it's true.

Roll the clock forward. I do not cry over broken objects. Not once. I have seen treasured items smashed to pieces and watched clumsy friends break special gifts. I have smashed many things myself, both precious and mundane. Usually, it's a wine glass shattering at my feet.

This childhood lesson impacted my whole life. That day I learned the value of stuff: stuff is not important. Living beings are important. Use stuff, value people.

#67

LET'S MAKE MX THE NEW X

CLIMATE COURAGE

IF YOU DON'T AUTOMATICALLY recognize the following acronyms, maybe you should count yourself lucky. In the world of technology, marketing, and sales, it's all about the experience. The X.

UX—user experience: what it's like to use something like software
DX—digital experience: what it's like to use an app
CX—customer experience: what it's like to be a customer interacting with a company
EX—employee experience: what it's like to be an employee working for a company

And I'm proposing a new dimension to the experience—MX, or Mother Earth experience.

This is the experience we have with a brand based on their commitment to the health of our planet. Commitment is the real actions they are taking, not their *greenwashing* efforts—which are plentiful. What are their products and their production and distribution processes actually doing to our earth?

Climate courage means changing the direction the world is going through our voice, our vote, and what we put in our supermarket trolleys. Putting our money where our mouths are is a good way to speak up and be heard by those in power. We need to put the politicians of the world on notice too, unless they do what's right. We can be the change our world needs, every one of us, by standing up and demanding it.

We've been given a chance that we won't get again. For ourselves and for our children, we have to claim this moment while the world is on pause.

While it may not be easy—witness my toothbrush challenge (**#How's your brand rage?**, *wisdom 46*)—our individual actions really add up.

So, what can you do?

You evaluate the MX of all the brands you use. If you work for a company, do it with your partners too.

Here is my Climate Courage MX guide and checklist for us, as individuals. This is just a sample of what you can do—get creative, think big.

1. Fashion and clothing

    *   The company I buy from respects all workers in its whole supply chain and is committed to providing a healthy workplace—without slavery, exploitation, sexual exploitation, physical dangers, and other forms of abuse
    *   The production process and supply chain pay a living wage
    *   It is clear of animal products that create suffering
    *   It uses natural fibers and has removed all plastics from its products
    *   The production process cleans up toxic waste like dyes or poisons from past practices, and today no longer uses dyes and poisons and has shifted to sustainable solutions
    *   The company has cleaned up its past impact in local environments around the world and is contributing to the health and wellbeing of the community creating its products

- The production process is healthy for the people working in this industry[36]
- The production process has been improved to reduce water waste
- The production process and supply chain are clear of child labor and slavery
- The company demonstrates full control and awareness of its supply chain and is committed to oversight for the long term
- Its marketing is not aspirational and encourages consumers to buy less, buy better, and make it last longer
- It no longer participates in weekly and monthly sales. Only two sales/year is standard for the industry again. It is not part of #FastFashion
- It sources its materials carefully, refusing to use products responsible for deforestation anywhere in the world
- The brand is transparent and shares independently audited data showing their true green actions

2. Food products and their brands

- Farmed and harvested foods are produced in a way that maintains the quality of the land and water used[37]
- This product's production and supply chain do not endanger animals or contribute to species extinction[38]
- The palm oil in this product (palm oil is in soap, laundry detergent, peanut butter, and many snacks) is produced sustainably (no burning off).[39] It proves this with verified, independent data

36 For more on brands failing to create a safe workplace, see: https://www.hrw.org/news/2020/04/01/brands-abandon-asia-workers-pandemic, https://www-image-ie.cdn.ampproject.org/c/s/www.image.ie/amp/fashion/boohoo-fast-fashion-leicester-garment-workers-207724 and the Bangladesh building collapse
37 Farmed land: are the farming practices sustainable? This covers crop rotations as well as fertilizers. Fertilizers get washed off by rain into the river systems and then into the oceans, creating huge problems. Seafood, in huge demand globally, is not only intensively farmed in ocean pens or done as trawl fishing, but also can be done by flooding rural farmland. This land can take decades or even centuries to become fertile for growing crops again.
38 For example, orangutans in Sumatra where oil palm is grown. They are considered collateral damage. Appalling! Or cutting down the Amazon to expand fields at the cost of putting more species into extinction. Atrocious MX.
39 https://www.yahoo.com/news/greenpeace-links-forest-destruction-palm-014916877.html

- The production process and supply chain are clear of child labor and slavery
- The company demonstrates full control and awareness of its supply chain and is committed to it for the long term
- The production process and supply chain pay a living wage
- Where possible, refill stations and bulk buy options are provided
- It is taking action to clean up its past negative impact in local environments around the world and is contributing to the health and wellbeing of the community creating its products
- The brand is transparent and shares independently audited data showing their true green actions[40]

3. Packaging of all products

- Do not buy products or support businesses that use excess packaging, including plastic and boxes up to 10 × the size of the actual product. Commit to businesses that commit to minimal packaging[41]
- The packaging—and creation of the packaging—is good for the environment (biodegradable mushroom packaging, hemp packaging, etc.)
- This product's production and its supply chain are healthy for people and animals
- The packaging is made from sustainably produced materials
- No excess packaging is used to attract consumers with gimmicks
- No low-quality freebies to lure in customers
- The packaging is designed to decompose in under 50 years once it is in landfill

4. Banking, insurance, and investments

- The provider of this service does not invest in environmentally damaging organizations

---

40 Some of the biggest players stand accused: Nestle, PepsiCo, Unilever, and Colgate–Palmolive, to name a few. So, let's do something. If they are not committed to providing excellent MX, then we must be committed to not buying their products. We can put pressure on them, too. Make them do the right thing by voting with your wallet.

41 I love my Bose headphones, but the packaging is 98% of what I'm buying. Why? It's the same experience with most products in the supermarket.

- The provider of this service invests in environmentally sustainable activities[42]
- The party offering this service looks through the layers of legal entities to find the full life production cycle impact of the investment on this planet[43]
- The provider of this service does not invest in greenwashing marketing activities
- The brand is transparent and shares independently audited data showing their true green actions

5. Lifestyle elements

- Fast food and takeaway: provided in simple, sustainable packaging or returnable packaging to be used again and again[44]
- Water bottle: carry and use your own refillable water bottle.[45] Do not buy bottled water unless there is no choice. Put a filter tap in at home and in businesses when possible.
- Make all businesses provide water taps for customers to refill water bottles on-the-go
- Air travel: thoughtful and fully offset its carbon impact, while committing to reduce unnecessary travel and taking greener options if available to you
- You are transparent and track your own true green actions ☺

The more each of us expect and demand brands to provide this sort of transparency, the faster they'll get into action on cleaning up. Our wallets and voices count (read **#How's your brand rage?**, *wisdom 46*).

I can promise you this: the more you do personally, the more responsibility you take in researching the brands you buy, as well as how you

---

42 Insurance companies that cover environmental damage make it easier for those who create the damage to pass the buck to others. Banks that invest in businesses that create environmental damage are profiting from it. Let such money stand up and be counted for the future.

43 Organizations that hide behind legal entities to be able to say "someone else is doing it, it's not us" are part of the problem. Close your account and make a stand—but don't forget to tell your social media community and copy or tag the bank too, so they hear your voice. Let's create a tidal wave so they are forced to act!

44 Unnecessary packaging is a no. Styrofoam is a double no.

45 Plastic bottles, while convenient, are clogging up landfill and part of that plastic that ends up in you.

interact in and support businesses in the world, it will give you great impetus to keep doing better for mother earth, and you'll feel great about it.

Please name and shame brands not delivering an excellent MX experience. The way to get them to change is to demand it. We can do this!

#68

SELF-PROTECTION AND THE CIRCLE OF TRUST

SELF-EMPOWERMENT

THE LONGER I LIVE, the clearer it is to me that the person most affected by my anger is *me*. Quite simply, I don't like the way anger feels in my body.

The reality is, life is full of disappointments and heartbreak, and by the time you get to 50, you have met plenty of people who let you down, in ways both big and small. How do you move past that? You adopt my circle of trust strategy, as I have, to avoid staying angry at all those people and carrying that anger in your body.

The circle of trust is a visual metaphor about self-protection and managing expectations. It's about not letting anger consume you.

I'll tell you how it works for me, and you can adopt this practice too, if it resonates. When I first meet someone, they start with a huge bubble around them—in my mind. It's a circle that represents full trust. If they do something that's disloyal or selfish or shows they are incapable of being a great friend, that's fine; I just shrink the circle and drop any expectations.

We often allow ourselves to be hurt by the same people over and over again. Families are brilliant for this, friends and communities too. Shrinking your circle of trust means you don't put yourself in a situation where they can do the same thing again, because that would be silly. You know now. You've got experience.

By shrinking the circle, you accept that they are just being who they need to be at that point in time. They can still be in your life, especially if they are a family member or other close contact, but you know what they're capable of and they can't hurt you anymore—because the circle is now smaller! The circle metaphorically protects you. It keeps you out of harm's way by helping you readjust your expectations of people.

The circle is basically how you minimize expectations. Expecting people to be different when they're not capable of is a waste of our precious energy.

Shrink the circle my friends, shrink it and create the space you need from those who would harm you.

The circle of trust is not a punishment for them. It's protection for you. You don't have to cut them off completely, but you don't allow them close and within range of hurting you again.

When I was younger, once I reduced that circle, it could not expand again. As I've gotten older and wiser, I've realized people change—they evolve, they grow. None of us are perfect. We're all trying to do our best. These days, when I see someone really making an effort to evolve, their circle can grow again. It's a dynamic thing, a little gesture of faith in us all.

USING YOUR CIRCLE WISELY

Who needs their circle reduced? Be honest!

Whose could be expanded a bit (on reflection)?

Think of the key people in your life, the ones you are constantly fighting with, or with whom the relationship isn't adding to your happiness. What are the expectations you keep putting on them that they can't deliver on? Think deeply.

What do you want them to do differently that they are not doing? Can you remove the expectation and accept them as they are?

Give it a try and check in 30 days later. How has the relationship changed/improved?

You actively shrink your circle every time you remove expectations. They can't hurt you when you expect nothing from them.

#69

BE
GENEROUS

EMPOWER OTHERS

GENEROSITY IS A DEEP VALUE FOR ME. There are so many ways to live it out.

We can be generous with money, donations, or material gifts. We can be generous with our time, attention and energy. We can be generous simply with our compliments!

Time is perhaps the truest form of generosity, when you get right down to its value to the recipient. However, have you noticed how the older we get, the harder it is to find the time to be generous with our time? Age brings more and more obligations, but it is also when we have the most to give. As we move into the age of wisdom, we need to pass that wisdom on.

The form of generosity that I've come to value greatly in age or experience is generosity of spirit. Sometimes it's just *seeing* another person—really *seeing* and appreciating them—because being truly seen by another can change a person's life.

Generosity is essential not just for the receiver, but for the giver, too. Practicing generosity of spirit has unexpected returns, as this generosity is another name for karma. It's about positive energy going out into the world.

In crisis it's easy to contract, to protect ourselves and our loved ones. However, I've learned that this is precisely the time to operate from a spirit of generosity. This wisdom has helped me move through crisis to thrive and to come out the other side flying.

The story of this time will be the stories of generosity, not self-protection. It's always been that way. Open your heart to generosity and go spread your generous heart everywhere. This has never been more important.

BE KIND

SELF-AWARENESS

I LOVE BEING ON THE BEACH IN PHUKET, Thailand with my golden retriever Freddy. It's not far from where I live at the moment. When the tourists are free to visit and the world isn't on lockdown, there's a hard-working team offering horseback riding on the beach, and the tourists love it. Who wouldn't? It's magnificent. One particular evening before the world changed dramatically, the people who had hired the horses this day were actually good riders, unlike most who plod along the beach.

But it's never the riders I admire. It's the guys working with the horses. They've got some work ethic, let me tell you! Typically, they walk along holding the reins of the horses while their customers ride, but on this occasion, they had to run. Full points to them. It's an endurance sport right there to run on sand, because sometimes it's soft, sometimes it's firm. This day it was soft. These guys are fit—our beach is 8km long!

Freddy decided to dash up to one of the horse handlers, who was running and trying to capture a video of his customer galloping down the beach.

Because of Freddy's interruption, the guy messed up the recording. A rambunctious dog will do that to the best videographer.

When the client came back to the handler and learned of the mishap, he reacted. "Why didn't you take the video? What is wrong with you? I asked you to take the video!"

I had some distance to make up, but when I made it over to them I pitched in, "Hey, this is all my fault! It's my dog and I'm so sorry it spoiled your video."

I got an obsequious, "Oh no problem, madam. It is not your fault. I just really want to capture this moment on video." All kindness and sweetness from up on the horse.

The handler gave me a grateful smile. I'd taken some of the anger away from him.

What struck me was how differently this man spoke to each of us.

I cannot stand this. *Everyone* deserves respect.

In my 30 years of travel, I've seen so many examples of people speaking badly to those they consider *beneath* them, while they speak nicely and respectfully to those they see as being their equals or superiors.

Often, the deference and respect are for something on the surface: skin tone, religion, nationality, perceived social status, etc.

If I could rid the world of one thing right now, it is this idea that some people are naturally superior and that the others are inferior. We are all human. Some among us were lucky to be born into great wealth. Others have created their own wealth. Many struggle week to week. Many more struggle day to day—especially at this time in history. Despite the differences in the way we experience life, under the surface, we are not different from one another.

So please, don't be nice to me if you're going to be horrible to one of my fellow humans. Kindness is meaningless when it's not given equally. No one is above you and no one is beneath you.

Be kind to everyone and watch life blossom.

PRACTICE

Have you been known to speak badly to people in your life? Whether it's people in your community, a different race or culture? Servants? Darker skinned people?

Do you come from a culture where these hierarchical layers are normal? And if so, are you aware of your participation in maintaining this status quo?

Or is this something you've never thought about? I appreciate that this is very often the case. But perpetuating these ideas doesn't serve us or make our community—and ultimately the world—a better place.

Do you think you *are* superior to certain people? Who and why?

Make a commitment now. Next time you feel yourself wanting to snap at someone or criticize them, take a breath and shift your words (and heart) to something kind, something designed to build them up, especially if they are traditionally considered "beneath" you.

Consider your culture and the idea of superiority and inferiority? Were you raised to believe you were above someone or below anyone? Do you think it's time we moved on from this? Is this a conversation you would be willing to start with your family and friends?

We are *all* equal and valuable. The good thing is you can change your perspective if you wish.

#71

BE A PERSON OF YOUR WORD

SELF-EMPOWERMENT

ASKED MY HUSBAND, STEVE: "You're a person of your word. How did that happen? How did you become a person who keeps his word?"

It was a serious question about something important to both of us. We were stumped trying to remember how we became this way. I don't remember ever being taught this principle. I don't remember anyone ever talking about it, either. Neither did Steve.

So, did it just happen?

After reflecting a bit, he said, "I got sick of people letting me down. They'd make promises and then they'd break them. I didn't want to be that kind of person."

Being a person of your word means that when you've made a commitment, no matter what, you do what you said you'd do.

It's so easy to say, "I'm not in the mood tonight," even for something as simple as a dinner with friends. I urge you, put yourself in the shoes of the person who made the effort to plan this evening. Think about their disappointment.

Dinner is a small commitment. There are many bigger ones in life. Your commitment to your word counts.

If your word is not firm, then expect to feel the people around you reducing their circle of trust (**#Self-protection and the circle of trust**, *wisdom 68*), because why keep inviting someone who keeps breaking their word? I know I shrink the circle when that constantly happens.

As a parent, I am actively teaching my children this idea. I'm also teaching them that when people make promises and then break them, we can't let that stop us from being true to our own word.

While we're preparing them for the fact that other people will let them down, we are also trying to help them understand that if the people around them fail to live up to this value, then it means they will stand out more, gain more respect and go further in life because they will be respected as men who are committed to their word.

We can resist giving into cynicism and deciding there's no point in honoring our word just because others don't. Hold to your word. Over a life span, you will find you attract the same quality of people into your world, and the added bonus is, they are people you can really trust.

REFLECTION INTO ACTION

When are you guilty of not keeping your word?

Pick one area in your life and decide to keep your word in that area. It may be social appointments, or it may be promises to call or to do something.

Focus on this area for a week.

Advanced: Pick another area. ☺

ROLLER COASTER OR MERRY-GO-ROUND?

SELF-AWARENESS

ONE OF MY HUSBAND'S favorite movies is *Parenthood*, with Steve Martin. At the end of the movie, which does such a great job of capturing the chaos of family life, there is a conversation where Granny shares her deep life wisdom with Gil (Steve Martin) after he finds out his wife is pregnant AGAIN!

Granny: *You know, when I was nineteen, Grandpa took me on a roller coaster.*
Gil: *Oh?*
Granny: *Up, down, up, down. Oh, what a ride!*
Gil: *What a great story.*
Granny: *I always wanted to go again. You know, it was just so interesting to me that a ride could make me so frightened, so scared, so sick, so excited, and so thrilled all together! Some didn't like it. They went on the merry-go-round. That just goes around. Nothing. I like the roller coaster. You get more out of it.*

It's a brilliant life metaphor, and there's no question in my mind—I definitely enjoy the roller coaster. I have fully embraced it and wouldn't want life any other way. The roller coaster is intense for sure, but it's exciting too. I sit in the front seat, holding the bars with a big smile on my face. The dips and swerves are in there too, and they don't always make me smile, but I know I'll head back up again.

However, the merry-go-round is another life option, and there are definitely days I look with more than a little envy at people living this life and obviously enjoying it. I know it can never be me, but I do admire them.

I see people living and loving both versions, but I also see people living in resistance to the ride they're on. They hate being on the roller coaster or they hate being on the merry-go-round, and it makes me wonder if the key is asking yourself: which life am I currently living, and is it the ride I want? If it is, time to embrace it all. If it's not, perhaps it's time to change rides?

As an aside, if you're in a relationship with someone who's on a different ride (one on the merry-go-round and the other on a roller coaster), is that a good idea for you? Maybe it is, maybe it isn't. But it's important to ask the question.

Or maybe you're on different merry-go-rounds? Probably not a big deal. Different roller coasters, well—that's another story.

#73

SEVEN TIPS FOR HANDLING SOCIAL MEDIA TROLLS AND NOT ACCIDENTALLY BECOMING ONE

SOCIAL LEADERSHIP

I HAVE BEEN BLOGGING and actively participating on social media for more than a decade. Over those years I've had some hideous trolling experiences, too. Being a woman with an opinion certainly attracts some interesting attention, as well as people who love to twist whatever you are saying into something it's just not!

Here's a few tips I've learned along the way. I hope it helps you claim your voice.

1. Never ever be unkind to anyone on social media. Don't criticize, don't judge, don't be an asshole. Ever.

    One of the ladies in my network had the color of her lipstick criticized by another woman—publicly. You don't like the lipstick? Send her a private message. Better yet, don't say anything, because how petty do you make yourself look when you comment on someone's appearance? Resist the need to comment on appearance, *even if it's positive*. It can distract from the conversation and diminish the message of someone who is participating seriously.

    If you don't agree with someone, keep scrolling. Even better, start a respectful discussion.

    A woman recently challenged my authority to blog on a topic I am very qualified to discuss. I've extensive experience in the area.

I could have got stuck into an argument, but I didn't, because I just don't understand why anyone would spend a second of their time commenting in the first place to argue with someone they don't know. I chose to scroll on.

2. What can you do when you see troll-like behavior?

    I have found the worst thing is feeling alone when getting trolled—especially if the attacks come in groups, which they frequently do. If you see anyone in your community getting attacked—male or female—come to their defense. Tell them you've got their back. Post something publicly in support of them (like a comment below the post).

    Engage with the haters if—and only if—you can cope with the fight that could follow. If you choose to engage, stay respectful regardless of how they respond. Block, hide, or mute as needed. The more support you give to the original poster, the better.

3. Don't join in attacking anyone online (aka cancel culture)—even really famous people, who may have done something truly horrendous. The reality is, we just don't know the truth—none of us. Now I totally appreciate the temptation and the righteous feelings attached to such stone-throwing, but the willingness and glee people seem to express when joining gossipy conversations and sharing horrible stories is what concerns me. This is *the mob* in action, and we can be better than that. We can express our disapproval for the behavior of public figures without stooping to viciousness.

    We must always remember there's a person at the end of that attack, so let's be kind. It feels nicer in your body when you are kind to other people, too. When you hate, your body produces and holds onto toxicity. Check out how terrible your body feels next time you are angry, and you'll see what I mean. (**#Epiphanies on anger**, *wisdom 26*)

4. Own a slice of the responsibility. I get it that social media platforms need to change—and social media has a lot to answer for in terms of nasty behavior. However, as a human being, if you want a better quality of conversation, you need to take part—and own your responsibility for that conversation.

    For example, if you can be the first commentator on a post, it sets the scene for a better class of comments. If the first comment on a post is judgmental in the eyes of other readers, they will up the ante—and that's how we get a feeding frenzy. But when you show up constructively, the bullies and the trolls have no place to go.

Equally important, positive support early on welcomes others to join in the conversation. If it starts off ugly, many people who may have been willing to comment back away. They don't want anything to do with ugly conversations.

If you want to be a social leader, attracting new audiences to you, succeeding in the broader social media world is part of that. We have a role as marshals in turning this around. We are all responsible for what happens on social media.

5. If you run a company or are in a leadership position, consider the role you play. So many "professionals" are being unkind online—even on platforms like LinkedIn. Businesses can and should take a more active role to set expectations on what's acceptable for those associated with their brand. It seems logical to me that people will self-censor, but it's not the case everywhere. I certainly wouldn't want to have an unkind person working for me—in any form.

If you see a colleague acting inappropriately online—being a troll or a bully—speak to them if you feel comfortable doing so, and explain how this looks for them and the company. If the behavior continues, it may be time to speak to their boss.

When I run my social leadership courses for companies, beyond the social media guidelines they all have access to, I recommend participating in alignment with company values. If you don't, you shouldn't expect to keep your job.

6. Gents, keep an eye on the ladies in your community—personal and professional—especially if they are actively participating with a strong voice on hot issues. The attacks can be relentless, and the world needs to hear their voice! The goal of these trolls is to silence women, and the world will suffer if these women stop speaking out. The early days of owning your voice can be hardest, so help them through. Keep them going. Help them believe in their message.

And ladies, it is not just men who troll women—women are horrible to each other, too. Please, do not participate in ripping down another woman—and I don't care who it is or what they've done.

Encourage those in your community not to engage in tearing each other down, either.

We can and must be better and more respectful to each other. If we don't, what sort of an example are we all setting for our children?

7. Don't support media and online platforms if they allow anonymous comments. I personally decided to no longer contribute to platforms like this long ago. Why? Because anonymity empowers haters and trolls. Simply put, if you can't stand by your words and identify yourself, then who cares what you have to say?

Platforms that allow this give trolls a powerful bullhorn while diminishing the impact of people trying to do something good. These platforms thrive on the feeding frenzy and the bitch-fest. That's how they attract huge audiences, and the numbers attract advertisers and funding.

A reality of our time is troll armies, relentlessly attacking individuals to silence their voices. We must stand up to these trolls and support each other through it. Many people have attempted or even committed suicide because of this ugliness. Report the trolls. Block their ugliness. Defend each other.

Bonus action: Start holding the media accountable for what they are contributing to the world. I am all in favor of excellent journalism and the journalists I admire are very fine people doing critical work. Free society needs journalism.

However, far too many media houses, media groups, and platforms are a huge part of the problem in the world today—giving coverage to those who use it to sow division and spread hate, fear, and misinformation.

My advice? Don't subscribe to or spend time on media that spreads hate. Don't even share that content to make a point. And if you are tempted to ignore this bit of advice, if you're going to share a post from someone spewing hate, it should be done in such a way that it's starkly clear to your followers that you're challenging that content. Your post should be your analysis of the content, rather than a re-tweet or share without commentary.

#74

SUPPORT THE YOUNG FIGHTERS

CLIMATE COURAGE

WE'VE GOT SOME AMAZING youngsters all over the world and their voices are rising. They're fighting for their future, and I love them and applaud their courage. However, it really annoys me when I see adults criticizing them and speaking about them as though they don't deserve respect.

There's also a milder form of criticism too, telling the kids to slow down, relax, and focus on going to school. Hello! Did you miss the memo? They're fighting for their future and they ain't going to stop.

These kids can't be kids. They're scared for their very future, the future we adults are leaving them due to our apathy, unwillingness to see what is before our own eyes, and the greed and corruption that has seen endless growth without regard for its impact on the planet. We have destroyed the foundation of our ability to live, and they will experience the brunt of that. It's a miserable-looking future right now, if we don't change. As we've taken more and more of what we want, their future is offering them less and less.

These kids are running a sprint, and they see their objective very clearly: a livable future for themselves. They also think the adults aren't listening—at all. I don't blame them. Not enough of us are, and the ones who matter are not standing up!

Who cares about education, sleep, or anything else when your very life is on the line? Many young people declare they will not have children,[46] because why would they bother?[47] Our youth are in an existential crisis and we have to wake up to it. Their despair is mounting. I feel this at home in the conversations with my two lads. One of the greatest concerns for their future—apart from misery of epic proportions—is extreme mental health issues. Let's be supportive to them in their fight. We owe them that.

So instead of expressing concern about whether they skip school or not, how about we get behind these amazing youngsters and help them succeed? Or better yet, let's raise our voices with them and take action, freeing them up so they *can* go back to school, because they'll know and trust that we're doing what needs to be done?

Not willing to join them on the front line? Support them in all other ways possible and help them get their message out. Vote for leaders who give a damn for the children's future, not the ones who make *you* feel safe today—that's short-term-ism, we need long-term thinking and planning now. There's sacrifice in voting this way, but it's beyond time we did that for the kids. Give them encouragement and positive reinforcement and help protect them from trolls and ugliness.

This isn't to say that it is *always* misguided to urge them to take care of themselves and get an education. (And let's not forget that by default, most young people will ignore anyone telling them how to live their life. Did you listen when you were young? I didn't.)

But we've got to start respecting and honoring the strength in their spirit and conviction. Before giving them advice on how they should manage their energy or their lives, we must understand what is driving them to stand up and fight. And then we must get behind them and stand beside them in this fight!

46 https://www.bbc.com/worklife/article/20190920-the-couples-reconsidering-kids-because-of-climate-change

47 https://www.huffpost.com/entry/climate-change-having-kids-children_n_5d493eaee4b024405 2e09033

IN SUPPORT

List 3–5 young folk you can support:

1.

2.

3.

4.

5.

MY COMMITMENT

What am I going to start doing to help in the fight for our collective children's future?

1.

2.

3.

4.

5.

#75

WHEN THEY GO LOW, WE GO ...

SELF-AWARENESS

WE GO HIGH, RIGHT? That's what Michelle Obama said in her famous 2016 speech.

Why, then, are so many going low? Why are so many people attacking and being horrible within their communities, which include their family and friends? That's not going to change anything or achieve a positive outcome, is it?

When we go low, it sinks into our bodies as negative energy, which makes us meaner and harder. We lose our love for life. It's self-sabotaging, really. When the majority go low, we guarantee more negativity in the world that we all have to endure. We don't want that!

Yes, the world is a challenging place. Yes, too many people are in deep pain and things are upside down. Yes, there are many people expressing horrible thoughts, but that should only tell us they're scared and are crying out for help.

We must remember, if we go low and they go low, we're all heading in the same direction—the opposite direction from where we should be heading.

The challenge is, the negative voices have only become more negative, and this is creating a bigger problem. Those who are typically positive or optimistic are finding themselves moving towards the negative. We're moving *towards* them, and that means, we're not holding the line! We must hold the line, or negativity will continue to gain a stronger foothold, and the balance will continue to be out of whack. Let's stop it in its tracks! The darkness is winning. Can you see it?

I know the only way to live a life of peace and contentment, is to hold onto your love for life. Because as soon as you lose your love for life, you sink into a negative frame of mind and it infects your days. It's not something we talk about enough, but every time I see it, I know it is a destroyer of lives.

This is an intense time for all of us, but that's all the more reason to take Michelle's words to heart and go high. Let's lift the global conversation and address people's fears with compassion. Let's collectively envision the future we want. We can't do this if we go low, we simply can't. When we go low, we move towards that which we don't like. We let the darkness win. Breath, relax, and share love!

#76

EXPLORE ALL PERSPECTIVES

SOCIAL LEADERSHIP

IN THE AGE OF A PANDEMIC *and* an infodemic,* it is time to challenge the foundations and rise to the moment. You and I have the power to influence the course of both through our behavior.

As far as the infodemic goes, we can stay the course by being mindful about how we explore and share knowledge. Rather than instantly rejecting ideas not aligned to an established view, we can open ourselves to all perspectives, even ones that make us uncomfortable. Otherwise, we live in an echo chamber.

---

* An infodemic is when we experience an overload of information—which is usually false or unverified (non-peer-reviewed). News and information ricochets around the world—in traditional media, on social media channels, on political podiums, and more. This massive torrent of conflicting information makes the challenge harder for us on the receiving end, because we're too overwhelmed to know what's true anymore!

An infodemic is a concept beyond information overload—which we've been dealing with for a couple of decades now. To give you context, we created more information in the first decade of this century than was created in *all* of human history, and since 2010, it's doubled every two years.

An infodemic commonly goes hand-in-hand with another crisis, such as a pandemic. The other crises that have compounded this pandemic—economic, social, political, and racial unrest—have created even more information chaos and reverberations. Essentially, we're facing an infodemic on multiple fronts. Arm yourself using the tips in this wisdom.

The algorithms of social media feed us what we view—please watch *The Social Dilemma* on Netflix! We are tracked through every click, so it's easy to be convinced of our virtuousness. But what it really means is we're living in an information silo. If we open our minds to other ideas, the algorithms will serve a broader feed of knowledge.

Critical thinking is one of those core skills required for us to create a better future. Critical thinking is how we see the woods for the trees in all this noise and deal effectively with the central issues of our time. And critical thinking depends on information—high-quality information, and lots of it.

This can mean confronting ideas we disagree with, ideas that go against our essential core. But it will equip us to better defend our own fundamental beliefs, or even challenge them—which is very healthy too.

Equally as important, if we don't understand how other people think and the language they use, how can we expect to engage in intelligent conversation or change their minds?

As someone who is both a communicator and a commentator, I use the following principles to guide me as I navigate the information landscape:

1. Be very focused in *how* you look for information; it will help you build a network of trusted providers over time. Follow and subscribe to news and media sites you value, companies too, and for business, follow the company social pages.

2. Follow thought leaders, experts, and futurists you respect, track key hashtags, and pay attention to your community. Who are the people consistently sharing amazing content? Keep track of them, engage with them. The quality of your daily information diet is based on the quality of who and what you follow on social media.

3. It's critical to be able to view both sides to ensure you remain objective and can continue to apply critical thinking. Deliberately seek out reliable sources that push your buttons, sources that bring you new, even challenging perspectives.

4. Know the difference between an opinion and fact. Verify all information back to the original source. If you want to find the source, it should be linked in the article. If there is no source attributed, then it's a sign you're reading an opinion.

5. This is where most of us get caught out: whatever data you want to back up your opinions, you can typically find it. It doesn't mean it is correct, so do a search using the title or the authors names and see what conversation has been generated. If it has been debunked, that's usually been done in a very public way.

6. Take your emotions as a signal for deeper enquiry and deal with them so you can look at multiple perspectives calmly. If you can succeed in taking the emotion out, you can view information dispassionately and logically. Strong, negative emotions are a good signal it's time to step back.

7. Do not share from an emotional state when possible. Work hard to take emotions out, especially before responding or sharing information.

8. One strategy to achieve neutrality is to absorb all information with the lens of history over it. When you put this lens on top, it helps determine what really matters. Ask the question, *what will be the story of this time when we look back?* How will we see today's breaking stories when we look back in five years, in ten years, or even in thirty years?

9. Become sensitive to the distractors. There are experts out there creating distraction information. Learn to spot it so it does not take you off course.

10. Appreciate that information, like scientific data, takes time. Always check for factual, scientific information to be peer-reviewed *before* sharing, or tell your audience it's not peer-reviewed yet. Scientific research is not a sound bite, it's not a headline, and it's not click bait. The same goes for political data. The processes for verifying research are arduous, but they ensure we get accurate information. Better to wait than act prematurely.

11. Stand back. See the patterns. Understand the divisions. When you feel an overwhelming negative emotion towards a group or idea, ask yourself why? Who sowed that seed? Who is benefiting? Is your life better or worse? Be really honest with that answer. Are you building more walls—physically or metaphorically?

12. Share the future you want. Envision it. Recruit your community into your vision too. Speak up for what you want to see in the world. Share the beauty, share the opportunity, share the craziness but position it in a way that is helpful versus adding to the negativity. Don't get baited into a fight. It hurts you, even if you think you can win it in the moment.

13. Let go of fear. Some parties are out there actively marketing fear to you. Recognize it, understand it is not good for you or any of us. It's hard to make good decisions or see deep insights from a place of fear. Commit to creating a better future, a future of hope. This is what helps me stay out of fear—hope! Identifying fear is the place to start.

14. Honor the feelings in your community. People in your circle may be feeling fear or overwhelm or even joy. Be sensitive to where others are when you speak out in your community. It's very important to be empathetic. Let your words be a balm to help your audience address their fears, so they can escape that crippling state of mind.

15. Stay in the game. Don't let the angry, the hateful, the dividers, or the trolls continue to have an outsized presence on social media. Just being present to counter this is why I won't let the infodemic overwhelm me. I see it as my duty. Let's flood social channels with goodness and powerful fact-based information.

16. Help your community. Commit to being a change agent and an educator. Raise your voice. Educate your communities. Understand the power of social leadership to drive change around the world. Open up a huge heart full of empathy, and then be present, stand witness, and contribute a beautiful vision for our collective future.

17. The final important tip is this: be kind to yourself. Data overwhelm is a real thing. Understand that burnout can strike even the most voracious news and information gatherer, because it takes an enormous amount of energy to do this and *face* it. Rest, relax, recoup, and come back when you're ready. It's so important to honor this need, but also to not let it defeat you.

#77

DOMESTIC VIOLENCE AND FEAR

SELF-AWARENESS

DURING THE PANDEMIC, domestic violence records have been shattered all over the world. What could be responsible for this dramatic increase in reported domestic violence? One of the contributing factors has been isolation: offenders can take their time, knowing no one can see their victim for weeks or months.

These days, we know that violence often comes from a place of fear. A fearful man is a dangerous man, especially if he has no outlet to express himself. There's plenty for the average man to be afraid of in this pandemic and the economic crisis it has set in motion. To move our society forward, we have to dig deeper than our judgment of men who have reacted with violence and help them move past their fear. (*see* **#From judgment to compassion**, *wisdom 12*)

And though domestic violence statistics are dominated by men, all of us behave badly when we're coming from a place of unexamined fear. Fear is a dangerous mindset, if we don't create the space to allow people to talk through their fears and help them understand that being violent towards another is a misdirected expression of that fear. Violence, whether physical or verbal, creates shame, and shame leads to more violence— a never-ending cycle deeply mired in fear.

Though taking it out physically on a loved one is a line most of us won't cross, we all know feelings of anger and frustration, especially at a time when the fears that feed them are getting extra oxygen, a time when many of us are cooped up with those loved ones in a way we haven't been before, all while facing a very uncertain future. There's a lot to be fearful of.

So, when you feel your anger flare up, take a time out to dig deep inside. Try to recognize and name what you are feeling for what it is. Find a safe place to discuss it and ensure you don't misdirect it towards someone you love. That's an action you can never take back, and from which a relationship may never recover. When we can identify the feelings underlying our thoughts and actions, we can address them, rather than staying trapped in them. Self-awareness is key to navigating this crisis.

A final learning from this pandemic: plans for future pandemic response must include separate accommodation for anyone convicted or accused of domestic abuse. Governments must define better communication strategies and put systems in place to address the real fear people have felt. We must provide outlets for people who need to speak about negative feelings in extreme situations. And we should be putting these structures in place permanently, for as a society we will be processing the fear and anxiety of this moment for years to come.

More than anything else, we must acknowledge the fear swirling around us right *now*. If you are feeling anxious, find someone to speak with about your fear. Men, don't be too proud to do this. Surely it's better to speak than it is to do something you will always regret?

REFLECTION

Step 1: How are your fear levels right now, on a scale of 1–10, where 1 is good and 10 is off the charts? How about those around you? Are they fearful?

Step 2: Reflect. Dig deep. What else are you feeling inside? List it all out and consider it!

Step 3: Identify what you can do about these feelings, like speak with your partner or a best friend. If you are really struggling, is it time to seek professional help? Let's face these fears, because when we do, we can overcome them.

INVEST IN MEMORIES

SELF-EMPOWERMENT

MANY YEARS AGO WHEN I was working full time in the technology industry, I was on a bus going to a corporate event with some colleagues. Everyone was talking about their share portfolios, houses, and other assets in which they had invested. Finally, someone asked me where I invested my money.

I told them I actually didn't have any investments in the traditional sense. I said I was a different sort of investor, I invested in memories.

The bus went silent.

I explained this is the way I decided long ago to live my life: I invest my money in memories.

My life has always been about seeking that next adventure, that next incredible experience, that next moment of awe. It's been about traveling and experiencing this amazing world. It's also been about putting myself outside of my comfort zone, so I stretch my thinking and expand my vision of life.

The returns are very favorable too, but they are different from financial returns.

You get to tell beautiful, rich stories! It can take weeks, months, or even years to be able to laugh at some of the unexpected predicaments you may find yourself in along the way, but with the right mindset you'll get there eventually.

Our real currency is stories. We humans crave them. And the best way to get stories (in other words, a great return on investment) is by getting outside your comfort zone.

Even the business world has gotten this message. Business leaders today know storytelling is key to success. It takes mastery, not simply a few good narrative outlines, to have good and compelling stories. But it takes life experiences to feed those stories.

So, if you want to lead *and* live an amazing life, don't wait until your mortgage is paid off and your car upgraded, or allow yourself to continue to be hooked on buying more and more stuff, because we know possessions don't make us happier. Invest in making memories. Experiences are top of the pops for living a happy life.[48]

48 It makes for happiness: https://edition.cnn.com/travel/article/travel-makes-us-happy/index.html, https://hackspirit.com/what-makes-people-happy/ and https://psychcentral.com/lib/what-makes-us-happy/

A TIME FOR REFLECTION

CLIMATE COURAGE

IT FEELS LIKE WE'VE ALL BEEN given a big time out since this pandemic began. We've been sent to our rooms and told to reflect and consider the world we create out the other side of this crisis.

While this is a very challenging time for everyone, it is much harder for those all around the world who were already struggling to stay afloat before it started.

Which means those of us who are lucky enough to maintain a comfortable quality of life through the pandemic have been given an opportunity to embrace a gift—the gift of time to deeply reflect. A time to reconsider how we live our lives and how we shape our collective future, so that all can live in dignity. We all have a chance, a beautiful opportunity, to create the world anew.

Will we, as a species, take this chance to reflect and change our ways? Or will we miss it and look back only when the next crisis hits, and the next, and the next?

With the climate crisis, the health crisis, the economic crisis and deepening global inequality all rising around us, it's clear that if we do not change, we are ensuring a permanent state of crisis.

We are ensuring a global atmosphere of injustice, violence, economic slavery, famine, poverty, and extended suffering. Some of this is directly affecting us in the "comfortable" world too. It's not somewhere out there for others to deal with.

It all begs the question—do we *want* permanent crisis? I certainly don't. We can no longer ignore the peril we are in. Scientists are predicting that major ecosystems are starting to collapse.[49] We were warned of this back in 2008.[50] It's not happening in 2050 or even 2030—the signs are here already, and the bigger it is, the faster it will fall![51]

Yet we continue to chop down life-giving trees. We glory in excessive consumption and the acquisition of stuff, all while the land gets warmer and the oceans get warmer too. Emissions are trending in one direction—up![52] We continue to pass nature's tipping points and don't seem capable of grasping the impact it will have on all of our lives.

Why should we care about tipping points? Tipping points are lines that, once crossed, make it even harder to fix things or reduce impact. It's pretty much irreversible. We have been over-indulging and gorging on our beautiful planet without thought for too long.[53]

But it's not simply about us. It is about today's children, and young people are frightened. When my son was 11, he said to me, "Mum, if it gets too hot to be outside because of global warming, I am going to commit suicide."

That was a devastating moment for me! Our children know, regardless of how we try to protect them from the worst truth. They see a future of unbearable hardship.

As adults, is that all we are prepared to offer them? We cannot wait for our children to grow up and act. We don't have time to kick it down the road yet again. The time to act was more than 30 years ago, but we still have now. Right now.

This time out we are all living through is a gift for us to claim a unique opportunity to rewrite our collective future, one where the sustainability and health of all life on planet earth are at the center of our values and plans.

49   https://www.nature.com/articles/s41467-020-15029-x
50   https://www.pnas.org/content/105/6/1786
51   https://news.mongabay.com/2020/05/climate-tipping-point-ecosystem-collapses-may-come-faster-than-thought-studies/
52   https://www.co2.earth/global-CO2-emissions
53   The following articles demonstrate how deep into this trend we are. https://www.nature.com/articles/s41598-020-75481-z; https://www.sciencealert.com/controversial-model-finds-global-warming-will-continue-even-if-we-stop-emissions-tomorrow

QUESTIONS FOR REFLECTION

With this gift of time, let's ask ourselves some searching questions and find the answers, together.

1. Are you happy with your life—family, home, community, and sense of achievement, contribution, and meaning? Even if you are, is it time for new directions?

2. Are you questioning the frantic pace of life we left behind? Do we want it to be like that when it's all over?

3. Are you proud of the company you work for? Is it contributing positively towards all life on earth, or is shareholder value overriding these needs? If so, what can you do to change it?

4. Do you believe it is time we demand business to change dramatically, to take into consideration the earth's finite resources and take responsibility for the waste left behind? What businesses—including your own, but also including those you patronize—can you begin to hold accountable?

5. Are we individually ready to face up to our part in the devastation and suffering going on in so many places in the world? Do we continue to accept children suffering in mines to make our latest phones or computers? And women suffering in the garment industry for fast-fashion? Companies like Ikea benefitting from (and ignoring until recently) illegal logging practices[54] to produce fast-furniture to feed our insatiable appetites for the new?

6. Are you wasting less, buying less, saying no to single use plastics, consuming less meat, shopping locally, and making plans to reduce your emissions?

7. Is your country polluted and full of rubbish? Are you ready to demand action from the businesses that have profited from it for decades?

---

54 https://www.eco-business.com/news/as-ikea-is-hit-by-illegal-logging-link-in-europe-furniture-firms-sustainability-function-in-southeast-asia-dissolves/

8. Is it time to close the wildlife markets, while creating new livelihoods for those reliant on them for income?

9. What about overfishing and destruction of the seas? What's the real impact? What's the risk to us?

10. Are you working to be part of the solution to end inequality, in all its forms?

11. What parts of life from before should we get rid of? I want the false, egocentric, hero-worshipping, sales-pushing nonsense gone. I want us to be real, to be meaningful. What about you?

12. And to the parents, are we acting and doing enough to ensure our children have a beautiful future?

We face big challenges.

Will you join me, so we can face them together? Will you raise your voice to demand change—on social media, in your communities, in your company, and on any platform or stage that you have access to? Will you join a rising chorus demanding better for all life on planet earth? Will we do the best we can to ensure our children do not face the worst possible outcome of the climate crisis?

SIGN the PLEDGE for a
BETTER FUTURE
I _____
pledge to REFLECT DEEPLY on the STATE of the WORLD, and to IDENTIFY where my POWER lies to CREATE CHANGE.

I will ADD MY VOICE to the CHORUS driving for this CHANGE.

Signed

#80

RECONSIDERING WORK

CAREER THOUGHTS

TECHNOLOGY PROMISED TO MAKE our lives easier, and it certainly has in many ways, but with 24/7 digital access and work from home becoming more and more common, sometimes it feels there is no escape from work. Not to mention the fact that cultural codes about disconnecting from work can be very different around the world.

However, another critical issue right now is the real fear people suffer because they have already lost their job or they feel that their job is not secure in this current global economic climate. This is creating deep anxiety, despair, and depression in those who are unemployed and in those working at all hours out of fear, rather than setting up healthy boundaries. It is not good for anyone.

If you want to consider how work interrupts our life in bad ways, all you have to think of is the angry email you received from your boss on a Friday evening, only to have the whole weekend ruined as you stress and stew over it. Has it happened to you? I can't stand stuff like that.

Or the relentless cycle of information and continuous messages, unclear work-home boundaries, and the expectation of instantaneous responses because the apps notify the sender if the receiver has opened the message. It's hard *not* to let our time with loved ones be impacted.

My hubby, Steve, reports to a US-based company, which means he's asleep when they work and vice versa. For years he would lovingly answer every email that came in before going to bed. The result? Poor sleep cycle, never enough sleep, irritable in the evenings and on weekends, among other challenges. Recently, he decided *no more*. He won't look at his email or work correspondence after 9 pm on weekdays, and he switches off for weekends. He's definitely less irritable thanks to these changes, a total *win-win* for our family and for Steve.

There are so many aspects of work that can be challenging for all of us, so many qualities of being in an organization that we struggle with, so the question we need to ask ourselves is—are we happy with it?

Once I realized that both my work and my husband's could be done digitally, we took stock. We moved countries, found a great school and community for our boys, and went digital as we rounded the corner to our 50s. It's possible at any stage of life.

With everything changing and up in the air right now, the way we work is changing and evolving, so we could sit and wait for the changes to impact us, or we can co-create the way we want to work moving forward. When we do that, we can also consider the way we live too.

Are you asking yourself how you want to work in the future? Do you feel empowered to follow different paths?

You don't have to make any changes right now, but a little daydreaming and planning can't hurt.

HOME-PLAY

Would you like to work differently?

What does that look like for you?

Where would you like to do it?

What would need to change for your family?

What are some of the steps you need to take to make this a reality?

1.

2.

3.

4.

5.

6.

7.

8.

9.

10.

#81

DIFFERENT SPEEDS, DIFFERENT AGENDAS

SELF-AWARENESS

DID YOUR MUM TELL YOU not to burn the candle at both ends? Mine did, all the time. She still does. But see, I was always going to burn the candle at both ends. It's who I am, and it's who I will always be. Getting older does tweak this a bit, as I rethink my energy levels and family commitments, but it's more about adaptation than change.

The truth is, some people come into this world to put their feet up and have a beer. Enjoy that life if you are one of them—I sometimes wish I could be that way, but I'm just not. I don't mind you being that way, though. Not at all.

Others are born already behind schedule and they come into the world going fast and hard all the time. Their minds are busy, and they're often the sort of people who believe it's important to leave a legacy, and they want to make the world a better place while they are here. These are the *both-ends candle burners*. They are driven by passion and they will burn those candles regardless of what anyone else says.

When someone is on a mission, they're not operating from a logical place. The way they see it, you should either get on board or get out of the way. They are driven by passion, driven by heart, driven by their soul.

What I see happening in the world is that one style of living resents the other, and vice versa. One style feels superior to the other and vice versa. They both think they are right, each looking down on the other, which provokes resentment on both sides. I don't believe this is useful.

I'm all guns blazing and I accepted that long ago. I love meeting and hanging out with people like me too, although we can be exhausting to be around. We are an *extreme* in the specter of human-styles—an arc of humanness that goes from the busy bees all the way across to people who are here to chill and enjoy life. Let's call them the easy riders. What I see is people calling these easy-rider folk bludgers, lazy, unmotivated, and so on.

Why can't we accept these people as they are? Why can't we make space for everyone to live as they want to live, and create societies that welcome that? Why do we place so little value on diversity of human experience? We're not all chilled, we're not all manic, and we're not all everything in between. Instead, it's a beautiful tapestry of life and possibility, if we welcome it.

If we really want to elevate humanity and consciousness, let's stop comparing ourselves to each other. Let's stop putting expectations that don't fit on each other, too. It's really important we learn to appreciate each other for who we are and who we're meant to be. It doesn't matter if it makes sense to us; we just need to get out of each other's way and get on with living our best life.

We each come into a life with our own path, and the point is to accept each other, not straighten out other people's roads for them. Our individual paths have deep meaning for the lessons they offer. It's a wonderful thing that they aren't all the same.

It is a game changer to see this. You can't look down upon someone or judge someone when you believe this truth. It's impossible. You just accept.

Judgment is a waste of time! The world would be a significantly more beautiful and generous place if more of us thought, "I'll do me and I'll let others do them."

THE GIFT OF ALL EXPERIENCE

SELF-AWARENESS

A **S A YOUNG PERSON I** lived through my parents' separation and divorce, as well as the many years of family turmoil that followed. It was a long bitter period. I was angry for a long time and hung onto that resentment deeply. Then I started traveling. I encountered different perspectives and saw different ways of living. I saw people living with so much less than what I had, and yet they had huge smiles on their faces and gratitude for every day they got to be alive. To encounter such people was amazing, mind-expanding, inspiring. These experiences taught me to look at life with completely different eyes. I decided happiness was something that should become a primary life goal!

Years after my parent's divorce, my dad apologized for all the pain he'd caused me while they were "sorting it out." I told him he had nothing to apologize for. By then, I'd moved well beyond those early feelings. And just as importantly, I'd learned to really value those painful experiences, which were such a gift of lessons. I was a stronger, more resilient, and definitely more independent person because of it. So, I thanked him!

I was bullied at school. I've been bullied in my professional life too. Rather than believing the bullies and allowing them to cut me down to the size they wanted, I decided to use that hurt for good. I used it to make me stronger and more determined when I was younger. As I got older, I learned to use it to be clear about my boundaries and push back. I'm not taking that shit from anyone. **#Stand up for yourself!** *(wisdom 90)*

These experiences also taught me to never bully anyone, and I have always stuck up for people who were bullied. This determination to be kind at all costs is a gift, a silver lining of those challenging early experiences.

The experiences we collect as we travel through life, whether we perceive them as good or bad at the time, are a gift given to us as well as an opportunity to learn and grow—*if we choose to see it that way.*

Psychiatrist and author Elisabeth Kübler-Ross puts it like this: "The most beautiful people we have known are those who have known defeat, known suffering, known struggle, known loss, and have found their way out of the depths. These persons have an appreciation, a sensitivity, and an understanding of life that fills them with compassion, gentleness, and a deep loving concern. Beautiful people do not just happen."

We can become the kind of beautiful she's talking about too, regardless of our start in life.

When facing hardships, embracing them as a gift of life experience *even in the moment* helps us come out the other side a better version of ourselves. That can be hard to do, naturally, and it can take time, as in my case with my experience of my parents' divorce. However, in the long run it sure beats the alternative—letting those hard experiences define our lives or diminish us.

I'll be the first to acknowledge it isn't easy, and for those who have suffered—especially at someone else's hands—this message is about setting yourself free, not about making light of your suffering or exonerating those who hurt you.

You will see light at the other end of the tunnel when you feel compassion for those who hurt you. I know that may sound impossible, but it's the goal. When we've suffered it's hard to imagine compassion and it's particularly difficult to view abuse of any kind as a gift—whether it's psychological, physical, mental, spiritual, or sexual abuse. How do you come back from abuse? How do you become a more beautiful version of yourself after what you've been through? How do you become compassionate towards people who hurt you?

At this point in the discussion, it's important to acknowledge that some experiences are best worked through with professional help. If you have been the victim of abuse in any form, you don't need to try to overcome it alone.

Whatever the nature of our hardships, we can look to role models who have gone through pain and come through with beauty in their hearts.

Be inspired by Malala Yousafzai, Waris Dirie, Sadio Mane, Fatima Siad, Turia Pitt, Kris Carr, Ruby Bridges, Rosa Parks, Mahatma Gandhi, Oprah Winfrey, and every person who has fought for human rights, equal rights, and civil rights around the world. I've named some famous heroes, but we can find people nearer us in life and be inspired to set ourselves free through their examples, too.

One way to redirect your pain toward the gift of growth is by taking your focus off the people who've done something to you, or the situation itself, and instead, look inside and ask what you admire in yourself: a hidden strength, a keen intelligence, a wry humor. Focus on what makes *you* great, not what makes the situation terrible.

While this may seem like a little thing, it can have outsized power to heal you. Each moment that you are focusing on something good about yourself is a moment where you're standing in your beauty and your power to decide how you want to see the world.

And if you have friends in pain, go out of your way to tell them what makes *them* great, too. When someone acknowledges the qualities we see in ourselves, it can be invaluable in terms of helping us overcome the feelings of being small or powerless that often make moving on from a hard thing all the more difficult.

To build a beautiful life despite what we have suffered, we must work to help each other not let the negative experiences diminish the light in our lives. We must always attempt to find the lesson of strength and resilience in hard experiences.

This is about you, not about what happened to you. If we let others diminish our light, we reduce our lives. Every step is a step forward to our best selves, and at the end of the day, that is what we're here to be.

HOMEWORK

Who do you admire that has suffered something similar to your own hardship?

Have they written a book, are they on social media, or have they created information you can dig into and learn from?

If they are someone you know or are connected to, can you speak with them and ask them to help you see the gift?

And finally, would professional help be useful to you? Never be ashamed to take this path.

An important note. This is not a quick fix. It can take a long time to break negative mental habits, so take your time and rest when you need to. Just remember to always come back and keep digging within to help you become the shining light you were put on this earth to be.

#83

SPEAK TRUTH WITH LOVE TO YOUR PARTNER

SELF-EMPOWERMENT

I OFTEN SAY TO MY HUSBAND, sorry I'm so annoying to live with. Sorry I'm not easy. Sorry I'm so intense. I could go on. It's not an apology in a traditional sense, it's an acknowledgement. My husband, Steve, appreciates it.

And guess what: he's not easy either. I think most people with a life partner have mental lists of their partner's annoying imperfections. How can we not? (If your partner is perfect—congratulations! They are a rarity. Or maybe *you* are the rarity, for seeing them that way . . .)

We all know habits or behaviors that make us squirm with discomfort inside. It could be a noise (like loud chewing), or not consistently putting the cap on the toothpaste, or perhaps they don't leave the toilet seat up or put it down, let alone replace the toilet roll. Sometimes there's more serious stuff—maybe they're quick to anger. Maybe you don't always like the way they think, and maybe you even find that they're racist, intolerant, or hateful towards someone or a group of people.

Feeling this discomfort doesn't mean you don't love them, for there are always challenges and differences when you're a couple! And if you've got teenage children, they probably feel the same way about you, or you feel the same way about them. Teenagers love to hate on their parents, right?

But 2020 saw even more pressure on couples and families. With the COVID-19 lockdown, we've all been placed into tighter quarters than we've experienced in a century, and well—it hasn't been too kind on many marriages. Reports indicate divorce rates have skyrocketed up 50%[55] around the world due to this forced confinement. Financial insecurity hasn't helped, either. Domestic violence has gone up too.[56]

For Steve and me, forced confinement brought many emotions up. I realized the only way to get through it was to be honest about our feelings. We have always been honest, but lockdown brought stuff to the surface faster, stuff that needed to be resolved faster, too. It was definitely more intense.

We agreed on absolute honesty. We knew if we weren't honest about challenges with each other, there was nowhere else for it to go other than to fester inside and between us. When you let negative emotions fester, every time the other person does the little thing you don't like, well, you hate them a little bit more. Over time this grows into something bigger and then it's too late.

It's impossible to talk these things out without a bit of unpleasantness, but I'm convinced frank communication is one of the keys to a happy marriage or partnership over time. All you can do is be gentle with your words but be honest with each other. It's even more powerful if you agree to it together that you're going to be open to talking. It will make your partnership stronger.

This practice helped us to survive our lockdown, and our marriage remains as strong as ever.

55 Divorce rate data https://www.law.com/dailybusinessreview/2020/09/23/marriage-and-divorce-in-the-time-of-covid/?slreturn=20210026020414 and https://www.divorcemag.com/articles/are-divorce-rates-and-custody-issues-linked-to-covid-19
56 https://www.webmd.com/lung/news/20200818/radiology-study-suggests-horrifying-rise-in-domestic-violence-during-pandemic#1

But it takes great self-awareness. You have to dig deep inside and see yourself and understand your actions. You have to connect the dots and stop projecting your fears on the people around you. If you are acting in anger and rage, that's about you. Go deep and be self-aware, and your partner will definitely appreciate it. (**#Ephiphanies on anger**, *wisdom 26* and **#Watch out for projection**, *wisdom 10*)

#84

BEWARE DRAMA KINGS AND QUEENS

EXTERNAL INFLUENCE

SOME PEOPLE LOVE DRAMA. We all have that friend or family member whose life is one big series of dramas—one after the other. Typically, they are surrounded by a group of people equally caught up in their dramas, but over time, many of those people get exhausted and step away.

I have drama friends. They are not bad people, but they often fail to realize that they are the only constant in the drama of their lives.

My greatest learning, when it comes to drama kings and queens, is to always keep a bit of distance. Never fully invest in someone else's drama.

There are typically two sides to every story, and taking sides is something I will rarely do, unless I have witnessed the issue myself, instead of hearing it second hand. Some friends have expressed frustration and even hurt that I did not support them. While I understand that expectation, if it's not my drama, it's really not my business. Please don't take it to heart if I don't jump in guns blazing.

When my parents got divorced, there was a lot of drama around it. Sides were taken and relationships destroyed overnight. And the judgments, oh the judgments. People who knew nothing of my parents' relationship had such strong views on it. It was quite remarkable. I think that was when I decided to sit in a more neutral position when it comes to other people's lives.

#85

BEG YOUR PARDON, DOLLY PARTON

SELF-AWARENESS

I LOVE DOLLY PARTON—LOVE her—but this wasn't always the case. Early in life, I actually rather despised her.

One day when I was 30, my boss played her new bluegrass album while we were driving to a client meeting, and on that trip, the song "Little Sparrow" entered my soul. I walked away from that moment stunned. Why had I not seen her incredible talent before? Oh, I could sing along to her hits, like "Jolene," but I had mostly just been judgmental of her.

I pondered this for a long time and realized my feelings towards her actually went deep. I also realized it was about me, not her. All my life when I looked at Dolly, I really struggled with her physical side—her *embellishments*. Mention Dolly in any conversation and at least one person will mention her boobs. Guaranteed. You may be sniggering right now, reading this, just as I always had whenever she was mentioned. And I'd never bothered to look past her boobs.

The beauty of the boob talk for Dolly is how much she makes a joke of it herself. She totally disarms the conversation when it comes up. I admire that tremendously. But boobs were a tricky issue for me.

I went from a scrawny, flat-chested kid to a 12-year-old with a DD cup almost overnight. Suddenly my boobs became a talking point in the background, in snide remarks—and I was always aware of it. Even as an adult, hearing friends speak of other large-breasted women in my presence, I figured this is how I was talked about behind my back too.

As a young teenager, I hated it. Really hated it. I didn't want boobs in the first place. I didn't enjoy the attention, and I definitely wasn't ready for it. Some girls grow up fast and relish being women; some, like me, grow up slower. But the world around us doesn't honor that because there is an obvious physical *contradiction.*

On reflection, I realized I pushed these feelings onto Dolly, because I couldn't understand why anyone would *want* to attract that attention to themselves. As a young girl with the older men in my life looking at me in ways they never had before, I thought this kind of attention was horrible. I blamed my boobs.

And because that's what I associated with Dolly, I dismissed her. I couldn't connect with this opposite way of being female. Not at all. She was proud of her femininity and went out of her way to draw attention to it. She was *proud* of having big boobs. I just couldn't understand it, so I judged her, and rather harshly.

Reflecting back on it today, I recognize that she was owning her own narrative. She was living on *her* terms, no matter who was judging. (**#Control your own narrative**, *wisdom 11*)

I appreciate Dolly so much for this lesson in self-awareness. Now when I notice that I have strong feelings towards other people, I try to understand which part of those feelings is about me and has nothing to do with them. Once you start looking at your own judgments from this angle, it's amazing what you uncover.

We are raised to pass judgment towards our fellow humans freely, but we are seldom encouraged to reflect on why we feel that way. Are our ideas the only right ones? Are our ways of living and being the only acceptable ones?

When you notice negative feelings towards someone, check in with yourself. If the real reason has something to do with you, then you can own that and stop deflecting it onto other people.

If we all took this approach to judgment, can you imagine what a difference it would make in the world?

REFLECTION

When you were growing up, what part of growing up, if any, made you really uncomfortable?

Who is someone that you do not know personally, but you may have judged?

Do you still think you are right and fair in that judgement, or does it require some deeper reflection?

#86

MOTHERING IS WEIRD

SELF-EMPOWERMENT

THE ONLY THING I'VE EVER DONE in my life where everyone has an opinion on it is mothering. There are opinions to contend with before you're pregnant, while you're pregnant, and after the kid is born.

And there is this idea that every single mother on the planet is going to feel the same way. Think of the representation of the archetypal Mother throughout art history. Really?

It's also the only job where you have zero qualifications but a world full of judgment upon you if you get it wrong, and if you dare raise another point of view, you'll be smacked down at once. It's a lot of weird pressure.

So, I'm going to say what I think about it.

I didn't like the baby years. Absolute emotional chaos and boredom like I've ever known.

Don't get me wrong, I loved my boys, and doted on them too, but when I saw a baby after my two moved beyond the baby stage, it made me feel nauseous. When Jax (my second) wanted to get down and move around independently on the floor, I was happy to let him go. It felt like I had people clinging to me, needing me, for years—and I was relieved to move beyond these stages.

Toddler years, ugh! More boredom. I would sit there, watching them play, bored out of my mind, and there was nothing else I could do. I dreamed of having a small computer I could set on my knees, so I could at least write something while they played, but guess what, the tech wasn't even close to that yet, even smart phones. How quickly technology has changed in a decade.

Loneliness was definitely a big issue for me. And yet I didn't enjoy mother's groups. I tried to give them a go, and it was one of the more miserable experiences of my life. When Lex (my oldest) was six months old, I took him to a mother and baby play group. He could roll and move already from four months, which I didn't know was early—it was just Lex. However, putting him in the middle of other babies the same age, all lying on their backs and incapable of rolling, let alone moving, well it made all of the other parents feel bad about their babies!

As a mother, it's hard being around people who feel excited their kid is achieving more than yours, or depressed when their kids aren't. Seriously, all kids get there eventually.

Another attempt at joining the mother's fraternity was the time I met a collection of mothers who were all beside themselves with boredom. There was no escape from it! They were there for their kids, no question, but some coped with the pressures of that moment in life by tending towards self-abuse: drinking, drugs, prescription medication, excess in all its forms. No judgment from me, I just couldn't let myself go there, because it was a place I knew I would only get lost in.

Mothering is definitely weird. It's not for everyone, and even for those of us who choose it, we do not all enjoy it equally. I'm not saying all of this to dunk on motherhood in any way, but because I think there needs to be more room to express how it really feels, the frustrations as well as the joys. It might make it less tedious and lonely for the mothers of the future, to be able to express ourselves fully about it.

#87

GOING WITH THE FLOW

SELF-EMPOWERMENT

DO YOU REALLY NEED TO BE in control at all times? And is being in control going to deliver the best outcome or experience? Will it allow surprises to appear in your life, which often happens when there is no certainty? Travel was the starting point where I learned to go with the flow. I then took the idea to another level and learned to trust my gut. My gut has saved me many times!

With work and life, when you know there is no way to really control the situation and so you go with the flow—with zero resistance—you might find everything turns out better than if things had gone according to a plan.

Going with the flow opens you to possibilities you couldn't otherwise imagine. In the total control option, the only option is what you already thought of. How limiting is that?

Openness can be more fun too; there's a joy in the spontaneity of putting yourself out there, into the unknown.

Even if going with the flow isn't in your nature, allow yourself to do it sometimes. Consciously let go of your desire to control everything. Try to leave something unplanned. Leave space for life to surprise you!

PS: My husband *hates* this phrase.

#88

OTHER PEOPLE'S BUSINESS

SELF-AWARENESS

HAVE YOU EVER NOTICED that pinched-lip style to conversations involving other people's business? They typically happen in hushed tones, with lots of furtive side glances. It's almost as though we don't dare open our mouths or look each other in the eye when we're obsessing over other people's lives—neighbors down the road or even complete strangers.

What do we gain from gossip-fests, whether in a whispered huddle or online? How can we ever really know someone else's story? How can we make the world a better place when we're tearing people down?

If you find yourself drawn into these conversations—even if being part of them is delicious at some level—make a conscious decision not to do it anymore.

Don't join in when other people gossip, bitch, or tear down another person—just say no.

Let's make a distinction between gossiping and bitching. I'm personally not a fan of either, but I know many who love harmless gossip, which is not destructive or dangerous. For many, it's a way to get updated on other's lives, and I get that. If you wouldn't mind being overheard by the person you are talking about, chances are you're doing no harm, though you can never be sure. We don't all have equally thick skin.

This wisdom, though, is about the destructive, ripping-another's-life-apart sort of gossip, which I'll call bitching. This form of gossip is often inaccurate and even when it might be factually true, it's the telling that is hurtful and mean.

If this kind of talk is something you've indulged in all your life, stepping away can be challenging and require real commitment. Not only is it a habit, but it may also be central to certain of your relationships.

When you break free of the "bitching circle" (as my husband likes to call it) you will definitely be happier and more whole.

As a bonus, you'll be freeing yourself from an ugliness that sits in your body. Pay attention the next time you think or say something awful. How does it feel in your body? Now, pay attention when you are praising and loving someone. Notice how differently that feels?

JOIN THE NO BITCHING FOR A MONTH CHALLENGE

Maybe we could show the children of the world adults actually behaving the way we ask them to behave. How would this be for role modelling?

The rules of the No Bitching for a Month challenge are simple. Keep in mind that they apply to our social media presence and online communities, too.

1. You are not allowed to criticize anyone for anything, and if you feel inclined towards bitching, you have to replace it with something positive, like, "She is an awesome person, who loves . . ."

2. You can't share any news that is derogatory towards anyone else, no matter what (famous people included). If you notice you want to slip up, and feel you must share it, you have to come up with a positive or compassionate angle.

3. If someone in your life does something horrible, stupid or insulting, be the bigger person. Walk on and smile, it's their issue not yours. Send them a bolt of loving light if you feel like it, just don't let them fester inside you.

For the advanced players, this includes your thoughts. You're not allowed to have negative ones. If one crops up, shake it loose. Monitoring negative thoughts is really a superb habit when you get into it. (**#Do you have voices in your head?**, *wisdom 4*)

Keep an eye out for comments or thoughts about the world around you. "Life is so miserable right now" could potentially be replaced with, "This is such an opportunity to . . ."

But most importantly, you can't bitch about yourself or even think bitchy thoughts. If you find yourself criticizing yourself at any moment, replace it with a compliment. *I am powerful, I am awesome, I am here to do good.* Join the challenge.

And if you like the way it feels, why not keep going for a year? By then it may be a permanent shift.

ACTION THOUGHTS

Step 1: List down the people you see as the ring leaders of your bitching circle, or the people who seem to be initiating or getting the biggest thrill out of doing it. Put yourself down if it's you.

1.

2.

3.

Step 2: Carefully watch your community and keep an eye out for those who seem reluctant to participate. Draw them out and tell them your concerns, asking for their advice on how to approach the problem. List reluctant gossipers:

1.

2.

3.

Recognize that approaching your friends could create division within your community, but if you can convince allies to join you, together you can start to build towards change, even if it means leaving the gossipers behind.

Step 3: If it's possible, speak to the whole group. Tell them you don't want to be part of those types of conversations anymore, because they make you feel horrible inside. Embellish on the reasons that make sense to you and the people you spend time with.

PS: None of us are perfect, but a commitment to not speak badly of others lifts us all.

TAKE ON THE CHALLENGE!

I completed a month of no bitching.

The challenge I overcame in achieving it:

The difference I've seen in myself:

A REMINDER OF THE RULES

1. You are not allowed to criticize anyone for anything, and if you feel inclined towards bitching, you have to replace it with something positive, like, "She is an awesome person, who loves . . ."

2. You can't share any news that is derogatory towards anyone else, no matter what (famous people included). If you notice you want to slip up and you feel you must share it, you have to come up with a positive or compassionate angle.

3. If a stranger is being stupid or insulting around you, walk on and smile, send them a bolt of loving light. Don't let bad feeling fester inside you.

4. For the advanced players, this includes your thoughts. You're not allowed to have negative ones. If one crops up, shake it loose. Monitoring negative thoughts is really a superb habit when you get into it. (**#Do you have voices in your head?**, wisdom 4)

#89

WINE TIME

SELF-EMPOWERMENT

FOR WINE DRINKERS WHO KNOW they'll never be a sommelier, yet want a good drop, here's a tip I learned from a British school mam many years ago that will guarantee you select a respectable bottle every time.

The first tip, when searching for wine, make sure it's 13% + alcohol for white wine, and for red wine it's 14% +.

No, it's not about more alcohol—it's about quality. The higher the percentage of alcohol, the better the wine. It also doesn't mean it has to be crazily expensive, either. And here's my most recent discovery: if you buy red wine over 15%, it starts tasting a lot more like port. So, 14.7% is the maximum I've found enjoyable.

Also, buy wine that's at least four years old. If it has been stored correctly, it'll be a winner. This rule has never let me down, and it's also impressed a few clients, bosses and friends. Not to mention, it helps in countries where you have no idea what you're looking at, especially if the label is in a foreign language. Typically, the percentage of alcohol and vintage are always numerical.

This tip has helped me buy excellent wine in any language in any country, and for a wanderer like me, that's been awesome. Give it a try and let me know how it goes for you.

#90

STAND UP FOR YOURSELF

CAREER THOUGHTS

WHEN SOMEONE SPEAKS TO YOU DISRESPECTFULLY, *don't stand for it*, no matter who it is, what title they hold, or what their status level is relative to yours, in work or in life.

I know it is ingrained in us to be respectful to our superiors, but if they are not treating us with respect, why should we be respectful in return? Expect, even demand respect from those around you.

Important corollary: you can't demand it if you are not respectful yourself.

Even when I was little, I wouldn't stand for it when somebody spoke to me in a way that I found disrespectful. It is a feeling that goes deep into my body. I cannot stay silent. Whether it was a rude uncle when I was a teenager or a rude chef when I was working in a restaurant as a waitress, I did not allow anyone to speak to me with disrespect.

Once I thought standing up for myself would lose me the best job I'd ever had. I was 23 and heading up communications for an aerospace company—a pretty incredible job for a person that age. One day the Chief Financial Officer (CFO) was really rude to me. I said to him: "You don't get to speak to me that way. Who do you think you are?"

I turned around to walk out, only to see my boss, the Chief Marketing Officer (CMO), standing directly behind me. He heard it all. "Great, there's that job gone," I thought.

The CMO followed me into my office and said, "Good on you for standing up for yourself."

The next day, the CFO came in and apologized to me.

Another instance happened in London a few years later. I was working for a public relations firm and there was a woman on another team who regularly tore strips off her "underlings" in the middle of the whole office. I found this behavior pathetic and couldn't understand how her bosses didn't pull her up for it.

One day, she decided to have a go at me. Brave lady. I instantly riled up and said: "How dare you speak to me that way? And if you have an issue with me or my work, you book a private room and we discuss it together without putting on a show for the whole office!"

The look of shock on her face was something I'll never forget, but I had had enough of her contemptible behavior. She never spoke to me that way again, nor did she do it so publicly with her team after that either.

It is never acceptable behavior. Do not put up with it. If you lose your job, so what! Better not to work in an environment where that behavior is accepted.

Whether it's a bully in the family, at school, or in the workplace, do not let anyone speak to you disrespectfully. Stand up for yourself.

While they may be shocked when you do, they'll respect you more. Since I've been sticking up for myself for so many years, people have this innate feeling that I should not be crossed. I don't project menace or threat, but bullies seem to recognize that I am not frightened of them and will not back down if they decide to go after me. And demanding respect gains you something ultimately even more important: self-respect.

I promise you one thing: if you stand up to them, bullies will always back down. Most people bully from a place of fear or pain. Standing up to them helps them reposition, which is good for them, too.

REFLECTIONS

When has someone spoken to me rudely and I did not stand up to myself?

How did I feel when it happened? What were the feelings coursing through my body?

The next time someone speaks to me, or someone I care about, disrespectfully, what am I going to do?

#91

GET FUTURE-READY

CAREER THOUGHTS

A FEW YEARS BACK I spoke to an American audience about automation and robotics—a casual chat, not a professional one, because it's definitely not my area of expertise. The response was, "But that's years and years away." I told them it was already yesterday's news. There are factories in China that have been run entirely by robots for years now.[57] This shift has happened, and the pandemic is only accelerating it worldwide.[58] It's just a case of getting the infrastructure in place to make it a reality in other parts of the world.

The next decade is going to be one of enormous change, of massive transformation and huge disruption in how we work, live, and earn money. With so many changes coming and so many trends in the air, it's hard to pay attention and work out what matters.

And this future is really anyone's guess. Futurists speak of two potential paths for humanity. One is a dark path of uncertainty, despair, and violence. But there is another path, a brighter path, which depends on global cooperation, breaking down walls, and coming together in unity to address the challenges of our time.

57 https://www.techrepublic.com/article/chinese-factory-replaces-90-of-humans-with-robots-production-soars/
58 https://www.cnbc.com/2020/03/02/the-rush-to-deploy-robots-in-china-amid-the-coronavirus-outbreak.html

Regardless of whether you subscribe to the futurist school of thought or not, what is clear is that our future is uncertain—and that it's time to get future-ready.

Globally, we need to get prepared for what is coming rather than allowing those dark-path uncertainties to come to fruition—which would guarantee war, immense suffering, and millions or billions of people with no place to go. Not being prepared for this is inexcusable and we must force our leaders to work with their peers around the world to find solutions now—not later, when the tragedy is full-blown. There is no excuse for lack of preparedness. None. We know what's coming, let's do what we need to do to ensure it is not apocalyptic.

On an individual level, we can look at our own work and skills, as well as looking to industries that are likely to prove resilient through several years of disruption and very low levels of travel. We can look at roles with an eye on the gig economy and make sure we can deliver our talents digitally if possible. Work from home or a café!

The key here is to pay attention to what's changing in your industry and in the wider world around you. Do your research and get yourself ready to embrace the opportunities that will open up for you.

The key to getting yourself future-ready is understanding what technological shifts are going to affect your industry and how. Become an expert and start creating opportunities by being ahead of the curve and learning new skills.

Major universities around the world have made their undergraduate curriculum available online. You do not need to pay thousands or hundreds of thousands of dollars for an education or to gain a new field of expertise.

Become known as a thought leader in your field through owning your voice on the digital stage as a social leader. It's where people and employers will look for expertise. It's where you build your credibility. Be creative about how you position yourself and be strong in your point of view. Take this seriously.

Those of us who live in Asia are ready to embrace the Asian century.[59] For decades it has been predicted that the Future is Asian.[60] And it makes

59   https://www.ft.com/content/520cb6f6-2958-11e9-a5ab-ff8ef2b976c7
60   https://www.mckinsey.com/featured-insights/asia-pacific/why-the-future-is-asian

sense. Sixty-three percent of the world's population lives in this region and it is growing on many fronts and advancing in ways that most people in the West can't even imagine. It's critical to understand the nuances between the many different countries and cultures that make up Asia. Such understanding can give you an important edge in getting ready for what's next.

We can get ahead on the sustainability curve, too. Start making essential changes now, in your business and industry. This will not only mitigate the impact of having to make many expensive changes very quickly later, but also positions you and your business in a leadership role. It is critical to ensure we are acting in anticipation, not reacting as we live through a constant state of crisis.

We can insist on greater equity and parity to accompany all changes, no matter our scale of operations. Equity and parity start at home and radiate out.

We can ask and push for intelligent answers to the big questions posed by the changes we know are coming. If companies are relying on AI and automation and thus hiring fewer people, how do we need to change the way businesses get taxed? Is it time for Universal Basic Income? How do we ensure we do this in a way that creates a utopia rather than a dystopia?

All of these are questions to be answered, but first, we need to make sure we're on top of what is coming and what it means to us personally, our community and the world. Let's get educated and more importantly, get ready.

We can be *excited* about the future, rather than full of anxiety and dread. Any time of big change can be exciting, and this moment presents us with an opportunity to shift the world in a better direction, especially in terms of equality, social justice, and the environment.

Go out there and embrace the future—because it's coming anyway. Become a voice defining the future of humanity. First envision it, then help your communities see that vision. And if you keep your eyes open for where the wave is coming from, you might just surf it for the ride of your life.

NO REGRETS

SELF-EMPOWERMENT

IT WAS A TERRIBLE DAY back in 1994 when I heard that Emma Pini, my ABBA buddy and childhood best friend, had died in a motorcycle accident. It was such bad luck, too. Her boyfriend came out of the accident with cuts on his face, whereas the way Emma landed broke her upper spine. She died instantly. She was 24 and left behind her adorable baby girl, Ruby—a divine young woman today.

Emma's death is one I can never fully get over. I have accepted it, but I'll always miss my outrageous friend and still wish I could share all of life's gloriousness and craziness with her. No question, Emma lives on in me and in so many others. She definitely made an impact in her short life!

At her funeral—which was awful—I was watching her coffin lowered into the ground and I reached inside my wallet, took out my brand-new motorcycle license, and threw it into her grave. I'm sure it is still there. For both Emma and I, motorbikes had a special attraction, but no—on that horrible day, I was done with them and have been ever since. Not worth it.

A few months after Emma's death, I packed up my life in Australia and started my journey around the world—which I'm still on, 26 years later. There's no question I was still grieving Emma at this point, because the manic-ness in getting ready to leave my entire life in Australia really didn't give me space to sit with my grief at that time.

The first stop of my glorious adventure was Nepal. I did a two-week Annapurna Trek and when I got to the highest point I was trekking to, I sat down, under the majesty of the Himalayas, and talked to Emma.

I said something along the lines of this: *Hey Emma, can you get over how bloody beautiful it is here? Just magnificent. Have a look around? And what a journey I'm having, but I am thinking of you every day. I've decided I want to make you a few promises today. The first is, I promise I will live life without regrets. If I set my heart on something, I'm going to do it. I also promise I will live the bravest and most courageous life I can. When you died, it really laid bare how precious life is and I will honor your memory by being a good person who gives generously, laughs a lot, and loves deeply.*

I'll also keep going on fantastic adventures too, always wishing you could join me on them. I know you would have if you were still here. That's my promise. No regrets. Fun, passion, and giving. I'll do that for you. I'll miss you forever, but I can still hear your laugh and think I always will. Thanks for being an amazing friend. We were lucky to have each other growing up.

If you have regrets, shake them off or just do that thing, but don't let them live within you, festering away into un-lived resentment. We all hear the stories of elderly people on their death beds—such posts are common on social media these days—but how many of us are really listening to this advice and then doing it? How many remain trapped in an idea of life, that brings no joy? Just busy-ness, always so busy, but busy doing what? If we're not doing something that brings us joy or makes the world a better place, we'll only regret it. If today we're living for possessions and status, we'll lose all of that one day, no matter how we live right now. What then? Was it worth it?

Please if you're ready to make a change, remember, if it's not making you happy, it's time to reflect and think anew. It's a great moment to reconsider all aspects of life. It's a great time for change. It's a great time to remember that life truly can be beautiful.

TWO QUESTIONS TO ANSWER

What have you always wanted to do that you have yet to do?

When are you going to do it?

#93

WHEN DID WE TURN INTO COMPLAINERS?

SELF-AWARENESS

I DON'T KNOW ABOUT YOU, but just because we have the technology to offer instant feedback on every experience we have today, it doesn't mean we should! I had a shockingly bad experience recently, and I won't go into detail about the experience or the venue, but I'll tell you what I did.

I sent them a raw, honest, nothing-held-back-while-still-being-respectful email.

What I didn't do is share that feedback publicly—even in gossip, but especially not online. How would that help anyone? How could that help them improve?

They were so grateful and passed my criticism onto the entire team with a promise to me that they will focus on fixing everything I listed out.

Now, if I go back in six months and it's still a shambles, then we have an issue on our hands. But the instant criticism we so often dish out online is not going to solve any problems. I know restaurant, hotel and bar owners who are regularly crushed by this type of feedback. And we seem to forget that there are people at the end of it, passionate people bringing a dream to life. Not to mention the fact that so much of the criticism has no appreciation of local culture behind it either. How things run isn't the same everywhere in the world, my friends—and that's a good thing!

Are we really going to allow ourselves to turn into a world full of petulant cry-babies? I hope not. Besides, the things that go wrong are part of the story moving forward. Learn to embrace it. Remember to laugh and enjoy life, especially when things that really aren't important go wrong. Please!

#94

LET'S ADDRESS SHALLOWNESS

SELF-AWARENESS

WHEN MY BOYS HIT THAT fear of zombies stage that creates nightmares and has small children running to their parents' beds at night, we kept telling them there was no such thing. But then I got to thinking, maybe there is? Between technology, social media, and the opioid crisis, we already have zombies living amongst us. A lot of them. Yikes!

Look around. We're skimming important information and spending our time on fluff. We are so distracted by shallow things that bring no value into our lives. In fact, much of the fluff we pay attention too makes us feel bad about ourselves. We're self-medicating rather than facing reality. And when we do get together—even after being locked in our homes for months—we still switch off from real life. It's zombifying and horrifying.

Long before the pandemic, this zombie effect was already creating huge epidemics of loneliness, isolation, and emptiness. In fact, much of what we spend our time on seems to be information or entertainment that makes us suffer emotionally, evoking jealousy, gluttony, and greed.

A wonderful example of shallowness was on display in the Netflix film *Fyre: The Greatest Party That Never Happened*. It made me want to put my head in my hands and weep. The part of the story I couldn't wrap my head around was the influencers, all beautified and, in my opinion, speaking utter drivel into their selfie sticks, while capturing themselves on the journey to the festival (jealous much?)—and then their complete outrage at the shambles when they arrived.

OK I admit it, *that* was quite amusing . . .

When they arrived and everything went to shit—what did they do? They all turned on each other and resorted to theft from similarly beautiful influencers. Interestingly, no one "lived" that part! No indeed. When the chips were down, it was each person for themselves and screw everyone else. That is not something to be admired! The fact that they are influencers begs the question: who watches these people? No really, who?

Are our children being influenced by this mindless, selfish, self-absorbed rubbish? Probably, and not for their own good or the good of the world.

Don't get me wrong, I do appreciate the need for escapism in our world right now, and besides, not all influencers are bad. There are many brilliant, meaningful influencers doing great work. But if escapism is what you're looking for, read a great fantasy series. Subscribe to *National Geographic* if you want to see the world. Listen to amazing podcasts or be inspired by TED Talks. I mean, surely we appreciate the importance of where we invest our time and attention? We're infecting our hearts and souls with this trash!

If I close my eyes and visualize the part of the world that's built on this sort of influence—like what I saw in *Fyre*—there's no craftsmanship in it. No elegance. No beauty. No inspiration. It's loud, ugly, greedy, desperate, and selfish. This kind of influence is not only potentially leading to our extinction as a species, it is also leaving people disconnected from what really matters. Like junk food, it feeds no purpose, and it touches little of what matters most on a deeply spiritual level—whatever that means to you.

When we want to justify indulging in something shallow, we call it "brain candy." Ask yourself, if you ate as much candy as you spend time consuming fluff on social media, what kind of shape would your body be in?

This junk food for the mind is leaving us spiritually malnourished and creating pain. Our pain shows up in rising suicide rates, especially amongst the young. Self-loathing and self-doubt are rampant, resulting in young people dying from trends like the latest plastic surgery that's so hot.[61] People don't just feel hatred towards themselves, they feel it towards others, often without even knowing them. Trust continues to drop. It's pretty bleak sometimes. No question, none of this is good for our wellbeing!

61 https://www.theguardian.com/news/2021/feb/09/brazilian-butt-lift-worlds-most-dangerous-cosmetic-surgery

It's better to invest our time in something that will help us grow, not suffer jealousy because we don't have what they claim to have! The Fear of Missing Out (FOMO) anxiety we feel is devastating huge swaths of people. It really does make me despair.

Too many have accepted a shallow dream that locks us into buying more stuff, which keeps us shackled with more debt and less happiness. And we're finally figuring out that neither stuff nor fluff can make us happy.

Everything has its place, but we're out of balance everywhere. Prioritize the information you take on board. If it makes you feel negative emotions towards yourself or others, it's not good for you and it's definitely not feeding your soul.

HOME-PLAY

Do a simple check-in today with these two questions:

1. How much of your time is spent on shallow content?

2. Did you do anything today that's driven by FOMO rather than by things that matter deeply to you?

Moving forward, keep an eye out for these two things . . . and gently, kindly reduce the time and energy you put into *splashing around in the shallow end of the pool*. Check in with what you value deeply (**#Integrity and values**, wisdom 8) and put more time and energy there instead. Feed your soul with beauty and inspiration. Feed it with service and giving. You will be thankful you did. Your life will be more rewarding too.

#95

DEATH
REFLECTION

SELF-EMPOWERMENT

WE DON'T LIKE TO TALK ABOUT death in many societies. It's one of the unmentionables. But living and travelling all over the world, I've seen how our perception of and relationship with death differs from culture to culture. It's not always a bad thing. And oftentimes it's a celebration of the life that has passed.

So here are my reflections on death.

I certainly hope my death is a celebration and not a somber affair. Can you promise me you'll party like rock stars when you know my time is up? I'd be so happy to know that's how it happened!

When it comes to dying, I'm not afraid of it. My exposure to so many different cultural approaches to death has probably influenced me in this. I can't wait to see what's next, and if there's nothing, I'm OK with that too, because I lived my life well.

I also don't want to be around when I can no longer do the basic things—like go to the toilet—by myself. I have asked my husband not to keep me alive, if it makes sense to let me go. I could not bear being a burden on anyone. I'd rather go. I have watched too many people suffer for too many years simply because technology can keep them alive, yet their lives are miserable. And it's not just miserable for them, it's miserable for those closest to them too. I don't want that at all. When the end is a certainty, don't prolong it, let me go please.

Turning 50 really brings that conversation into perspective, as death and serious illness start to become a little more common around you—and even more so during a global pandemic. To me, reflecting on death is a space for thinking on what I leave that lasts beyond me. It's about legacy.

Acquiring stuff has never felt important to me, and I spurn the societal expectations and marketing pressures we all endure. From a young age, consumerism struck me as a noose around our necks that got tighter and tighter as we got older. No, I wasn't a buyer of that dream. As you know, I believe it is better by far to **#Invest in memories** *(wisdom 78)*.

When it comes to reflecting on death, I want to encourage you to think about yours. Who knows when it will come?

I've included a reflection process here to fuel your life now.

Use it to help you focus on living your very best life and to become the very best version of yourself. This should always be our goal. Shake off anyone or anything that won't let you live the life you want.

I personally find this a very powerful exercise. I've included it below, if you are interested to try.

Do it from an intention of love, not fear. Accepting that we will all die is an important part of the cycle of life, but the goal here is to make sure we live in the first place.

REFLECTION PRACTICE

Step 1: Close your eyes and spread loving energy around and within you. Smile if you can. Relax. Then visualize your funeral—with you in a casket (open or closed), urn, or whatever else is culturally appropriate and aligned with your wishes—and ponder these questions:

1. Have I lived the life I wanted to live? Did I do it? Did I do it all?

2. Look at the people attending your funeral, are they the people you wished to see there? Who is a gift in your life? Who isn't?

3. How do people think of you at this moment? Have you left a powerful legacy where you touched people's hearts? Or are people ambivalent towards your contribution?

Step 2: Write down what comes up.

Step 3: Pause and reflect. Step back from what you've written.

Step 4: Decide the past does not define you.

Step 5: Set some goals for the path ahead.

Bonus Step: Let go of the people you saw who are not a gift in your life, even family members. Be brutal. Be courageous. It's your life, and you only have one. Give it your all and leave the world a better place than how you found it. That's a gift each of us can leave for future generations.

The best legacy is to have given it our very best shot while we're alive and healthy.

Practice note: Recognize the thoughts that have held you back from overcoming your goals. Break free of them. If you need to, hire a coach or a mentor to help you break free.

Whatever you do, listen to the insights that come through and then act on them!

#96

THE RIPPLE EFFECT

SOCIAL LEADERSHIP

TIMES ARE TOUGH. Challenges are everywhere. Some people speak up to call attention to the issues we face without necessarily having the solutions. Sometimes they get discounted or ridiculed for it, because there seems to be this idea that speaking up is not as important as solving problems.

There is something wrong with that idea.

Firstly, being able to find a solution is not the same as having the gift of impactful speech—which is why smart politicians surround themselves with experts. Those who do have the gift for speaking can raise issues. They can get millions to listen, follow, and believe. They begin the ripple effect of knowledge and awareness, which is fundamental to driving solutions.

It's time to acknowledge that these raisers of awareness are as important a part of the equation as the people who are coming up with solutions and strategies for change.

The role of influencers is to prepare the ground for solutions. Those who speak out clearly change people's minds, change their hearts, and create momentum for investment in solving the crisis. Both locally and globally, those who speak out begin changes for important movements. They multiply the reach of important messages, because they are *insiders*, and they reach people no outsider could. They reach them because they are trusted.

You and I have the ability to create positive ripples of change within the communities where we have influence, we are all like a stone tossed into a pond. The more of us who take part reach more people, create more ripples, which reach more people. The ripple effect is incredibly powerful, and it is critical for driving the awareness which creates change. Even better if you help link up other influencers and solution creators, too, which makes the ripple move faster.

If you want to create ripples of change, how do you do it? You step into your voice and start sharing relevant and powerful information. You help raise awareness and speak out in your community—to people who love you, trust you, and believe in you. If you can influence a few people in your community and they start doing the same in their communities, it's exponential—and that's powerful. The ripples of impact can only multiply!

We need the multiplication of ripples more than ever. We need everyone, in every corner of the globe, to hear this call to action for the sake of our future, for the sake of our beautiful planet. Believe in your voice. Be a change agent. The ripple effect is the way. The ripple effect is how we get everyone on board.

HOME-PLAY

What topic do I want to speak out on?

How can I participate in a meaningful way?

Where can I participate to get my message heard—social media, speaking, within my company, or beyond?

What trusted information sources do I need to start following?

How often will I commit to sharing information with my community?

IN GOOD TIMES AND BAD, LOOK TO SERVE

CAREER THOUGHTS

WE ARE ALL STRUGGLING THROUGH a rough patch during the pandemic, but the other catastrophe grinding many down to their knees, especially in the developing world, is the extreme economic downturn. It is brutal for far too many of our fellow citizens. And while it might feel like the time to focus on you and yours, those who fly highest in times like these are the people who embrace a service mindset.

Why serve? Whenever I've engaged in service, I've received far more than I've ever given. I've volunteered since I was a child. It was an important part of my family's culture, I suppose. We just did it without thinking about it. I can't remember a time of not getting stuck in, not going the extra mile—for my communities, friends, or anyone who really needed it. It's rewarding on too many levels to count.

Many of us have been taught that life is about looking out for yourself—that a *me-first* attitude is the road to success. Some people are self-centered out of self-defense, because they have been hurt and let down in a society that has been going in the wrong direction for a very long time. Other people think that service is a distraction that will derail personal ambitions. Some professionals don't want to go the extra mile for their organization or the associations they are part of.

They're missing the fact that relationships are the key to all success. I wholeheartedly recommend a service mindset for building a fantastic career and life—one that makes your heart sing. After all, what's the point of having a big bank balance if your heart's not singing?

I have witnessed many inspiring examples of service lately. One lady who manages our life in Phuket, Khun Bo Choomanee always had a service mindset. She always went the extra mile, even before things went bad. Because of her attitude before, we are doing everything we can to support her now—with work and connections—because we are so grateful for her service mindset.

On a bigger, corporate level, the Marriot Group has been a stand-out in its service mindset, and IBM and Microsoft too. The programs they are launching to help the broader community have really been outstanding.

Whether you're an individual or a corporation, a mindset of serving your community matters and helps when times are good, and when times are bad.

Individually service means investing in a community that will help you when you need it, too.

Service means building more powerful and meaningful relationships with people that matter to your career.

Service means understanding the pulse of an organization or association, which means you become a more valuable employee or member.

Service means growing and flourishing in ways you can't even imagine right now.

When your service helps others succeed, by default, you succeed too.

Do you sometimes get let down when you serve? Yes, as in many other areas of life. When you give, you have to do it with no strings attached, accepting that you may be let down.

Sometimes it's people taking too much and not being respectful of your time. Others take your intellectual property or get angry if you don't give them more. Many will take and never even say thank you or acknowledge your existence.

Me, I let them go. I don't cut them out. I don't speak badly about them. They have shown me who they are, and I believe them. And then I move forward. (**#Self-protection and the circle of trust**, *wisdom 68*)

You see, when you let yourself get bitter about giving and being let down, you sacrifice a beautiful part of yourself. If you truly want to be of service and to be a giver, you continue to be the giving person despite the takers. I know it can hurt. I know it's painful. But gently send them on their way and keep going. Don't hate. Let go of any anger. Be at peace and move forward. Keep giving. Keep serving.

Over time, the magic starts to happen. You attract more and more like-minded people to you. People who relish the experience of being givers. And when you have a huge community like that around you, life is pretty good.

The damage that a *me-first* attitude can cause to society has been very apparent lately, with people behaving selfishly and ignoring risk to their families and communities. Our collective failure to put our concern for each other first has made this pandemic harder for everyone and worse for longer.

All we can do is lead by example, showing people who are behaving selfishly that there's a better way. If they get the message, they'll start to shift a little too, and that's how real change happens, in ever-increasing ripples. What we build together will be far more meaningful, powerful, and substantial, than if we approach life with an "each to their own" mentality.

When times are tough, serve. Serve your community in whatever way makes sense to you. There will be great riches for you, though they may not be financial, but rather in the form of mutual support.

WHAT'S NEXT?

Step 1: Identify where you can be of service. In your community? In your bigger world?

Step 2: Reach out and serve. Join a committee, volunteer your time, set up video meetings with communities you can help. Look around and work out where you can serve. Make a note of what you're going to do next.

#98

LET'S ADDRESS POWERLESSNESS

EMPOWER OTHERS

POWERLESSNESS IS EVERYWHERE. Single mothers, retirees on pensions, our indigenous brothers and sisters, people with intellectual and physical disabilities, job seekers, the incarcerated, people with addictions, the children of people with addictions—and on it goes.

We have created societies centered on amplifying powerlessness. People who have no power over their lives become stuck in a cycle of never-ending misery and poverty. Society seems to have been built to ensure they cannot escape and become their highest selves. Only a tiny percentage get that lucky break and a way out.

Who benefits from this?

Some think the wealthy and the powerful must benefit. Yet they are fearful too (which is another form of powerlessness) as they build higher walls and invest in more technology to protect themselves and their way of life. Don't forget, the more you have, the more you have to lose! But their children are not safer either, nor are their communities, because the imbalance in society makes life worse for everyone.

As a voracious reader of history, I know that the idea of keeping our communities separate has never proven successful. Walls have always been useless—even metaphorical ones, like the partitions we create when we divide up our towns and cities. As humans, we know how to find each other.

The way things are, there is no winning for the powerful and there is no winning for the powerless. So why do we keep holding onto a broken system?

It's high time to rebuild our societies with human dignity at the heart of what we create, and with a foundation that values a new concept of what is powerful. That which unites us is our true power, not that which builds walls to drive us apart. That just makes all of our lives a little bit worse.

Look around, the evidence is everywhere: it's time for change.

#99

SPEND TIME ALONE, IN SILENCE

SELF-EMPOWERMENT

SILENCE CREATES SPACE TO investigate our thoughts and beliefs. This is powerful practice toward self-awareness, and it helps with so many of these other wisdoms.

I'm talking about intentional solitude. It is only in silence that we can define and clarify our personal values and to really get to know ourselves, without external input.

The challenge is, we're surrounded by noise—television, social media, kids, cars, machines, community, even the noise in our own heads! We seldom give ourselves the space to really go inside and reflect. So, the first job is to be conscious of the noise levels around us and be honest about how they affect us.

Then set aside moments in your day when you are not confronted by the noise of living—turn off the TV, turn off the music, YouTube, podcasts, and everything else. Set a reading hour or a quiet time in your home. Use that time to step back from your life and question or reflect in a relaxed way.

Book time alone and away from your daily routine. A week off, a month off—whatever is possible. I am eternally grateful for my youthful travels, which gave me my first real dose of silence.

However, you don't need to get away from it all to spend quality time with yourself on a daily basis. You can do it anywhere and still make it a game-changer.

When you really go into places of silence regularly, I believe you will be surprised by the things you learn about yourself, when you take the time to listen deep inside. You may discover that your inner voice is louder or meaner than you realized. (**#Do you have voices in your head?**, *wisdom 4*) You may find deep pools of gratitude. You may find deep pools of anger—and wade through them to the other side. You may find space for forgiveness—for others or yourself.

Dig deep into the silence of you. Don't be scared of it. There is so much wisdom there. So much opportunity for personal transformation. (**#Have you met your soul yet?**, *wisdom 37*)

MY COMMITMENT

I will dedicate .... every day to silence OR I will take time out of my life in silence, alone.

My silent place will be ....

My silent practice will include:

1.

2.

3.

I hope to achieve

1.

2.

3.

#100

WERE YOU TAUGHT TO HATE SOMEONE YOU NEVER MET?

SELF-AWARENESS

A **WOMAN I ONCE WORKED** with in London, who hated "Pakis" with a passion (by this she meant anyone from the Asian subcontinent—India, Pakistan, Bangladesh, Sri Lanka—all countries lumped insultingly together). She'd grown up in Birmingham, a city whose considerable social and cultural challenges at that time were the source of her horribly racist attitudes towards anyone with darker skin.

I often found her opinions disturbing and ugly, so I challenged her views regularly, and I went at her pretty hard. She was a tough lady, so she could cope with it. My campaign included introducing her to my "Paki" friends, talking about my wonderful experiences of travelling around India (still my favorite country in the world), and constantly asking her opinions on people and challenging her views. I didn't think I made one bit of difference, but as I was doing my "Farewell London Drinking Fiesta" before moving to Boston, she thanked me.

I said, "What? I didn't think you listened to a bloody word I said."

And she said, "No, I really did, and thank you. I really appreciate it."

I was thrilled to have made a positive impact, if only on this one person. It's definitely been a mission of mine to surround myself with people from all walks of life and if someone expresses anything racist, ageist, sexist, or offensively judgmental in any way, I try to take the time to find out where that belief comes from. Not everyone is open to my probing questions, so I choose my battles well, but I do think that a regrettable number of people never question or grow beyond what they were taught.

The great news is when someone does move beyond what they know, it is a beautiful thing to see.

Another friend, a woman from India, told me how growing up, not only was she taught "caste" hatred and superiority, but also hatred towards Pakistanis. It wasn't until she was an adult that she realized her prejudices might be worth revisiting and revising from a new perspective.

As she had gone out into the world, she met people from all walks of life, including meeting and making great friends with Pakistanis and with "low-caste" people from her state. It really helped her to reassess her thinking and to realize that she is lucky.

She is lucky because she was able to move beyond the stereotypes she was indoctrinated with as a child. But she can also see that the people who made her think this way aren't ignorant, they just haven't had the opportunities to see the world through "new" eyes.

So much of the thinking that's holding us back, globally, falls into this category of unexamined, *received* prejudice. Think where we could go if each person examined the ideas given to them and asked, *do I believe this? Is it even my own thinking? And if not, do I want to keep believing it?*

Growing up, I got lucky. My dad didn't have a racist bone in his body and everyone in the world fascinated him—he was open to everyone and took every chance he could to speak with people from other countries. That was how he "travelled" the world long before he got on a plane.

His way was contagious—I grew up feeling open and fascinated by everyone, too. It also turned me into a bit of a fighter against racism and prejudice, because I learned that most people really are wonderful, when you get to know them.

And beyond my dad's open mind there was a moment that really helped me see the world through new eyes. When I was a young teenager, two Laotian sisters came to attend our school. They entered Australia as asylum seekers and eventually ended up at our rural school through Catholic sponsorship. We were intrigued by these girls when they arrived, because our almost exclusively white town didn't have too many people who looked like them in the early '80s. However, they quickly settled in and became part of our community. At that age, you really don't see differences. You just make friends.

One day, the school invited the entire family to come in and tell us their story. My memory of their story is that to escape the unbearable suffering the family was enduring, the father had tied all 11 children, their mother, grandma, and himself to the bottom of a train, and they escaped the country overnight. On the very long and uncomfortable train journey one of their brothers died, as did the grandma. Eventually, after what must have been terrible months of uncertainty and hopelessness, the family made it to Australia. I still remember sitting there thinking, wow, I cannot imagine anyone having to go through something like this—it was an amazingly brave and heartbreaking story.

Their story made me curious and made me wonder what I could do to help find solutions to the challenges facing so many people in our world— a commitment that's especially important now, as the number of asylum seekers and refugees worldwide is only going to grow. We must do what we can to create a better system, so our fellow humans caught up in real horror can be safe and live with dignity.

So many of crises in the last decade have been caused or compounded by the refugee crisis. The extremist right has reemerged, and we are allowing anger, division and resentment to grow, instead of saying: let's bring the brightest minds together and FIX THIS!

Let's tap deeply into our humanity and look at this challenge with bold ambition and determination. We can solve this challenge if we can muster the will!

What about *you*? If you haven't already, how about sitting down with yourself to do an inventory on any views you've never questioned?

Do you have strong feelings about Muslims? Would you rather not have Blacks or Jews in your neighborhood? How do you feel about associating with gays, lesbians, or transvestites? Do you find yourself pronouncing judgment on your local indigenous community? Do you think all white people are arrogant, patronizing turds? Do you think all Malays are lazy? Do you think Chinese people are unfriendly? Do you despise Evangelical Christians? Do you think African Americans are violent? Do you think the Dutch are tight with their money? Do you think Germans are humorless, overly tanned Nazis? Do you think all Russians are gangsters and prostitutes? Do you think the French are arrogant? Do you think the English whine too much and have pasty skin? Do you think all Americans are noisy, over-religious racists? Do you think Australians are big-mouthed and self-opinionated, always claiming superiority based on our high number of Olympic medals per capita? (Steve, my English husband, insisted I added that last one!)

Maybe you hate rich people because your parents told you rich people get rich off the backs of others? Or you hate all alcoholics, druggies, and street people, because you've been told they're pathetic or lazy? Or perhaps you have strong feelings about top-paid "fat cat" executives or blue-collar workers or single mothers?

Everything above is something I've heard from someone I know. We love to hate!

If you've somehow made it through life without accumulating any unexamined prejudices, you probably know someone who hasn't, who has never done this inventory on themselves. Can you help them think about this? Yes, it can be challenging. It requires delicate probing to see if we can get them to open up to a new way of thinking.

One of the great privileges of my life is the opportunities I've had to be touched by people from all walks of life. I've heard stories of joy and pain, I've heard views I'd never considered, and I've understood beliefs that never made sense to me before. I believe that these encounters have given me greater compassion for all people, but also a greater under-standing that we're not that different. Human values across the world are essentially aligned. We all want the same thing, but where we live often determines how that plays out.

In my travels I've seen more great people than bad, and this is the absolute truth! I agree with an amazing and very funny friend in Sydney—the great Gavin Warring—who once said something along the lines of, "Let all the asylum seekers in. I'd rather have someone who'd been through all that shit as my neighbor than the lazy bastards who whine about them stealing our jobs. These folks have been through complete shit, they work harder than anyone at building a new life and giving opportunities to their kids, and every one of them is welcome in my country."

We all need to be more like Gav!

Your assignment is to get out there and meet someone you've been taught to judge or even hate. Do it with an open mind. Spend time with them, talk to them, and, if you feel like it, let me know if they change your mind! Hey, you never know, maybe you'll change *their* mind about people like *you* while you're at it? That would be amazing, huh?

When we stay focused on hating our neighbors, we're not paying attention to the bigger issues or looking at who is really responsible for our pain. I can assure you, it's not your refugee or other-raced neighbor. They are merely a distraction the power players want you to focus on. But more than that, when you live with hate in your heart, you can never truly be in love with life. To really love, you've got to love it all.

#101

PRINCIPLES HAVE A PRICE

SELF-AWARENESS

AM A PRINCIPLED PERSON. I always have been. I'm not sure where it comes from, but I know what I will accept and what I won't accept, no matter what. My principles are always central to who I am as a person. A principle is a core value that governs our behavior. (**#Integrity and values**, *wisdom 8*)

When you are strongly principled, it can be challenging to spend time around those who are not. They can feel wishy-washy, insincere, or uncommitted.

Principles come with a price, though.

You can't take that job because you don't believe in the company. Your truthful speaking, even if gently done, can alienate those around you. You're exhausted but you made a commitment and have to see it through to the end.

As for me, I have always found the price worth paying. It might be annoying sometimes or even draining to be a person of principle, but the only important question is, can I raise my head in pride at my contribution to my family, community and the world? Can I look at myself in the mirror in the morning and be happy with myself? Most importantly, I want my boys to look at me and say *mum was awesome. She never quit fighting for our future.*

I believe the exchange is fair, even if a little challenging sometimes. The truth is, you can't put a price on standing proudly in your shoes and looking both forward to the world your principles will help build and back at the legacy you'll leave behind.

#102

CALM DOWN, SLOW DOWN

SELF-EMPOWERMENT

LIFE IN THE 21ST CENTURY and before COVID-19 was fast, relentless, brutal, and disempowering. We allowed ourselves to be overcome by noise, nonsense, shortcuts, comparisons, and FOMO (fear of missing out).

No space. No silence. No peace. No balance. Just rushing everywhere, never able to keep up—too much coming at us, families fractured, passions lost, money to be earned, things to buy, always more, more, MORE.

Nowadays we are waiting for the pandemic to be over, and everywhere people are pining for what was. Getting back on planes, back to the office, back to the pub, back to what we left behind.

Why do we so badly want that way of life? Was it amazing for you? Did it fill your soul? Did it make you burst with love for life, your family, your friends, your community, the wider word?

Or has this pandemic *breather* helped you see other possibilities? New ways of living? More peaceful ways of living? More connection with those you love the most? A different way of working? A different way of existing?

While we're on our breather, let's not forget to consider what we want after this. Let's not go back to what we left behind. Let's create a better world. Mother Nature—and our own worn-out natures—will thank us.

#103

REMEMBER TO SEEK AWE

SELF-EMPOWERMENT

TUDIES SHOW THAT IF YOU take the time to be awed by the world we live in, you can be a happier person.[62] Awe or a sense of wonder makes you kinder and more loving, and your social behavior is elevated because awe helps you appreciate things greater than yourself.

With the enormous global challenges we're experiencing right now, including the drastic shrinking of the spheres in which we live our lives, many of us are looking back at past memories and sharing them digitally. I love this, I actively participate this way too. It's what makes social media glorious.

The outpouring I'm seeing online puts me in the mood to share some of my awe-inspiring moments. I'm hoping to prompt you to remember similar moments in your own life, but also to ensure you seek more awe— the big moments and the small ones—moving forward. We need to love the world if we're going to save it. Awe reminds us of what there is to love.

Please remember I'm an **#Investor in memories** *(wisdom 78)*. This means that when everyone else was growing up and doing sensible things, like buying homes and nice cars and essentially securing their futures, I decided to take a different path and invest in my memories. This was a very focused decision, and while I've got an amazing memory investment

---

62 https://www.apa.org/pubs/journals/releases/psp-pspi0000018.pdf

414

portfolio, when the chips are down financially, I don't have any backup plan. This is a risk I've always been prepared to take, and even though it has exposed my family and me to some challenging years, I wouldn't live life any other way.

Here are some examples of the moments when I've been awestruck.

Glorying in man-made structures—the Taj Mahal, the great monument to love, took my breath away, it was so delicate and beautiful. Abu Simbel in Northern Egypt—the statues and the way man came together to move these monuments in order to save them when the dam was built is simply awe-inspiring. I couldn't believe how beautiful Edinburgh was. Standing on the Great Wall of China—watching it weave through the mountains in both directions. Standing in Managua, the capital city of Nicaragua, and being gob-smacked by the cathedral that was standing there in ruins after an earthquake more than 20 years before. It was beautiful in its destruction, and the fact they'd never rebuilt it. Walking through the colossal mountain paths and coming face-to-face with the first temple at Petra in Jordan. Indiana Jones had been here! The immense history of Varanasi, an ancient city on the Ganges in India: the vats where they burnt the bodies, families swimming in the holy water, dead bodies floating in the water because they couldn't afford the vats.

Glorying in nature—flying into Nepal, and seeing the Himalayas popping through the clouds then having them as my backdrop for the next month—majestic is an understatement! Sitting in a hot spa in Costa Rica while the volcano heating the water was exploding, with lava flowing down the mountain. It was scary and powerful at the same time. The full moons in Australia, big, beautiful orange moons. The Milky Way from my dad's old farm outside of Wodonga, Australia. My first time diving off the Island of Utila in Honduras, a "fever" of stingrays swam by. Standing on Mount Sinai, where Moses received the Ten Commandments—an incredible view over a desert mountain landscape. Or swimming in the Dead Sea for the first time—the Dead Sea!

Glorying in love—falling in love with Steve was truly awe inspiring. It consumed us for years and we were so happy about that! Every time I have gone to Paris I've loved it, but it was extra special when Steve and I went six weeks after we met. If you fall in love, go to Paris! It was equally special to take the boys there in 2019. And later, the pleasure we gave everyone who came to our wedding and the fact people still talk about it. Falling in love with my sons Lex and Jax. When Lex was born, it took some time to feel it and then *wham!* Number two, Jax, was instant. Pure magic. I am regularly in awe of my children as I watch them grow into men.

Glorying in global moments—coming into NYC on the train from Boston a week after September 11, and the twin towers were not there . . . That whole experience in NYC at that time was something I will never forget. Understanding the scale of the destruction the Tsunami wrought from our balcony in Phuket, when we lived there for a few months in 2009. The entire village of Kamala Beach, which we overlooked, was wiped out. Or back in time, to the fields of Gallipoli, walking among the tombs of the young Antipodean solders who died here, hearing the immense respect the Turks continue to have for our ancestors to this day, as well as towards the young people of ANZ who come all the way across the world to visit this very moving place.

While awe isn't always travel related, one thing that has helped me during this time when travel isn't possible is to go into my memories and remember these many moments of awe. It has certainly helped when the days are dark and somber.

One day the roads will be open again, and while I would love nothing more than to get on the road again, it is time to face the fact that global travel must be reduced worldwide to ensure we reduce global emissions. Until planes can fly emissions free, that is—which isn't expected until the 2030s. However, the number of travelers needs to be reduced too. The growth of the travel and tourism sector cannot continue to grow without careful planning. It just can't. Our natural wonders cannot cope with the number of people wanting to stomp through them for selfies, and the statistics show growth doubling from where it was before the pandemic!

Still, I pine for awe inspiring travel experiences. A dream has always been to stand before the Gates of Babylon. I want to visit the Maldives too, the Russian Steppes, Siberia, the African Savannah, and more. Maybe I'll never do any of these things. Maybe it is time to recognize my travel time is past, for the sake of our planet.

When it comes to awe, I think the greatest learning I've had, is you need to **#Get out of your life** *(wisdom 1)* to see it. My awestruck moments came after I left Australia, because I always took things for granted growing up. Returning to Australia now, I'm definitely inspired to awe by my beautiful country.

The power of your first awestruck moments is something you'll find yourself addicted to. It's such an incredible feeling to be awed by something—whether it's natural or man-made. Life takes on bigger meaning when you experience this.

Make awe a part of your life. Seek it out. Recognize it when it happens. It doesn't have to be the big things; small things are awe-inspiring too. Have you ever seen a firefly or your first hummingbird? Small and awe inspiring. Share awe with your community and help them fall in love too. This feeling makes life worth living.

AWE INSPIRING

List as many awe-inspiring places or moments as you can remember—try and list 20 to start with, across all aspects of your life.

What can you experience where you are? Awesome moments are more than travel!

Now list your top 10 bucket-list experiences to seek after this pandemic is truly over.

JUST SAY YES

CAREER THOUGHTS

WHEN THE FIRST REQUEST CAME IN, a bolt of fear ran through me so deep, I wanted to say NO, straight away! Me, speaking at industry events? Why would anyone care what I have to say?

Yes, fear was my first response. I deftly side-stepped a few opportunities—phew. And then one day I said: why do I keep saying no? I'm forever sitting the audience, disagreeing with what is being said onstage. So, why don't I say yes, get onstage, and put my own opinion forward? How will I ever know if it will resonate if I don't have the courage to share it to a wider audience?

I put this *aha* moment into play and decided to just say yes to requests to speak. When I started, I wasn't great. But I found myself getting better at it. I started to learn how to shape my thoughts more succinctly. I joined a professional speaking community, Asia Professional Speakers Singapore (APSS), so I could learn from established speakers. The opportunities kept coming in.

Not long after joining APSS, I was asked to emcee an association event for the first time. I wanted to say no. But I knew I had to take this opportunity. Speaking in front of a room full of professional speakers— how daunting is that? I was a bundle of nerves that night, but I made it through and learned a lot. Since then, I've spoken in front of this community as a speaker, panel host, and more. I still get a little bit anxious, if I'm completely honest.

Saying yes is not just about being on stage for me. It's about what it opens you up to. For example, you have no control over photos of yourself anymore. Oh my word, people can get you at weird angles and make you look hideous, can't they? Interviews too—the sort you don't get to read before they are published. However, my biggest challenge was video. When cameras were thrust in my face, I ran for the hills.

When I finally stopped running, it was because I remembered what my heart yearns to do.

It wants to help people find the magic within themselves, find their voice, find their self-belief, understand the tools they have to amplify their voice, and finally, get out there and live the largest life they can, making a huge, positive, impact on those around them.

This is what I want to do. With that goal in mind, playing small is not an option. Staying in the shadows isn't an option either. I can't do what I've set out to do from there.

So, I started to just say yes. It's that simple.

"Andrea, would you be willing to speak at this event on content marketing?" Yes!

"Andrea, can you MC our event?" Absolutely!

"Andrea, can you work with our senior executive team on their personal brands?" I'd be delighted to.

"Andrea, can we get you on video?" Why not!

Don't get me wrong, I still squirm inside.

Courage is about making brave decisions, and sometimes saying yes is the hardest of them all.

I want you to ask yourself—what can you say yes to? What makes you squirm, but if you said yes, everything could change?

Side note: please, make sure you're able to say no when it's necessary, too!

HOME-PLAY

When I say no, what am I reacting to?

What could I say yes to (even if I am squirming inside)?

What's the dream that I would get one step closer to if I started to say yes?

#105

CHEERS

SELF-AWARENESS

EVERY COUNTRY IN THE WORLD has a ritual and different words for expressing good wishes before drinking. In English it's *cheers*, but there are many variations. *Salud! Prost! Saude! Živjeli! Skål! Kippis! Egészségedre! Pro! Sláinte! Tcin tcin! Kampai! Togtooy! Gezondheid! Saude! На здоровье! Chai yo! Şerefe!* So many glorious words for clinking glasses and wishing each other health and happiness!

When I left Australia in 1995, I had not yet learned the most important rule about this ritual. I'm sharing it in case you've not heard it either.

In my Australian community, *cheers* was often done as a group with no eye contact, or everyone went around the circle too fast to look at each other. With a little more life experience under my belt, I now understand how much more meaningful and joyous these occasions are when we take our time, make eye contact, and savor the moment together.

You must look the person in the eye as your glass connects, while saying *cheers*. It's not a flippant exercise—it must be done with deep meaning and intention. You can't rush a good *cheers* moment, because it needs to be slow and provide an opportunity to individually connect with everyone you share it with. In Europe they say that failing to look others in the eye when saying cheers means risking seven years of bad sex. We don't want that now, do we?

So, if you join me for a festive occasion and you do not look me in the eye when we say cheers, you can expect to be asked for a do-over.

Thank you for those who taught me this wisdom, but especially Saskia Wurpel and Nathalie Dassas. Love you, ladies.

#106

LIVE LARGE AND HAVE FUN

SELF-EMPOWERMENT

GUESS WHAT: YOU'VE MADE IT to here, the most epic showing-up of my life!

Congratulations. I hope you enjoyed this journey together, or took something away, or feel calmer and more content, or happy?

I have been writing this during a somber and scary time for our world. But we were not in good shape before the pandemic, if we are honest with ourselves. Society everywhere has been getting far too close to reading like dystopic fiction. It's tempting to close the book and chuck it at the wall. I see many people around me expressing feelings of hopelessness and helplessness, disengaging because the world has become so negative. At least we kicked off 2021 with some renewed hope in the world, yes?

We know the hard times are not behind us, and based on what the economists are saying, we're not moving back into good times anytime soon.[63]

But please, good people, let's not give up. Let's stick together and envision a better future.

Let's think, plan, get involved, and be activists together. Let's start the people's revolution to create the future we want, a future with a rich life for everyone, not just the few.

---

63 https://theconversation.com/world-economy-in-2021-heres-who-will-win-and-who-will-lose-152631

This is the future all life on earth deserves, and I refuse to believe it's out of reach.

In the meantime, there's something simple but important we can do to make the world better. Even if life feels extra small right now, we can live large *today*. The other thing we've got to make sure we remember to do is have fun, too! Because if life is devoid of fun, what's the point?

Embrace the moments as they pass and enjoy everything you've got as much as you possibly can, especially the people in your life. The greatest pleasure and privilege of my life has been the people in it, from the amazing people I grew up with to all the fabulous people I've met as I've lived, worked, and traveled my way through this beautiful world. It's been such a privilege to have so many people touch my life for the better.

Open your horizons. If you're surrounded by a community of people that you've known all your life, expand it. Seek out people from different cultures and different religions. During the time when face-to-face meeting and mingling is limited, let's take advantage of the possibilities in the online network. That's what it's there for.

People are brilliant. The world is brilliant. The differences between us are brilliant.

Living large means living generously, giving as much as you can of your time, energy, and knowledge. When you're giving of yourself, you always feel like your cup is running over.

Let's not build walls, let's build bridges. Even tunnels, if needs be.

I think I've been fairly committed to that on my journey of life. I hope I pass it on to my boys, because that's really what it's all about. So much of what we're taught and brought up to believe in is not important, in the long run. It's the people in our lives that matter. It's the earth that sustains us that matters.

Let's create the future we want. This is living large. Let's make the '20s the time that we redefined the future of humanity.

And let's enjoy the hell out of this life while we're at it. Smile, laugh, party, enjoy. Open the champagne. Don't save it. Life is about, right here, right now.

Don't forget to be kind too. Walk the world with a gentle heart my friends. It's much nicer that way. If you've forgotten to do it, love life again. All of it!

#107

WISDOM FROM MY 100-YEAR-OLD GRANDMA

SELF AWARENESS

MY GRANDMA DIED PEACEFULLY in her sleep at the grand old age of 104, a phenomenal length of time to live. She was three months off 105. This means she was alive back in the days of the Spanish Flu!

Living in Asia for nearly 20 years has taught me to value my elders differently than before. In Australia and many other Western societies, we've forgotten that our older generations might have something to say that's worth listening to.

Grandma was born into a time when life was very hard, and that heaviness is something I saw her carry through life. It was such a different generation—especially for women. I was lucky enough to be able to ask her a few questions in her 100th year of life. I wanted to share her wisdom with you here.

GRANDMA TOTTIE'S LIFE ADVICE:

Q1. What do you think is the meaning of life?

The meaning of life is to keep God in your life because sooner or later we will all have to give an account of our life when we meet God face to face.

Q2. What have you learned in your 100+ years?

- To treat people as you would like them to treat you.
- To help the underprivileged; for example, I sponsored Tottie's Chooks in Mannya, as well as the worming program for the village children, both in Uganda. I have done this sort of thing all through my life.
- To keep up with your religion—please don't think that I am telling you what to do.
- Save some money for a rainy day so you won't have to depend on other people in your old age.

Q3. If you could give your children, grandchildren and great-grandchildren any advice on life, what would you say?

- Live a good life, don't take drugs, smoke, or abuse alcohol and then you can die with no regrets.
- Always pay your way and don't rely on credit cards. I have always paid cash for what I wanted.
- Keep God in your life and remember what you were taught as a child. The world might change but God doesn't.

Some good, solid life advice in here, and I think my Grandma will be happy to know that I pay cash for everything too. Debt is a burden I choose to avoid whenever possible!

When it comes to God, I think Grandma's idea of God is very different from the way many of us practice spirituality today. I certainly won't be re-joining the Catholic Church based on her advice. However, I'm pretty sure my grandma wouldn't be disappointed with my idea of spirituality. I believe in being a good person in the world and doing the right thing by everyone I meet. That's what religion has come to mean to me. Charity is important to me as well. I believe we can help wherever we can.

One of the things I love about my grandmother's advice is its simplicity. We've overcomplicated so much about our lives, and getting back to simple is a good idea for our moment in time.

Grandma, whether you're facing your God, or just finally resting in peace, I must say, a jolly good innings, Tottie. Well done.

#108

LET'S SHOW UP

EMPOWER OTHERS

IF YOU MADE IT THIS FAR, thank you so much for joining me on this journey as I unravel some of the learnings I've taken onboard in this life, testing them out on myself as a case study. I'm sure there were some that did not resonate with who you are, but hopefully others were exactly what you needed to hear or were in alignment with how you already feel. All I can hope is that there was value here.

If you're like me, observing the global discourse, you know we have a lot of work to do, but if we allow human society to continue unravelling, it will be so much harder to bring us back together, united for the challenges ahead. This is something we need to prioritize.

I believe we have been heading in the wrong direction for decades, prioritizing individualism and confusion over global unity and compassion. We need to take stock and say: hang on a minute, if we don't turn this around, we will guarantee more misery, more despair, and unbearable suffering for our children and future generations. None of us want that. Even those we disagree with don't want that. They have their view of the world, as do we; the challenge is that our views are so different.

Protecting ourselves, our family, and our community is a natural instinct. However, the bigger problems are not local, they are global,[64]

---

64 https://e360.yale.edu/features/the-age-of-megafires-the-world-hits-a-climate-tipping-point?
fbclid=IwAR1EAMHv4Pp-CzjjjOQWXIkfW2BhCCCZdmLFcwgsMIkjN2mBazLMUMCg4wk

and we need to get ready to face them and solve them before even more human misery is unleashed.[65]

I wrote this from my heart—as I hope you can tell—in my quest to be one of the people contributing to the bigger global discussion we must have about raising humanity to a higher level. When enough of us rise, we will be more in tune with the greatest challenges the world faces.[66] The only way we can succeed is by working together. Our divisions within countries and around the world are distractions from the bigger challenges we face, and truthfully, it is *old* thinking and needs to be a part of history, not the future.

We must unite and plan. If we have one billion climate refugees turning up on our doorstep[67] and we haven't put in place ways to manage this certainty, it means they will have no place to go for shelter or safety and they will have no dignity. Half of all the displaced are children, which is something we should not accept. We must prepare. We have to do this for the kids, as they are our leaders of tomorrow.

And just as they will be in misery, so will we. While we are less directly impacted by the impending crises, our lives will be worse too. All you need to do is look at the rise of extremism around the world compounded by the refugee crisis. It ripples out and consumes us all—it's not good for anyone. It makes everyone's life worse.

Listen to the futurists, scientists, researchers, social commentators, and certain politicians, like Lee Hsien Loong of Singapore. He's one of the politicians who get it. Listen to the people who can clearly see where we are heading if we do not act now. They speak of more war, more walls, and scarcer staple food supplies, which will result in widespread starvation and famine, as well as higher food prices all around. We face water scarcity in every corner of the globe, ongoing economic crisis, unlivable heat, extreme weather events, warming oceans, and ecosystem collapse. None of us are safe in this. We can't protect ourselves from the impact. We must prepare and look at this from a global perspective, because it is a global problem.

---

65   https://www.livescience.com/oldest-climate-record-ever-cenozoic-era.html
66   https://www.nytimes.com/2020/09/22/climate/climate-change-future.html?referringSource=article Share
67   https://www.nytimes.com/interactive/2020/07/23/magazine/climate-migration.html

Please scan this QR code, which will take you to my website. It features regularly updated content covering all aspects of the crisis humanity faces.

WHAT CAN WE DO AS INDIVIDUALS?

While many brave people are ready to face into the huge challenges ahead, far too many of us still choose to bury their heads in the sand. It is hard and frightening to acknowledge these challenges and I fully appreciate the personal struggle as we all attempt to come to terms with what is happening in our world. The climate crisis, waste crisis, famine, starvation, refugees, climate refugees, social breakdowns, children who do not have enough to eat in rich countries and poor, human slavery, extinction, ecosystem collapse and its impact—the road ahead is not an easy one.

One of our primary challenges is a feeling of hopelessness. And that is really what I wanted to address in putting this book together.

Because one way we can prepare for the work ahead is to do the work within, to ensure we move into a higher level of consciousness, where we are more open, loving, accepting, generous and kind. If we can move enough of us into this higher mindset, we will be an unstoppable army in the fight for a better life for all.

When we operate from within this higher mindset, we are more in tune with humanity and we have more compassion for each other, regardless of where people are geographically, what faith they follow, or the color of their skin. If we elevate our consciousness, we will only see fellow humans in crisis and will commit to working together, united, determined to overcome and help.

If you noticed the common threads in what I've written, the first and most important is self-awareness. If there is a spiritual crisis we face as humans, it is this. We do not spend the time or create the silence to go within and reflect on our emotions, reactions, responses or fears. We lash out, we do not question ourselves. Why do I feel this way? What is the essence of my anger? Am I acting out of fear?

This lack of awareness is creating great unhappiness across the world. You can't be in fear, uncertainty, and anger and be happy at the same time, so the cycle of frustration grows, the anger grows, and even when lashing out at others and causing harm—in words or deeds—people still do not feel vindicated. This is because the reason for the unhappiness lies deep within. Expressing it externally does not satisfy the emotion driving it, which creates more frustration, more anger, more unhappiness, and more pain. This is playing out around the world as we speak.

Having the courage to face ourselves makes our lives better, because we finally understand our habit of projecting onto others, rather than recognizing why we feel that way in the first place. It's about taking the opportunity to explore the foundation of that negative emotion within and remembering how it even got there. When we do, we can release it. When we really understand the negative emotions that drive us, we can move to a place more in tune with life around us.

In the age of disinformation and fake news, the chasm between us is widening too. So many people no longer trust the institutions that created information within a structure of rules. The collective scrutiny typically applied before broad-based acceptance is, unfortunately, no more. Without proper scrutiny, new information creators have been unleashed on the knowledge economy, many becoming famous and rich because of it. Of course, some people are contributing to the global conversation in a positive way, but as we've seen during the pandemic and on the world's political stages, there's a lot of damage being done as well. The infodemic has confused whole countries and has increased and extended the challenge of overcoming the pandemic for everyone.

However, I do not agree that social media is the problem. It's just a channel, a tool. It amplifies information within our social media silos, but we had infodemics before social media came into our lives.

No—the challenge is much deeper. It's about profound distrust, for our foundation of trust has been eroded very badly in the last 20 years.[68]

---

68   https://www.edelman.com/trustbarometer

This is causing deep anxiety and disempowerment, and it's why conspiracy theory acceptance is on the rise. People are looking for something to believe in and for communities to be part of, because they feel alienated by the world in which they live.

We have a massive global responsibility to address this and put trust front and center in the world we build from here. To rebuild trust, radical transparency will be required—a level of transparency we have not had before. This alone will be a huge societal shift.

And it is why we need to raise our voices in this confusing time. If you have an intelligent point of view, a well-researched perspective, and the ability to understand the information that matters and you step away because of the noise and chaos on social media, you are abdicating your responsibility to your human neighbors. People believe in crazy ideas these days, and the media is not helping in this fight for truth, so we all must rise up and get the conversation back on track. There are more of us than of them, many more. Raise your voice. We need you, and we also need to tackle the media and its negative impact on the world today.

I've discussed many emotions and ideas that I've experimented with and sought to understand across my life. If there's a central message I hope you take away, it is this: we need to prioritize harmony within ourselves, so we can achieve it out in the wider world. Humanity has been out of balance for so long, and regaining balance starts within each of us.

In essence, I'm speaking of a constant mindfulness and vigilance of our thoughts—paying attention to how they got there, asking ourselves if we will continue to accept them as our own, and being conscious of the actions we take that come from these thoughts. So many people do not see or own their thoughts. It's the centerpiece of this book. It's where I believe we unlock ourselves.

We have all heard the idea that our thoughts define our reality, right? Well, if our thoughts are taught us by others, then never questioned, never challenged, never even noticed, is that the reality you want? Dig into your thoughts. Pull them apart. Are they even you?

And when we, the lucky ones, achieve this level of self-awareness and when we get this essential message of the power of our thoughts by being fully aware of them, we can then be in a position to lift up those who are screaming for our help and attention around the world, because we will be able to really hear them at last. We'll have renewed energy for the challenges too, and if enough of us get on board, think what a world we can create together!

Let's rebuild our world anew, with dignity for all life at the center of our priorities, and in alignment with that which sustains us—our beautiful earth. All throughout history we have evolved to a higher consciousness. It's part of our story, but what is required right now is the greatest evolutionary leap we've ever taken, across every corner of the globe. I believe we can do it. It's big, bold, and ambitious, but every wonderful achievement is.

It is time for that which is uncommon to become common. I'm talking about courage. Will you be courageous with me and help lead this world towards a beautiful future for everyone? Are you ready to show up with me?

With love always,

Andrea

AFTERWORD

FULL DISCLOSURE: I'm Andrea's husband, and as such you might think that I am biased. The truth is, the ideas she expresses here have helped me conquer so many of my own demons—and continue to do so. When she decided to capture her "wisdoms" in the book you've just read, I honestly didn't know if her philosophy could translate onto the page to resonate as powerfully as it does in the way she lives her life. I think she's nailed it—and hopefully after what you've read here, you agree she did too.

As a partner in her case study (and life), and as someone who's sat beside her through the intensity of creating *Uncommon Courage*, I want the world to know that this book can transform your life. It's thought provoking, scary and exciting, all at the same time.

We know most people claim to want to be the best version of themselves, but many of us hit the common roadblock of where to start and how. The default reaction is to go "get" knowledge by buying a book. However, with so many books out there claiming to be life-changing, how do you know the advice you are reading is genuine and legitimate? It's very simple—get your advice from someone who has actually done it and lived it, rather than using data to make the arguments. A lived experience is always more powerful and relevant—and Andrea's book is lived experience distilled.

Uncommon Courage is unfettered access to the knowledge gleaned by a normal person from ordinary beginnings who's lived an extraordinary life—all of her own making. In this book, Andrea has taken us along a journey as she unpacks her 50 years of life experiences, recounting amazing and humbling interactions around the world through the lens of her boundless and unquenchable curiosity. She has laid bare her findings with so much vulnerability and courageous candor that hopefully—right here, right now—you can't help but feel like you have caught some of her infectious enthusiasm and love of life.

Don't shy away from soul-searching questions about yourself and humanity in general—face into them. Andrea does not claim to have all the answers. However, her rare thirst for knowledge and getting to the bottom of the big questions is part of what inspires the rest of us to keep striving to live our best life through empowerment, self-awareness, and a humanitarian outlook that is sadly diminished amidst the current environmental tailspin we're in today. Now that you have done some foundation work as you read this book, it's time to get stuck in, as Andrea would say, and get involved!

Uncommon Courage is packed with practical takeaways you can apply immediately in your daily life. This manual for the soul is an invitation to all of us to make a start—pure and simple. Pick something you can change today and just start. Who knows—if enough of us answer Andrea's invitation, just think what can we collectively achieve together!

STEVE JOHNSON, sales and marketing professional, business leader, proud (and very patient) husband of Andrea Edwards

ACKNOWLEDGEMENTS

WHERE DO YOU EVEN START to say thank you with a book like this? Especially when everyone who has ever touched my life is part of the stories I'm sharing here! I suppose it must start with the family I was born into. A completely dysfunctional family, it was our crazy family vibe that really gave me my wings. From my dad, Peter Edwards, mum Kathryn Edwards, and my two brothers Paul and Mark, as well as my fabulous sister, Phillipa Edwards—life was always big and noisy and I felt unlimited possibilities were always available to me. If there is one definite thing about my family and growing up in country Australia, it's that life was never boring. And while we weren't a wealthy family, we had wide exposure to hobbies, passions and ideas that were richer than anything money could buy. My childhood gave me the courage to embrace a big life and to have no fear of discomfort or change. It's a gift that served me well.

Then into the world, from my friends in the neighborhood—Emma Pini (who I talk about in this book) and her sister Claire Kielty, and friends at school—Dunny (aka Megan O'Bierne), Sally Hart, Lisa Kieghran, Kaz Stahl, Nicole Lockhart, Nadia Dosenko, Suzie Josic, Kath Fraser, and so many more, plus the boys who joined us in the last two years of school. What a crazy bunch of fabulous mates and an awesome influence you were. Not to forget my musical community in the Wodonga Citizens Brass Band and the Victorian State Youth Brass Band, the cycling community when I raced bicycles, and the gyms I used to work out in. So many people touched my life. Of course, not everyone was great, but everyone gave me something to work with. I relish my memories of growing up with all of you.

After my Monash University days, where I finally grew up and started opening my mind thanks to the people I met then, and onto my Army Days—which taught me more than anything about how to relate to people from all walks of life. It was at this time I started traveling the world. I wandered every chance I got, then I moved away. Living and working in London, then Boston, then New York City before September 11, when the ecommerce crash forced me to put my backpack on again to go take a look at Central America. Beautiful. Every step of the way, people came into my life, influenced my thinking, changed my ideas, exposed me to new thoughts, and to all of you, I am so grateful.

I attempted to return to Australia, which gave me a chance to enjoy a year with my amazing pals in Sydney (centered around Lorna Pringle and Carl Schwartz), only to be offered a job in Singapore. I didn't want to take that job, but the one thing I knew by this point was, keep following the path and see where it takes you. Australia was wonderful, but the wider world was always calling me back.

So I jumped on a plane and moved to Singapore, and four months later I met Steve Johnson—the love of my life. Beautiful new friendships were made in Singapore, and as I traveled the world for work and fun from that home base, always growing, evolving, changing. However, the financial crisis of 2008 sent us moving again.

With two small boys in tow (Jax at 15 months, Lex at two and a half) we landed in Phuket in 2009 and within a short period of time Jax was electrocuted, so we knew this wasn't where we should be. Our problem is we never had a plan B. We went to Perth, didn't like it, Brisbane, didn't like that either, Noosa north of Brisbane and, well, it wasn't a great experience for us as a family, so we headed back to Singapore to take our chances, minus any security.

It was a grueling time getting back on our feet in Singapore, with our own faith in ourselves the only backup we had, but I eventually ended up at Microsoft (which was awesome), then a content agency (which was awesome for different reasons) and finally my own business—The Digital Conversationalist. In Singapore, through my work and my community, I met an incredible group of people who inspired me, showed me new ways of living, and opened doors to new opportunities.

One of the prime groups of influence was the Asia Professional Speakers Singapore (APSS), which opened me up to the global community of professional speakers, and once again, I have friends and an amazing community all over the world because of this! They also opened doors to new possibilities and ways of life. They stretched me and made me want more from life, and to contribute more to create a better world. To everyone in this community, thank you. You have taught me so much and supported me beautifully. I am beyond grateful.

And of course, the most recent chapter, nearly four years living in Phuket, Thailand, again, but different this time. We came so our son Lex could attend Arrowsmith at United World College, Thailand. Both of our boys are flourishing in this beautiful school and life is good for all of us, with a new community around us, which brings many new gifts. Everyone is in Phuket for very different reasons, so we have a wide community of fascinating people, from all over the world. I am a sponge for their thoughts and ideas. I have more quiet and peace in my life, which has meant I can focus on the ideas I'm sharing in this book and beyond. So, to our fun crowd in Phuket, which is also a deeply thinking crew, thank you. We love you guys and couldn't imagine a better group of people to experience these strange times with. We really are in the one percent of luckiest people in the world during the time of COVID-19, but we don't rest on our laurels. We are all doing what we can to ensure no one in our community is left behind #OnePhuket. Thank you for embracing and loving our family. Thank you for being awesome.

Huge gratitude to Tiffani Bova for taking the time to write the forward. I feel so honored you were happy to support me with Uncommon Courage!

To everyone who reviewed this book, David JP Philips, Shirley Taylor, Andrew Bryant, Tanvi Gautam, Tara Moody, Lindsay Adams, Wendy Tan, Wendi Stewart, Dr. Frank Hagenow, Kerrie Phipps, Vicky Coburn, John Vincent Gordon, Sha En Yeo, Anupama Singal, Niklas Myhr, Natalie Turner, Ferenc Nyiro, Samantha Gayfer, Sally Foley-Lewis, Kevin Cottam, Rebecca Kynaston, Pravin Shekar and Phillipa Edwards. Thank you. I know it is so much to ask, but I am deeply grateful to each of you who did it gleefully, providing feedback, ideas, and of course, your testimonials.

Big shout out to Vicky Coburn, who really pushed me to take my original 50 Wisdoms and write a book, and my pal John Vincent Gordon, who didn't just read and review the book, but spent time with me to help me make it better. Legend. Also, Samantha Gayfer and Wendi Stewart, two ladies who've given me incredible support on this journey—massive appreciation.

Also, Tim Hamons and his team at Art of Awakening. Tim is one of my friends in the Asia Professional Speakers Singapore (APSS) and he is a brilliant speaker and creative artist. I knew I wanted to illustrate some of these ideas, and it's been a wonderful opportunity to collaborate together. Do check out Tim's work beyond this book. He will inspire you.

Priscilla Joseph, you beautiful lady, and my very patient virtual assistant. I know I drive you nuts, but I can't do what I do without you. Love you babe.

Arewa Lanre, my design god in Nigeria. Thank you for giving my brand-vision the wings to fly. I love working with you and I love what you've done to bring the *Uncommon Courage* design to life.

Also to Bo Choomanee, the lady in Phuket who makes our life run smoothly, our Phuket Manager. How could we do this without you?

A huge hat tip and a BIG hug to the fabulous Joanne Flinn, whose Project Wings Author Services I brought on once again after an amazing experience editing my first book—*18 Steps to an All-Star LinkedIn Profile*. Joanne is a thought leader, professional speaker, author, business consultant, artist and so much more, AND she has amazing talent for the written word too. This was a big and complicated project, and she has been by my side since the beginning. Thank you so much Joanne—you're an amazing professional and have helped me bring *Uncommon Courage* to life. I am immensely grateful to you.

My sister from another mother, Vicky Minguillo, you take work off my hands that frees me up to express myself, and spend time on work that I hope matters in the world. Not only did you teach me to be a mother, but your gentle wisdoms every day of my life have taught me to be a better person. I love you, woman.

And of course, the three main men in my life. The mini ones—although not for too much longer—Lex and Jax. You guys rock! Thanks for being so interested in my work. I know so much of what I do and say doesn't make sense right now, but I hope one day you can think back on all the things I've said, and maybe read the words in this book, and it really will help you to be courageous, bold, brave and magnificent. I want you to both be **#manbassadors** *(wisdom 31)* who respect all life, understand that living is about joy and contentment, but also that when you forgive, you move on. Don't be shackled by past baggage. Don't be shackled by fear or hatred towards anyone. Beauty is everywhere, my loves. Look ahead, dream big, and make the world a better place for me.

And finally, my husband Steve Johnson. You accepted this journey with me, and while you have never shied away from challenging me or how I think about things (which I always appreciate). You've been with me all the way. I know it's a bit bonkers sometimes, but it's never boring, right? We have had so much fun together, explored the world, and produced two fine fellas. You really are proof of the power of my recipe for love. I visualized you until you turned up and you were just perfect, in all of the messy ways that perfect love is. Thanks for loving me. Thanks for believing in me. Thanks for sticking by me. You give me courage boosts every day! I couldn't have done this book without you. You are not only a huge part of the story, but you supported its creation in every way that matters. I love you more and more everyday my sweetheart.

To everyone who has touched my life, thank you. The greatest privilege of my life is the quality of people who have walked it with me. I feel like the luckiest lady in the world.

18 STEPS TO AN ALL-STAR LINKEDIN PROFILE

Check out my first book to learn how to put your voice out into the world in a more powerful way!

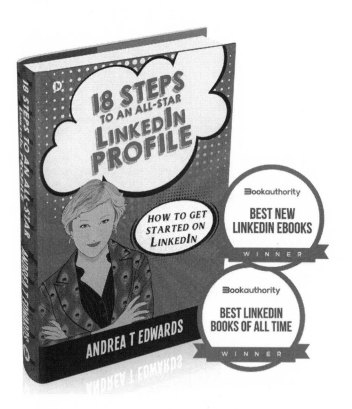

ABOUT
ANDREA T EDWARDS

ANDREA T EDWARDS, The Digital Conversationalist, is a Certified Speaking Professional (CSP), and a globally award-winning B2B communications professional. Andrea works with the world's largest companies on the transformation needed within to maximize business growth in our digital future. She is a change agent, provocateur, author, passionate communicator and social leader. Andrea's book *18 Steps to an All-Star LinkedIn Profile* was added to two Book Authority's listings as the "100 Best LinkedIn Books of All Time" and "22 Best New LinkedIn eBooks To Read In 2021."

With *Uncommon Courage,* Andrea hopes to inspire conversations which change the direction of how we live.

You can join her for more insights with special guests on the podcast/LiveStream *Uncommon Courage* and at her Websites **www.andreatedwards.com** or dig into the section **www.Uncommon-Courage.com**

CONNECT WITH ME

If you would like to connect and join my community, here is how you can do it. I'd love to have you join the Facebook group *Uncommon Courage*, where we can dig into these and any other ideas relevant in the world.

Facebook Group Uncommon Courage

For every book you buy, I plant a tree.